Two week loan

Please return on or b—
date stamped below.

MANAGEMENT DEVELOPMENT
· · · · STRATEGY AND PRACTICE · · · ·

Jean Woodall and Diana Winstanley

Copyright © Jean Woodall and Diana Winstanley 1998

The right of Jean Woodall and Diana Winstanley to be identified as authors of this work has been asserted in accordance with the Copyright, Designs and Patents Act 1988.

First published 1998

2 4 6 8 10 9 7 5 3 1

Blackwell Publishers Ltd
108 Cowley Road
Oxford OX4 1JF
UK

4 JUN 1998

Blackwell Publishers Inc.
350 Main Street
Malden, Massachusetts 02148
USA

British Library Cataloguing in Publication Data

A CIP catalogue record for this book is available from the British Library.

Library of Congress Cataloging-in-Publication Data

Woodall, Jean, 1950–
        Management development: strategy and practice / Jean Woodall and Diana Winstanley.
            p.   cm.
        Includes bibliographical references and index.
        ISBN 0–631–19866–0
        1. Management–Vocational guidance.   2. Career development.   3. Executives–Training of.
    I. Winstanley, Diana.   II. Title.
    HD38.2.W66   1998
    658.4'07124–dc21   97–22032
                                                                    CIP

    ISBN 0631 208402 (hbk)
    ISBN 0631 198660 (pbk)

Commissioning Editor: Catriona King
Desk Editor: Paula Jacobs
Production Manager/Controller: Lisa Parker
Text Designer: Lisa Parker

Typeset in 10/12pt Galliard by Photoprint, Torquay, Devon
Printed in Great Britain by T. J. International, Padstow, Cornwall

CONTENTS

•••• PART I ••••
THE PURPOSE OF MANAGEMENT DEVELOPMENT

Introduction • Learning Objectives • What is Management Development? •
Why Management Development? • The Current Context for Management
Development • Overview of Chapters • Exercise • References

Introduction • Learning Objectives • Management Development: the Link
with Organizational and National Economic Performance • Management
Development and Strategic Fit: a Critique • Meeting Business Needs
Outside the Large Corporate Sector • Demonstrating that Management
Development Adds Value to the Business: Evaluation • Demonstrating that
Management Development Adds Value to the Business: Auditing •
Summary • Exercise • References

Introduction • Learning Objectives • The Subjective Career and the
Evolution of Models of Managerial Careers • Organizational Careers and
the Evolution of Career Management • Changing Organizational Contexts
and Career Development • Bringing Together the Individual and
Organizational Perspectives • Summary • Exercises • References

•••• PART IV ••••
MEETING DIFFERENT MANAGEMENT DEVELOPMENT NEEDS

·····FIGURES·····

·····TABLES·····

·····ACKNOWLEDGEMENTS·····

The origins of this book are many and diverse. We have both been involved in management education for several years and since 1991 Jean has taught a specialist masters option on management development at Kingston Business School. In addition we have both independently been involved in research on management development, Diana within the NHS and Jean elsewhere in the corporate sector. Although at the stage of completion we might ruefully wonder why we agreed to take on such a mammoth task, we nonetheless enjoy the stimulus of working with one another, as we have indeed in the past, and shall no doubt do so again.

We would like to thank Pat Stevens for her professionalism and painstaking efficiency and calm in the face of chaos, in wordprocessing the manuscript.

Jean would like to thank all the family and friends who provided support and welcome distractions during the long process of writing this book.

Diana would like to thank Nick, Victoria and Julian for allowing her to juggle work and home.

We should also like to thank colleagues in our own institutions and elsewhere. Above all, we are grateful to those practising managers whom we have taught and supervised on masters and diploma programmes over the last ten years. Without them, this book would actually not have been written.

The authors and publishers gratefully acknowledge the following for permission to reproduce copyright material:

Ashridge Management College, Audit Commission, The Body Shop, Blackwell Publishers Ltd, Bloomsbury Publishers, Business in the Community, Butterworth Heinemann, Cambridge University Press, Greenwood Publishing Group Inc., Gower, Harper & Row, Her Majesty's Stationery Office, The Institution of Electrical Engineers, Institute for Employment Research (University of Warwick), Institute for Employment Studies, International Book Distributors, Investors in People, IPD Enterprises Limited, John Wiley & Sons, Inc., Journal of Management Studies, Kendall/Hunt Publishing Co., Macmillan Publishers, Management Charter Initiative, Management Development Review, The Management School (Lancaster University), Marks and Spencer, Office for National Statistics, The Open University, Oxford University Press, People Management, Personnel Publications Ltd, Prentice Hall, Philip Allan Publishers, Routledge Publishers, Royal Mail, Saville and Holdsworth, Simon & Schuster.

The publishers apologize for any errors or omissions in the above list and would be grateful to be notified of any corrections that should be incorporated in the next edition or reprint of this book.

PART I

The Purpose of Management Development

CHAPTER 1

Management Development – Purposes, Processes and Prerequisites

•••• Introduction ••••

It is universally recognized that organizational management is a vital ingredient in securing improved business performance. The training and education of the UK managerial workforce has been on the UK Government agenda for over 30 years. Yet while governments, company-level HR staff and managers themselves might all agree that management development is a priority, there is little agreement about how to go about this, and too many glib exhortations are made which pass without comment. For example, assertions such as 'what is needed is more on-the-job, relevant training', 'development for employability is the way forward', 'identifying competences is the best way to approach development' seldom receive critical scrutiny.

This book provides an overview of our knowledge of what is happening in management development in theory, research and practice. The text is intended to take a more critical approach than many standard textbooks on management development in identifying the themes and contradictions. The focus is on the strategic organizational level and the role of management development in contributing to organizational aims as well as individual objectives. Although much of the information will be useful to those designing management development programmes, this is not a nuts-and-bolts book about how to go about setting up a management development process from scratch.

We hope that this different perspective will be a refreshing and stimulating way of helping those interested master the subject, but we do not offer easy answers and panaceas. It is not always possible for management development solutions to meet both individual and organizational needs, and there is no single right way or perfect solution. It is even possible that management development may not be an appropriate solution at all. In this chapter we begin by looking at differing definitions of management development and examine its purposes and aims, its varying processes and how it is delivered, and the prerequisites which require a strategic approach contingent on organizational and individual manager circumstances. The chapter then focuses on the changes taking place in the current context for management development and concludes with an overview of the chapters in this book.

•••• Learning Objectives ••••

As a result of reading this chapter you should be able to:

- define management development and distinguish it from management education and management training, and be able to describe its links with organizational development and self development;
- be aware of and be able to compare and contrast some of the key approaches to management development;
- give an overview of the management development process;
- identify some of the reasons why there is not a single perfect approach to management development and be able to suggest at least three factors which may affect the type of development which would be appropriate.

•••• What is Management Development? ••••

Management development has been defined in a myriad of different ways. The following extracts illustrate definitions of management development used in the literature.

> An attempt to improve managerial effectiveness through a planned and deliberate learning process. (Training Services Agency, 1977)

> The terms and processes of 'management education', 'management development' and 'organisational development' merge into one another both in understanding and practice . . . I use management development to describe the total process by which managers learn and grow in effectiveness . . . Management development is perceived as an attempt to increase managerial effectiveness through planned and deliberate learning processes . . . We have to take account of both formal and informal processes. (Mumford, 1989)

> At the personal level, [management development] is the process by which you and the others gain the skills and abilities to manage yourself and others . . . At the organization level, management development involves all issues listed on the continuum (recruitment and selection, induction and training, work allocation and objective setting, on-the-job learning, performance appraisal and review, leadership training and development, career management, promotion assessment and planning, team management and development, self development), but it is more than just that. Management development is a way of doing business. It is an integral part of management. It is a way of life where challenges are being faced every day and confronted as learning opportunities. (Margerison, 1991)

> I define 'management development' as the management of managerial careers in an organizational context. (Burgoyne, 1988)

> The aim of management development should be to increase workgroup and organizational effectiveness which, in turn, is a function of the interaction between characteristics of the organization, its environment and people . . . For the high performance competencies, management development is a process of expanding the range of contributions based on competency strengths that a manager makes to workgroups. (Schroder, 1989, 28–32)

[Management development is] the planned process of ensuring through an appropriate learning environment and experiences the continuous supply and retention of effective managers at all levels to meet the requirements of an organization and enhance its strategic capability. (Harrison, 1995)

To make these competing definitions more intelligible, it is possible to divide them into two types. Authors have defined management development with respect to its **purposes** and aims, or with respect to its **processes** and how it is done. Here these two approaches are combined and incorporate a third element – its **presuppositions** or, in other words, its requirements for effectiveness (see table 1.1). These are all discussed below.

Table 1.1 The purposes, processes and prerequisites of management development

	Purpose	Process	Prerequisites
Organizational development	Processes to develop organizational structures, culture and management systems to enhance the achievement of organizational objectives, especially with regard to enabling organizational change	Action research based around formal work teams working on their values and beliefs and trial-and-error learning with and from each other	Work in developing corporate objectives. The creation of a sense of purpose and acknowledgement of the need for change. A theory Y approach to the workforce
Management development	Primarily oriented towards developing individuals in ways which are complimentary with the organization and its objectives and appropriate for meeting the individual's own career and development needs	Formal and informal activities and processes which provide opportunities for individuals to develop cognitively in their understanding of management and behaviourally in their managerial skills and competences	A positive attitude towards learning and a willingness to develop and change in the learner. Capability on behalf of the facilitator or developer. Support from the organization
Self-development	Primarily concerned with interventions to further the setting and achievement of an individual's own personal development plans and future career aspirations. Usually instigated by the individual, albeit within a supportive organizational framework	The development by an individual of their own personal development plans, an individual devising their own programme of development activities. This may include MD activities and career-planning exercises	Some self-motivation to develop on the part of the individual, and an ability to take initiative in this area. Requires some external support

PURPOSES OF MANAGEMENT DEVELOPMENT

The purposes of management development may be many and varied, for example Storey (1989, 1994) identifies the following five objectives, which are then discussed further below:

(1) a device to engineer organizational change and 'culture' change;
(2) to forge a common identity and approach following company merger or acquisition;
(3) to structure and change attitudes;
(4) to assist in changing and widening the role of line managers;
(5) a tool in pursuit of quality, cost reduction and profitability.

For example, beginning with Storey's first point, using management development to enable organizational change and transformation is highlighted by those who advocate a learning organization or learning company approach which is discussed in chapter 7 (see, for example, Garratt, 1987; Pedler et al., 1991; Schon, 1971; Senge 1990). Learning organizations enable continuous transformation, and do so by engaging all individuals in continuous learning so that their knowledge, energy and creativity is harnessed to meet, shape and develop their strategic goals. Although as we show in chapter 7, there are few organizations that achieve this, there are many that have embarked on this approach, and for these management development is only one part of the learning culture and practice.

Whether or not they are learning organizations, many organizations are under-going radical change. Former public utilities have been privatized, public-sector services have been restructured and subject to internal markets and competition, small firms may cope with growth, mature firms with decline, and many companies in the private sector are subject to merger, acquisition and global competition. The context of organizational change has led to a literature which focuses on behavioural and attitudinal change, as reflected in the burgeoning literature on transformational leadership. A host of writers advocate the need for development to incorporate skills and attitudes related to transformation, instability and discontinuity, dating back to literatures on previous decades of organizational change (for example, see Bailyn, 1993; Drucker, 1969; Tichy, 1993; Wheatley, 1993). However, the methods for achieving these may be many and varied, and management development is thus supposed to allow for the diversity of learning styles and ways of bringing together these skills. Although it is asserted that employees at any level in an organization can be trained to be more transformational, transactional and charismatic (Bass and Aviolo, 1993), such an approach brings leadership theory full circle back to an assessment and development of leadership qualities even if they can be nurtured rather than being immutable.

Requiring individuals to be capable of managing change, and also to cope with continual change, requires development not just of various qualities and skills but also the structuring and restructuring of attitudes, cultures and values. As we and other writers have noted elsewhere, (Ackroyd and Crowdy, 1990; Fitzgerald, 1988; Woodall, 1996), changing attitudes may not be as simple and straightforward as is implied in the organizational change literature, work cultures are highly resilient and resistive to change, and as Willmott (1993) points out, culture change literature has overtones of George Orwell's *Nineteen Eighty-Four.*

Returning to Storey's (1989, 1994) objectives of management development, one huge area where management development is used for change is to help line managers to adapt to downsizing and delayering as their role is changed and widened. These circumstances have left many middle and line managers worried and disorientated over their careers as they see the traditional career ladders disappearing. Instead they are expected to be involved with a more lateral acquisition of skills, and move away from a directing role and towards that of coach and facilitator (for example see Ebadan and Winstanley, 1997; Herriot and Pemberton, 1995). This is examined further in chapter 3.

Storey's (1989, 1994) list of purposes and aims of management development also included enabling an organization to meet its strategic objectives, whether these be quality, cost reduction or profitability. Whatever the specific objective of the organization and the means by which management development can help an organization achieve this objective, the key point is that management development is justified, in the final analysis, by its ability to contribute to the organization and its objectives whilst at the same time developing individuals in ways which may be complementary with their own aspirations. Chapter 2 examines in more detail the relationship management development has with business strategy and objectives.

There are also a number of contradictions in any attempt to meet all the purposes placed on the label 'management development', deriving from mixed messages in the rhetoric. Some areas where purposes are not always compatible are management development for:

(1) developing and valuing diversity versus supporting team working and under-pinning common corporate values and culture;
(2) meeting role requirements versus promoting innovation and transformational leadership;
(3) personal development versus steering performance in an organization's interests.

Such mixed messages introduce the element of political agendas, as management development may be pursued for different ends by different actors and, where these ends differ, the outcome may be the result of power plays and manœuvring. For example, an organization may send a manager on an MBA to develop them for current or future positions within the company, whereas a manager may use it to gain a job at another firm. In most organizations there is likely to be a lack of consensus over the purpose of management development, and its aim may depend on the perspective of the stakeholder.

MANAGEMENT DEVELOPMENT PROCESSES

Management development can also be defined by its activities and processes. Such definitions of management development have largely expanded out from a narrow definition focusing on formal programmes, as evidenced by the Training Services Agency definition above, to include informal and on-the-job processes, as suggested by Mumford's (1989) and Margerison's (1991) definitions above. Storey (1994, p. 368) goes so far as to suggest that definitions which overemphasize the formal and deliberate planning processes which are discussed in chapter 8 are now out of fashion, being replaced by organizational development, self-development and informal methods explored in chapter 9.

Our definition includes both formal and informal activities and processes, on-the-job and off-the-job variants, and learning which includes opportunities for both cognitive and behavioural development, and the acquisition of new skills, competences and understanding. The range of processes available we examine in chapters 7–9, and activities targeted at specific markets in chapters 10–13.

It is quite common for the process approach to follow a systems model or a training-cycle model with the emphasis on processes appropriate for each stage; for example analysing individual or organizational management development needs, approaches for designing and selecting interventions, processes for delivery and processes for evaluating developmental activity. The main shortcoming of the process approach is it is easy to get sidetracked into specifying best practice in the processes themselves, at the expense of fit with organizational context and strategy. For example, emphasis on a well-designed development centre in an organization where the overall career opportunities are very unclear.

PREREQUISITES FOR MANAGEMENT DEVELOPMENT

It is not enough to pay attention to systems and processes alone, we need also to take account of individual's motivations and capabilities to learn, and the developer's own capacity to deliver. In order for the management development processes to be effective in achieving their purposes, a number of such prerequisites have to be in place, as outlined in table 1.1. On behalf of the learner, there has to be a positive attitude towards learning and a willingness to develop and change if management development is to be effective. It may be the case that such an attitude is developed through the process, as learning to learn and learning to like learning is all part of the process. On behalf of the developer, there has to be some planning to identify the most appropriate vehicle for that manager's needs, and this requires diagnosis and assessment both of the current competencies of the individual and of their future aspirations in terms of roles and tasks. There has to be an assessment of the competence gap between the competencies demonstrated and those required both now and in the future. Fonda (1989) goes beyond this and suggests that, for it to be successful, critical success factors need to be identified and the activity needs to be future orientated. Chapters 2–6 are designed to clarify this activity and ensure the learning is appropriate both for the individual and the organization.

•••• Why Management Development? ••••

A question which needs to be answered at the outset of this book is why management development is chosen as the topic. This question can be posed in one of two ways. First, we could ask why not management education, or management training? 'Management education' is a term usually reserved for that type of learning that takes place in a structured, formal, institutional framework, such as a university or college (Deloitte et al., 1989). It often involves working towards the achievement of certain qualifications, for example honours degrees or MBAs, and may be taken by those without any prior experience. It is usually dominated by learning away from the workplace, decontextualized learning in the classroom, and places a great emphasis on intellectual problem solving and conceptual understanding. For our purposes this was too narrow a framework, as we also wanted to include the informal and on-the-job aspects of learning. 'Management training', on the other hand, has in the past referred to vocational-oriented education, or hands-on skill development where skills are developed through practice which is guided by formal structured means. Management development may include one or both of these, but is used more comprehensively to encapsulate all types of learning which enable an individual to develop their skills and understanding to meet current and future organizational needs.

In reality, the boundaries between management education, training and development are quite fluid. Changes are occuring and these definitions are no longer as discrete as they may once have been. Management education is now more often than not linked to management development where, for example, a junior manager may take a part-time MBA at university but one which requires considerable contact with their work environment through project work, as described in chapter 8. Likewise, management training is no longer seen as the lower-status end of the educational system where practice is taught rather than theory. Instead, it is seen as one string in the bow of management development which can be taught alongside management education.

The second question begging to be asked is why we inserted the word 'management'; why not human resource development, organizational development or self-development? 'Organizational development' tends to emphasize the needs of an organization to grow and change, and 'self-development' focuses on ways in which an individual can help themselves to grow and change in ways which are of benefit to their own career aspirations. Management development in a sense bridges and acts as a nexus between the two (see table 1.1, figure 1.1). It has the twin aims of developing the individual for their own and the organization's requirements, in line with Burgoyne's (1988) quote above; it is 'the management of managerial careers in an organizational context'. We have chosen the title of management development for this book because of its inclusiveness and its place at the crossroads of organizational development and self-development, and of education and training.

More difficult to answer is the more political question: why focus on management development at a time when layers of management are being removed from organizations, and 'managerial' decisions are being supposedly pushed down to the front line? One criticism here is whether there is such a thing as management development any more that is distinct from 'human resource development'? Our answer to this is threefold. First, there are still significant numbers of people viewing

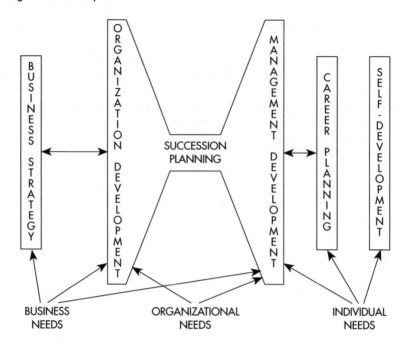

Figure 1.1 Management development in the context of organizational and self-development

themselves as 'managers', as evidenced by the membership of management institutions such as the British Institute of Management and the policies pursued by such organizations as the Management Charter Initiative (MCI) and the Institute for Personnel and Development (IPD). These institutions continue to call for more emphasis on management development. Second, any pushing of managerial decision making down the line does not remove 'management', it merely expands the numbers of people involved in this activity. Although the managerial capacity of an organization is more diffuse, it is none the less essential to achieving strategic objectives. These changes can be seen in a historical context as being developments in the 'profession' of management. This started with scientific management in the style of Taylorism, bureaucratic management epitomized by the work of Fayol and others, with the centralization of management supported by computer technology and large transnational corporations, and was superseded by various forms of the decentralization of management, for example in strategic business units, and by the introduction of the internal market and self-managed units in the public sector, and by the expansion of small businesses in the private sector. The widening of the management franchise in the 1980s and 1990s as more people are viewed as engaging in 'management', along with moves to professionalize management, has led to a greater, not lesser, requirement for a book on management development.

Third, although there is a significant overlap between management development and human resource development, both contain activities which exclude the other.

For example, human resource development may include greater specialist and technical skill development, such as in customer care, and in functional skills such as sales, marketing and finance. It also includes a wide range of behavioural and attitudinal change and organizational development. Management development may place more emphasis on decision making and activity at the strategic level, such as in top team development. However, the overlap includes areas such as the use of competence frameworks, and appraisal, coaching and team-building skills.

•••• The Current Context for Management Development ••••

There are a number of changes in the economy which have reinforced the value of management development, although there are also conflicting forces. First, there are changes in the nature and composition of management. In 1992 the Institute of Management decided to review progress in management education, training and development since the major reports by Constable and McCormick (1987) and Handy (1988) (discussed in chapter 9), and they set up a working party under the leadership of Professor Tom Cannon. The Cannon Working Party Report *Management Development for the Millenium* (Cannon, 1994) drawing on published quantitative data and qualitative data drawn from semi-structured interviews of senior managers responsible in a quota sample of 41 firms, identified a number of contextual factors which are changing and affect the number of managers in existence. They argue that the managerial pool is shrinking since Handy's (1988) research from about 3 million down to about 2.25 million as a result of the downsizing and delayering activities in the corporate sector already mentioned. However, others, such as Bevan et al. (1995), argue using projections made on some earlier labour-force surveys, that employment is growing within the corporate managerial and administrative categories at a rate of about 2.7 per cent per annum, with a growth rate for managers and proprietors being about 1.25 per cent, resulting in about 5 million people in both categories by the year 2000.

Clearly there are huge contradictions in the data as to whether the number of managers is increasing or decreasing, and how many there are. This is partly due to the fact that there are conflicting forces at large. On the one hand, many organizations are downsizing, rightsizing, delayering and cutting back on their managerial head-count. For example National Power alone reduced its head-count from 17,000 in 1989 to 5,300 in 1994 (Ebadan and Winstanley, 1997). However to retain competitiveness they still need to develop those that are left, but for what? As fewer organizations offer permanent job security and as we are told that organizations of the future will be 'shamrock-shaped' networks of self-employed and short-term periphery with a very small core if one at all (Handy 1989), then how meaningful is it to talk of management development? The part of the workforce which is downsized will not want firm-specific skills, and in any case the organization does not necessarily want to develop staff to go and work for their competitor; and those that are left within the organization have little hope of climbing a ladder up the managerial hierarchy, as this no longer exists. So what are we developing these managers for? Is it for employability, or for horizontal development and flexibility?

Although downsizing and delayering may mean fewer middle managers, there has been a growth in team leadership roles at such organizations, and thus there is the counter-argument that there are pressures for growth in managers with greater requirement for management development. For example, there has been a growth in the numbers of self-employed of about 6 per cent per annum resulting in a population of about 2.9 million, and of small business managers. The numbers of managers in the public sector have grown to over 50 per cent of the total, and also the number of professionals entering management has increased, particularly in the public sector, such as in the National Health Service and education. Many people have had their jobs retitled and reframed as managerial ones, such as ward sisters becoming nurse managers and lead consultants becoming clinical directors.

There are also discrepancies in the figures as a result of whom we include in our category of managers, and whether it includes team leaders, administrators, small business proprietors and the self-employed, and whether figures are based on managers employed or in the labour market.

Whatever our conclusions on the size and composition of the managerial labour force, there are other reasons for the increasing value placed on management development. Certainly the Government have asserted its importance, not least through the development of national management competences and standards for junior and intermediate and now also for senior managers, via the Management Charter Initiative (MCI). The introduction of Investors in People, sponsored business links, and in the introduction of the broader qualification framework General National Vocational Qualifications (GNVQs) further illustrates this. The White Paper *Competitiveness – Helping Business to Win* (HMSO, 1994) emphasized the importance of management development in improving the quality of UK managers. It identified the role of the Government as being to identify and disseminate best management practice and encourage information sharing and cross-fertilization, as well as to encourage companies to improve managements' skill base and provide effective access to a wide range of business services.

Although there are huge differences between the movements identified above, and work on learning organizations, they all have one thing in common: the belief that managers should be encouraged to take responsibility for their own development, that organizations should provide a framework in which managers can learn in a participative and relevant way through applying knowledge to practice and demon-strating competence in the workplace, as discussed further in chapter 4. As we noted earlier, there is increasing interest in highlighting the organization as a learning environment, with learning being seen as a more integral part of organizational activity rather than just a support function.

There are also changes which have occurred and others projected which directly affect both the modes of delivering management development and the skills needed to be developed. Cannon (1994), when reviewing existing changes to the delivery of management education, identified four types of provider – academic, organizational, consultancy and institutional (i.e. professional associations) – and suggested there had been the following changes:

- an increase in academic provision, with a massive increase in MBAs, about 85 per cent of which are part time or distance learning;
- persistence of undergraduate business education as an initial qualification (despite Constable and McCormick's (1989) reservations);
- an increase in organizational provision, but mainly in large firms, with continuing under-provision for small and medium-sized enterprises, for the self-employed, women, older workers and ethnic minorities;
- increased use of independent training organizations for in-company development, with less use of business schools for this, and limited progress on accreditation of in-company management development (e.g. for MBAs);
- a rapid increase in market share by consultancies, with an estimated 12,000 providers;
- variable provision of management development by professional institutions.

In terms of the changing skills required through management development, we can question what skills and competencies should we be teaching the managers of the future? Taylor's (1994) working party, set up by the Institute of Management, looked to the future and identified strategic thinking, responding to and managing change, and orientation towards quality and customers as priority skills for development for the future, and Bevan et al. (1995) identify a number of future management skill needs concerned with the changing business environment, emerging management roles and skill implications (see table 1.2 for details).

Again, the advice over future skill needs is conflicting, and demonstrates the lack of utility of some aggregated survey data. As Taylor (1994) comments, it is not possible to provide a comprehensive list or template to suit all managers, as the nature of environmental compexity means that the skill needs are very varied.

The reports over the changing nature of management development and its context also point to a number of problems and challenges for management development. An under-resourcing of management development in most organizations, a shortage of suitable qualified academic staff, lack of integration between organizational and academic provision, weak links between individual investment in management development and promotion and reward strategies, (Cannon 1994); problems dealing with ongoing issues such as contracting out, empowerment and delayering, and the need for individuals to take more responsibility for their own development (Taylor, 1994). Watson (1994) identifies six main challenges for the future.

Table 1.2 Future management skill needs

Changing business environment	Emerging management roles	Skill implications
Globalization	Coach and counsellor	Project management
Technical change	Team builder	Staff development
Business unit focus	Assessor	IT management
Stakeholder focus	Leader	Customer orientation
Change management	Project manager	Languages
		Process improvement

Source: Bevan et al, 1995 p.12

(1) Organizations still need to be educated to recognize that investment in management development contributes directly to long-term competitiveness.
(2) Managers need to commit themselves to life-long learning.
(3) Senior managers need to provide commitment and leadership.
(4) Standards and qualifications need to be transferable and widely acceptable.
(5) Providers need to recognize and respond to diverse training and development needs of users.
(6) We need a more coherent infrastructure for management development.

This boils down to two main points: ensuring the commitment and motivation for learning of those involved, organizations and individuals alike (not an easy task); and having flexibility to meet specific needs. This requires having available appropriate tools for identifying the needs of the particular situation, as well as integrating this with the diverse needs and capabilities of those in the process. Organizations are required to go beyond providing standardized solutions to the diverse problems and situations faced by individual managers. The approach we develop through the ensuing chapters is aimed at identifying specific needs in context. In particular, chapter 2 focuses on identifying the strategic needs of the organization and chapter 3 the various needs of the individual.

In the current context, management development has to be strategic and flexible, and needs to be linked with the objectives of the organization and the individual. To borrow Lawrence and Lorsch's (1967) terminology, we believe both **integration** and **differentiation** are issues which need to be tackled in strategic management development (see table 1.3), and this creates many contradictions which are illuminated in the ensuing chapters.

Table 1.3 Strategic management development: integration and differentiation

Integration	Differentiation
Compatibility with organizational development	Compatibility with self-development
Compatibility with the aims and objectives of business strategy	Compatibility with people's future careers
Proactive; forward looking and forward planning from top	Left to individual initiative, in terms of the what and how
Uniformity of objectives	Enabling choice to suit career, individual's personality and own situation and learning style
Top down	Bottom up

Both integration and differentiation are needed for the development to be fully strategic.

•••• Overview of Chapters ••••

Part I of the book focuses on the purpose and *raison d'être* of management development. This introductory chapter locates management development within a changing context, and debates over changes in managerial work, and has explored its links with concepts such as management education, management training, human resource develoment, organizational development and self-development.

Chapter 2 examines the importance of management development and its fit with business strategy, suggests that there is a huge gap between theory and practice, and questions the feasibility and desirability of many of the underlying assumptions of the models. Although there are good reasons for it to be part of a strategic armoury, there are also creative tensions between integration and differentiation, cohesion and fragmentation, formality and informality, and, of course, between the strategic organizational needs and an individual's own desires for self-development. In particular, the need for formality is questioned, and the difficulties of providing a close fit with business strategy are raised. The assumptions made over business strategy may be flawed, with over-emphasis on clear and detailed plans to which management development can be hitched. In view of this discussion, we examine ways in which management development can be evaluated in terms of its contribution.

Where chapter 2 focuses on the link between management development and business strategy, chapter 3 moves to the individual level, to look at the connection between management development and individual careers. We examine the management careers literature and explore the changes taking place and their impact on the design of management development.

Part II of the book is concerned with identifying and diagnosing development needs. Chapter 4 locates development needs within the context of managerial roles and competencies, and explores the changing nature of managerial work. In chapter 5 methodologies are examined which have been used to identify managerial roles and competencies to see how these can be identified as a basis of development. Methods for job analysis are discussed in more detail, and we pose the problem that it is much harder to identify future than current roles and jobs. Realistically, when identifying development needs, the individual as well as the role is assessed, and a form of gap analysis is required to clarify what development needs to take place. Chapter 6 therefore examines the tools available to identify individual learning needs and tools which provide insight into a person, their current skills and qualities. We tackle the thorny questions of reliability and validity of methods and outline the recent debates which have flared up on these issues.

Part III of the book is concerned with the availability of different management development interventions and the desirability and problems with each for different uses. Chapter 7 places these in the learning context and examines the theories surrounding the learning process. Chapter 8 focuses on those areas and methods traditionally associated with mangement develoment, the formal and off-the-job approaches. It is suggested that contrary to various obituaries written for them, these methods are alive and kicking, with management qualifications in particular becoming the cash-cow of many universities. Chapter 9 explores the more recent fads for work-related learning and those methods thought to be particularly successful and valid, particularly when research is conducted comparing UK approaches with those which are held up as shining examples elsewhere.

Part IV of the book turns to management develoment for various contexts and to meet specific development needs. Chapter 10 examines the difficult role of professionals in management, the problems they face balancing professional and managerial objectives, and the constraints existing for anyone wishing to design development programmes targeted at them. Chapter 11 focuses on women, and discusses the difficulties women face in management and in breaking the 'glass ceiling'. The role of management development in tackling some of these equal opportunity issues, and in helping women to be effective in management, is discussed. Chapter 12 looks at the issues involved in developing international managers and those methods particularly suited to supporting cross-national development. Chapter 13 hones in more closely on the top team, and the various development needs of chairmen and women, chief executives, non-executive directors and senior directors.

EXERCISE

Write down your own preferred definition of management development. Does it relate to the purposes, processes or prerequisities of management development, or all three? Defend your definition by explaining why it is useful.

•••• References ••••

Ackroyd, S. and Crowdy, P. A. 1990: Can culture be managed? Working with Raw Material: the case of English slaughtermen. *Personnel Review*, 19, 5, pp. 3–13.

Bailyn, L. 1993: Patterned chaos in human resource management. *MIT Sloan Management Review*, Winter, pp. 77–83.

Bass, B. M. and Aviolo, B. 1993: *Improving Organizational Effectiveness Through Transformational Leadership*. Thousand Oaks, CA: Sage Publications.

Bevan, S., Toye, J. and Frost, D. 1995: *Managers for the Millenium*. IES Report No. 285, Brighton: Institute of Employment Studies.

Burgoyne, J. 1988: Management development for the individual and the organisation. *Personnel Management*, June, pp. 40–4.

Cannon, T. 1994: *Management Development for the Millenium*. Canon Working Party Report: Progress and Change 1987–1994, Corby: Institute of Management.

Constable, J. and McCormick, R. 1989: *The Making of British Managers*. London: British Institute of Management/Confederation of British Industry.

Deloitte, Haskins and Sells/Training Agency, 1989: *Management Challenge for the 1990s*, Sheffield: Training Agency.

Drucker, P. 1969: *The Age of Discontinuity*. New York: Harper and Row.

Ebadan, G. and Winstanley, D. 1997: Downsizing, delayering and careers: the survivors' perspective. *Human Resource Management Journal* 7, 1, pp. 79–91.

Fitzgerald, T. H. 1988: Can change in culture really be managed? *Organizational Dynamics*, 17, 2, pp. 5–15.

Fonda, N. 1989: Management development: the missing link in sustained business performance. *Personnel Management*, December, pp. 50–3.

Garratt, R. 1987: *The Learning Organization*. London: Fontana.

Government White Paper 1994: *Competitiveness: Helping Business to Win*. London: HMSO.

Handy, C. 1988: *Making Managers*. London: Pitman.

Handy, C. 1989: *The Age of Unreason*. London: Business Books.

Harrison, R. 1995: *Training and Development*. London: Institute of Personnel and Development.

Herriot, P. and Pemberton, C. 1995: *New Deals: the revolution in managerial careers*. New York: John Wiley.

Lawrence, P. R. and Lorsch, J. W. 1967: *Organization and Environment*. Boston, MA: Harvard University Press.

Margerison, C. 1991: *Making Management Development Work*. Maidenhead: McGraw-Hill.

Mumford, A. 1989: *Management Development: strategies for action*. London: Institute of Personnel and Development.

Pedler, M., Burgoyne, J. and Boydell, T. 1991: *The Learning Company*. Maidenhead: McGraw-Hill.

Schon, D. 1971: *Beyond the Stable State*. London: Random House.

Schroder, H. 1989: *Managerial Competence: the key to excellence*. Iowa: Kendall Hunt.

Senge, P. 1990: *The Fifth Discipline: the art and practice of the learning organization*. New York: Doubleday.

Storey, J. 1989: Management development: a literature review and implications for future research: part 1: conceptualisations and practices *Personnel Review*, 18, 6, p. 5.

Storey, J. 1994: Management development. In Sisson, K. (ed.), *Personnel Management*, 2nd edn, Oxford: Blackwell.

Taylor Report 1994: *The Way Ahead 1994–2001* report of the Taylor working party, Corby: Institute of Management.

Tichy, N. 1993: Revolutionize your company. *Fortune*, 13 December, pp. 114–18.

Tichy, N. and Devanna, M. A. 1986: *Transformational Leadership*. New York: Wiley.

Training Services Agency 1977: *Glossary of Training Terms*. London: Manpower Services Commission.

Watson, T. 1994: *In Search of Management: culture, chaos and control in managerial work*. London: Routledge.

Wheatley, M. 1993: *Leadership and the New Science*. San Francisco: Berrett-Koehler.

Willmott, H. 1993: Strength is ignorance, slavery is freedom: managing culture in modern organizations. *Journal of Management Studies*, 30, 4, pp. 515–52.

Woodall, J. 1996: Managing culture change: can it ever be ethical?. *Personnel Review*, 25, 6, pp. 26–40.

CHAPTER 2

Management Development and Organizational Strategy: Justifying and Evaluating the Business Focus

···· Introduction ····

Making the business case for human resource management in general, and management development in particular, often sounds like common sense. Arguing that 'people are the key to the business' and so it is logical to invest in the development of managers, does not get us very far. Yet it is intuitively obvious that the way in which managers are developed within an organization could be central to corporate success. What is needed is some careful analysis and practical suggestions for ensuring that management development relates to organizational strategy. In this chapter we will explore the ways in which management development might fit business strategy, and also outline approaches to auditing and evaluating the appropriateness of this 'fit'.

···· Learning Objectives ····

After reading this chapter you should be able to:

- evaluate the relationship between models of management development and models of corporate strategy;
- identify the difficulties encountered in creating strategic management development for diversified organizations and small businesses;
- identify and critically evaluate at least four methods for evaluating and auditing the strategic 'fit' of management development;
- design a framework for auditing management development in a specific organizational context which takes account of the required purpose, scope and criteria for the audit.

•••• Management Development: the Link with Organizational •••• and National Economic Performance

From time to time, over the last 50 years, UK Government policy makers have turned their attention to the 'making' of managers. In contrast to other advanced industrialized countries such as the USA, Germany and France, until 1945 training for managerial work was not taken seriously (Sadler and Barham, 1988). Most companies were owner-managed, and so managerial succession planning was a family affair. Also, the anti-industrial culture and social snobbery about work in 'trade' as opposed to the professions, meant that very few university graduates were attracted to managerial jobs. There was a great deal of evidence to suggest that a public school education or professional qualification in accountancy were a better passport to entry into senior management positions. This disregard for the benefits of higher education meant that the prevailing norm was to praise the virtues of the self-made man (not woman) who made his own way by means of natural ability or personal connection to managerial office.

After 1945, things started to change. There was a growing awareness that investment in higher education in general, and in management education and training in particular, were associated with successful national economic perform- ance. But until the first major inquiry resulting in the report of the Franks Committee in 1962 (Sadler and Barham, 1988), there was very little publicly provided management education and training, and British universities continued to resist the creation of their own business schools on the grounds that business education was insufficiently academic a subject. This obstacle was overcome only with the creation of new universities and polytechnics, after the mid 1960s. Very little undergraduate business education was ever provided by the older universities.

Concern about the quality of management education and training persisted throughout the 1970s, with strong division between those who believed there was a place for management education, training and development within higher education, and those who felt that company-based learning was the most valid. This concern was further fuelled by the onset of economic recession in the 1980s. The UK Government commissioned a number of reports, including *Competence and Com- petition* (IMS, NEDC/MSC, 1984), *A Challenge to Complacency* (Coopers and Lybrand and Associates, MSC/NEDO, 1985), Constable and McCormick (1987), Handy (1988), Handy et al. (1987), Mangham and Silver (1986). Charles Handy's (1987) report made the greatest impact because he presented evidence that compared UK management education and training unfavourably with its major industrial competitors (USA, Japan, Germany and France). One note which particularly struck home was his pithy comment that the British approach to management development is like giving driving lessons as a reward for passing the driving test – and that what is provided is generally 'too little, too late, for too few'. These reports suggested that management development activity was largely peripheral and irrelevant to British organizations and needed to be more grounded in what managers need to know and the development of what has come to be known as 'managerial competence' (see chapter 4).

Over the last ten years, then, the contribution of management development to organizational and national economic performance has been reaffirmed (Training Agency and Deloitte, Haskins and Sells, 1989), and competence-based standards for management education and training have emerged from the Management Charter Initiative (see chapter 4). The significance of management development to individual business and overall national economic performance has been recognized for a long time. Successive government-sponsored investigations have diagnosed the short-comings of management education and training, and of recommended solutions, and in turn have subsequently subjected these solutions to a trenchant critique. From the 1940s until the 1980s and the publication of the reports mentioned above the focus has been on the volume and type of management development activities. However, at the end of the 1980s research into company practice has revealed that neither the volume nor the quality of management development activity itself is as important as the strategic fit with the organization's overall business strategy (Institute of Management, 1994).

•••• Management Development and Strategic Fit: a Critique ••••

The notion of strategic human resource management that complements an organization's corporate strategy was developed in the 1980s and has influenced thinking about management development. However, the gap between rhetoric and reality has been wide. Research carried out by Ashridge Management College (Barham et al., 1988) with leading-edge companies found out that for the majority, management development policy and practice was 'fragmented'. In a number of other organizations it was, at best, 'formalized', but it was seldom, if ever, 'focused'. The inference was that strategic business-led management development should always be focused and integrated with the rest of human resource policy, and that organizations that did not aspire to this could be neither effective nor efficient in their use of human resources.

The Ashridge model (exhibit 2.1) is particularly interesting for what it has to say about both the content of management development programmes and the way in which they are managed. In the case of fragmented management development, its very *ad hoc* nature means that it is difficult to justify as an investment as opposed to a cost (albeit necessarily incurred), and that its status in the organization is low in the eyes of practically everyone except the person in charge of management develop-ment, who themselves holds a peripheral position in the business.

However, the desire to raise the status of management development too often results in a formalized solution. This was often encountered in the traditional bureaucratic organizations found in both the public and private sectors. A status hierarchy and division of labour in the management development team mirrored the organizational structure. Typically it would be headed by a management develop-ment manager with assistants and specialists in management development. The

•••• Exhibit 2.1 ••••
The Ashridge Model: the role of training and development

1 The fragmented approach

- Training is not linked to organizational goals
- Training is perceived as a luxury or a waste of time
- Approach to training is non-systematic
- Training is directive
- Training is carried out by trainers
- Training takes place in the training department
- Emphasis on knowledge-based courses
- The focus on training (a discontinuous process) rather than development (a continuous process)

2 The formalized approach

- Training becomes linked to human resource (HR) needs
- Training becomes systematic by linking it to an appraisal system
- The emphasis is still on knowledge-based courses but the focus of the course broadens, with greater emphasis on skill-based courses
- The link which is made between training and HR needs encourages organizations to adopt a more developmental approach
- Training is carried out by trainers, but the range of skill demands placed on a trainer develops with the new breadth of courses offered
- Line managers become involved in training and development through their role as appraisers
- Pre- and post-course activities attempt to facilitate the transfer of off-the-job learning
- Training is carried out off the job, but through career development the value of on-the-job learning gains formal recognition
- There is more concern to link a programme of training to individual needs

3 The focused approach

- Training and development and continuous learning by individuals is perceived as a necessity for organizational survival in a rapidly changing business environment
- Training is regarded as a competitive weapon
- Learning is linked to organizational strategy and to individual goals
- The emphasis is on-the-job development so that learning becomes a totally continuous activity
- Specialist training courses are available across the knowledge/skills/value spectrum
- Self-selection for training courses
- Training is generally non-directive, unless knowledge-based
- New forms of training activity are utilized, e.g. open and distance learning packages, self-development programmes, etc.
- More concern to measure effectiveness of training and development
- Main responsibility for training rests with line management
- Trainers adopt a wider role
- New emphasis on learning as a process
- Tolerance of some failure as part of the learning process

Source: Barham et al., 1988.

procedures and routines of everyday organizational life were reflected in the policies, plans and range of management development solutions offered. While on the surface it seemed very systematic, it was so easy for the content of management development to become quite divorced from the strategic needs of the business and for those who enrolled, not to be those that needed it most. This is most often seen in organizations that operate a menu-driven system of generic management training courses for which departments are invited to nominate participants. It frequently results in the wrong people attending a course for the wrong motives.

Hence, the virtues of focused management development which is linked both to overall business and human resource strategy, and individual career development. This usually involves a departure from hierarchical departments of management development specialists to more flexible teams of highly qualified advisors who act as internal consultants and whose main task is to review management development needs continuously and to identify appropriate solutions. With focused management development, the actual delivery of management development is as likely to be subcontracted to outside organizations as delivered in-house. The main instrument for delivering in-house management development is likely to be the line manager or project manager who is entrusted with analysing development needs and where possible meeting them through everyday work situations. At the same time the individual participant is also a key stakeholder in the process by means of the personal development plan they 'own'.

This position was echoed by Burgoyne (1988) who argued that it was both possible and desirable for organizations to move up a ladder of organizational 'maturity' in management development, and that it was possible to integrate both organizational and individual needs (see table 2.1).

Both of these models assume that organizations are able to articulate a clear strategic vision. On this basis management development can both derive from and feed into organizational strategy: it can be both a tool for implementation, and an engine to drive the change. The practical way of achieving this is to conduct some sort of gap analysis of the difference between current individual capacity and organizational needs. This would enable a plan to be drawn up based on an appropriate mix of internally and externally sourced management development activities, providing both on- and off-the-job development. However, both models are based on the experience of large, relatively stable corporate-sector organizations, and it is questionable as to how universally applicable they are. In the 1990s, the reduction in managerial job security, associated with corporate downsizing and delayering, and talk of new psychological contracts centred around a guarantee of employability rather than a job for life (see chapter 3), mean that for many individual managers the possession of a transferable management qualification such as a DMS (Diploma in Management Studies) or an MBA is of greater personal worth than 'focused', work-related development opportunities within the organization (see chapter 8).

Obtaining a close fit between management development and human resource and business strategy is also easier said than done – especially given the variety of organizational forms that exist in the business world. It is easiest to achieve in unitary, functionally organized bureaucracies. However, this is no longer the norm

Table 2.1 Levels of maturity of organizational management development

1 No systematic management development	No systematic or deliberate management development in structural or developmental sense. Total reliance on natural, *laissez-faire*, uncontrived processes of management development
2 Isolated tactical management development	There are isolated and *ad hoc* tactical management development activities, of either structural or development kinds, or both, in response to local problems, crises, or sporadically identified general problems
3 Integrated and co-ordinated structural and development tactics	The specific management development tactics which impinge directly on the individual manager, of career structure management, and of assisting learning, are integrated and co-ordinated
4 A management strategy to implement corporate policy	A management development strategy plays its part in implementing corporate policies through managerial human resource planning, and providing a strategic framework and direction for the tactics of career structure management and of learning, education and training
5 Management development strategy input to corporate policy formation	Management development processes feed information into corporate policy decision-making processes on the organization's managerial assets, strengths, weaknesses and potential, and contribute to the forecasting and analysis of the manageability of proposed projects, ventures, changes
6 Strategic development of the management of corporate policy	Management development processes enhance the nature and quality of corporate policy-forming processes, which they also inform and help implement

Source: Burgoyne, 1988

for organizational structure, and where functional bureaucracies existed, as in the public utilities, the NHS and local government, the advent of privatization and internal markets has brought greater diversification. Multidivisional matrix manage-ment structures are now more the norm, and the diversification, divisionalization, decentralization and divestment associated with this makes a close strategic fit with management development very difficult (Purcell and Ahlstrand, 1994). In these organizations human resource management responsibility is more often than not located below even the divisional level, in the strategic business unit, and is thus far removed from the sight of corporate strategists. In these circumstances, the implementation of a common management development strategy or achievement of coherence among different business unit policies may be difficult. The modern multidivisional organization may well be creating obstacles to the very goal it is seeking to achieve: focused management development. Tension often arises between the needs for management development identified by the strategic business unit, and those identified at divisional or corporate level. In this case a coherent corporate management development strategy may not be a realistic goal. Similar problems may be encountered in organizations assuming new structures, such as networks.

The structural impediments to achieving a close fit between management development and organizational business strategy are compounded by the nature of corporate strategy itself and how it is understood by corporate strategists as opposed to human resource managers. Starting from the corporate strategy perspective, it has been argued that the focus and methodology of business strategy in the corporate sector has undergone a change in response to business environment pressures. The transition from stability and growth in the 1960s through the knock-on effects of the energy crisis in the 1970s to cutback and rationalization in the 1980s have been paralleled by a transition in corporate management practice from long-range planning to strategic planning, and eventually strategic management (Taylor, 1986). Methodologies have changed from long-range forecasting and, later, scenario and portfolio planning to a total business approach to strategy formulation and implementation. Today, clear detailed plans for the different products in the business portfolio, let alone for the whole business, are rare. The talk is currently about declaring a broad 'strategic intent' and viewing strategy as an 'emergent' process (Mintzberg, 1987).

For example, Whittington (1993) identifies four different theories of strategy along two axes, relating to its objectives and outcomes and whether they are profit maximizing or pluralistic, and to processes and whether they are deliberate or emergent. The four perspectives are 'classical' (which sees strategy as deliberate with profit-maximizing objectives), 'evolutionary' (which sees strategy as emergent, and with profit-maximizing objectives), 'processual' (which sees strategy as emergent, but with pluralistic objectives), and 'systemic' (which sees strategy as deliberate but with pluralistic objectives).

Thus it can be very difficult for human resource specialists to make sense of what is understood by corporate strategy in practice, and their grasp of approaches tends to lag well behind current understandings. The academic literature on strategic human resource management abounds with efforts to relate human resource strategy to outdated concepts of business strategy that one suspects were not widely nor consciously adopted. For example, Miles and Snow (1984) identify three basic types of strategic behaviour and supporting organizational characteristics: 'defender', 'prospector' and 'analyser'. However, even though they spend a great deal of thought envisioning the human resource demands of each strategy, their very assumption that strategy is deliberately formulated into such generic, relatively unchanging types poses practical problems for relating human resource management policies to strategic requirements in a dynamic business world.

The same point applies to the use of the Boston Consulting Groups's product portfolio planning growth share matrix to identify which employees should receive development (Storey, 1989). The classification of employees as 'workhorses', 'stars', 'deadwood' or 'problems' does not take us far along the road of strategic decision making. It also perpetuates the elitist view of management development being about 'polishing stars' which the Handy Report (see Handy et al., 1987; Handy, 1988) so eschewed in the traditional British model. Nor are organizations likely to adopt generic strategies 'off the shelf' (as suggested by Porter, 1985), be it cost minimization, diversification or the pursuit of quality. Similarly, the distinction between a 'first-order strategy' relating to decisions on the scope and range of activities, and 'second-order strategy' (the type of interrelationships and control systems employed by the corporate centre, or the distinction between long-term, mid-term and operational strategies corresponding to each level of the multi-divisional corporation) still perceives corporate strategy as a rigid system of classification (Miller, 1987; Purcell, 1989; Purcell, 1995). (See figure 2.1.)

The recent switch of thinking in corporate strategy has moved towards a 'resource' view of strategy. The central tenet of this view is that for sustainable competitive advantage (doing better than your competitors over the long run) the firm must be able to have resources and utilize them in ways that are rare and cannot be copied. Thus the possibility of sustained competitive advantage is seen to lie in the strength of intangible resources, which are most often people. The best-known exponents of this view are Hamel and Prahalad (1991) and Prahalad and Hamel (1990) who argue for a corporate strategic process centred around the identification and development of 'core competencies'. Core competencies are essentially strategic resources and should be distinguished from the more common use of competency by HRD specialists (see chapter 4). They are more than just a bundle of skills and technologies, but are integrated in some way to deliver a customer benefit that is of unique and sustainable value to the organization. Examples of these could be speed of technical innovation, project management, logistics or management development.

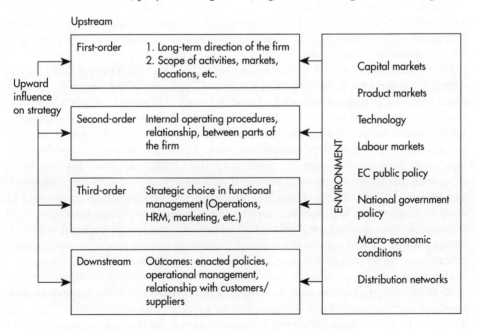

Figure 2.1 Three levels of strategic decision making
Source: Purcell and Ahlstrand, 1994, by kind permission of Oxford University Press

Thus management development may constitute or make up part of a core competency or help to sustain a core competency that applies across strategic business units. It may be one of a set of other resources that give an organization a corporate as opposed to a product-based competitive advantage. This has interesting implications for ensuring a fit between management development and organizational strategy, as it will usually involve identifying a distinctive group of employees whose development will constitute the intangible strength. However, as yet there is very little evidence of organizations intentionally identifying a human resource component as a core competency.

•••• Meeting Business Needs Outside the Large •••• Corporate Sector

Much of the academic discussion about strategic human resource management has stopped with the multidivisional corporation, and research still lags behind other organizational developments. Yet management gurus (Drucker, 1988, Handy, 1984; 1994; Quinn, 1992) have enthusiastically heralded the appearance of even more fluid organizational structures: the 'contractual' (or 'network'), 'federal' and 'information-based' organizations. While much of this has yet to withstand more sober academic scrutiny, ensuring that management development fits these newer, flatter, more flexible structures can be even more challenging than in the multidivisional corporation. For example, how is it possible to ensure that a common management development practice reaches the remote or outsourced functions in a 'network' or that managers are 'empowered' through development to enable them to participate in cross-functional team working?

Finally, in discussion of the link between management development and business strategy, it is too easy to overlook the fact that 97 per cent of UK businesses employ fewer than 20 people and in 1989 these firms accounted for 35 per cent of all employment outside central and local government (Department of Employment, 1993). Many managers in these small businesses will be in even greater need of management development in comparison with their counterparts in the corporate sector. It is also important to remember that many of these are acting as subcontractors to larger organizations, and therefore their management capability is seen as crucial to the success of their corporate clients. It is a mistake to assume that small business is a fairly homogeneous category in respect of human resource as well as business concerns (Abbott, 1995). Many staff are already highly qualified (e.g. in design, marketing and advertising), while in other occupations, such as construction or catering, those in small business are not likely to have had prior technical or professional training.

Nonetheless, small businesses do tend to exhibit some common features in their approach to human resource management in general (Vickerstaff, 1991). They are less likely to have a business plan and make provision for training budgets. Human resource policy and practice in general is likely to be conducted in an informal and *ad hoc* manner. The cost of hiring a human resource professional means that very often the responsibility is spread between the owner–manager and another manager, neither of whom are likely to have an HR background and who may well be resistant to advice on 'good practice'. It is thus understandable that most management development in small firms occurs experientially – people often learn on the job without necessarily having access to a coach or mentor within the organization.

However, management development in small businesses is of great strategic significance for a number of reasons. When they start to grow, they are most likely to recruit managerial talent from the external labour market. These are often people with existing functional or technical skills. However, in time, many growing small businesses need to think about succession planning, to develop additional managerial talent, often from people in supervisory-level positions. In turn, retention and career development of managerial talent in the small business is particularly problematic. If the business is in a niche market, the risk that the manager may leave and set up a rival business is a major concern. The problem of poaching as a disincentive to development is thus magnified in the small business. Finally, while most development will be experiential and work related, management education can be particularly attractive to the small business manager. It can be a valuable means of networking and benchmarking against best practice which takes small business managers out of the rather insular environment in which they operate.

Returning to the theme outlined at the start of this chapter, achieving business-focused management development is in practice a difficult task for which there are few clear guidelines to follow. What is understood by strategy and the process by which it is developed and implemented is an important starting-point for anyone responsible for management development. At the same time, it is essential to understand the constraints of organizational type, and in particular those of multidivisional and network or federal structures, as well as the much more diverse world of small business. Yet, all of the preceding discussion in this chapter has assumed that it is self-evident that management development should be strongly related to business strategy. Perhaps, then, this assumption needs to be challenged and the question posed: 'how does management development add value to the business?'

•••• Demonstrating that Management Development Adds •••• Value to the Business: Evaluation

In the contemporary organizational context human resource professionals are continually having to collect and analyse data to prove that human resource management adds value to the business. There has been an upsurge of interest in the skills of human resource auditing and evaluation. While a great deal has been written on the evaluation of training, this has usually been done in terms of the training system being envisioned as a closed cycle as illustrated in Bramley's systematic training cycle (Bramley 1991, p. 6). This cyclical trainer-centred model has become the dominant framework for evaluation via which the training intervention can be assessed at different levels.

- *Reactions* of participants immediately during and after the intervention
- *Learning* that takes place after the intervention, from the perspective of participants
- *Behaviour* of participants after the intervention as assessed by themselves and those for whom they work (and occasionally their direct reports)
- *Results* – the discernible impact on business performance

This is the standard model used by most professional trainers. However, despite its formal rigour, most of it is not easily applied to informal development activities and is more suited to assessing the reactions of participants during a formal training or education programme, and the subsequent transfer of learning to the workplace. Most traditional evaluation theory is difficult to apply to management development as it was developed mainly with task-specific craft and operative-level training. Given that managerial work is less task-specific, that managerial roles are contingent (see chapter 4) and that the distinction between learning and working is often quite blurred (see chapters 7 and 9), it is not surprising that the dominant approach focuses on process. Easterby-Smith (1986) led the way with his model (see exhibit 2.2).

Even so, Easterby-Smith's (1986) approach is still primarily geared to structured training and education events, and has been criticized for an over-focus on the procedures of development rather than the learning processes involved (Mumford, 1987). An alternative consultancy-based approach (Robinson and Robinson, 1989) has argued for a 'training for impact' approach which claims to:

- be driven by business needs;
- help the organization to achieve its goals;
- provide people with skills and knowledge needed to improve performance;
- assess the readiness of the work environment to support learning skills;
- achieve management acceptance of responsibility for a supportive work environment that encourages skill transfer;
- have measurable results that can be tracked.

This approach emphasizes **process** rather than **content** of training and development interventions. In many ways it is akin to Process Consultation (Schein, 1988), as the emphasis is on:

- the establishment of a close collaborative relationship between line manager and trainer at all stages on a consultant–client basis;
- building in analysis of participant performance effectiveness at early stages;
- feedback to line managers for joint interpretation and action planning with participants;
- joint identification of expected outcomes as the basis of reaction and learning evaluations and for establishing baseline information.

Only after these processes are in place is there any attempt to deliver a training or development intervention, followed by systematic evaluation against the expected outcomes and joint interpretation of the results and follow-up action needed. The Training for Impact model is presented in a flow diagram in figure 2.2. The action-orientation and general systems methodology of the Training for Impact model is

•••• Exhibit 2.2 ••••
Easterby-Smith's model of evaluation for management education, training and development

(1) Clarifying the purpose
- *Proving?* Demonstrating that the cost of delivering management development interventions were more than covered by additional contributions to business performance, or that the chosen interventions met pre-set objectives
- *Improving?* Establishing the ways in which the type and delivery of management development interventions might better meet individual manager and organizational needs
- *Learning?* Establishing who actually does take advantage of specific management development interventions, and their experience of them
- *Controlling?* Establishing that the management development activities have taken place in the planned manner

(2) Choosing the methodological approach
- *Scientific:* which tests hypotheses about what should happen by means of a controlled experiment
- *Systems:* which identifies the inputs and their relation to the way in which they were implemented to result in specific outcomes
- *Goal Free:* disregarding the ostensible aims and objectives of the programme and stakeholders, to establish what in practice these turned out to be.
- *Illuminative:* allowing the evaluation process to focus progressively upon interesting issues and practice, rather than just address preconceived criteria.
- *Responsive:* involving the various stakeholders in the evaluation process, by letting them set the agenda of what is to be evaluated.

(3) Adopting a framework (the CAIPO model)
Context – identifying the reason for the programme and stakeholders.
Administration – the mechanisms for nomination, selection and briefing of participants before the intervention, and the follow-up mechanisms afterwards.
Inputs – the contributions of various methods, techniques, and people.
Processes – the record of what happened, and the experiences of trainees and trainers.
Outcomes – the impact of the programme on participant perceptions, learning, behaviour, etc.
Data collection
   Ensuring that the methods and techniques capture information from those closest to the intervention.
Implementation
   Using methods to ensure commitment from appropriate stakeholders such as action plans, tasks forces etc.

Source: adapted and elaborated from Easterby-Smith, 1986

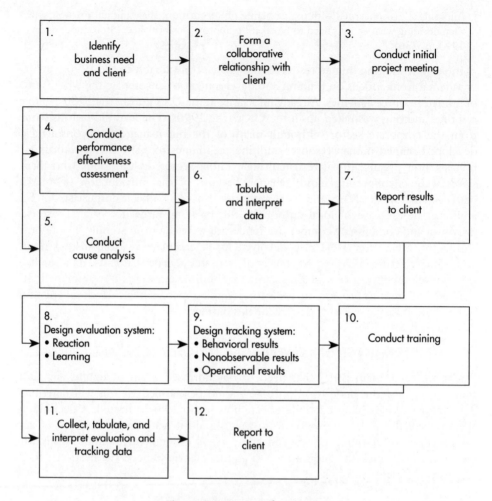

Figure 2.2 Training for impact
Source: Robinson and Robinson, 1989

very appealing. The involvement of several stakeholders makes individual follow-up and action planning, as well evaluation, more achievable.

•••• Demonstrating that Management Development Adds •••• Value to the Business: Auditing

Here we turn to the process of auditing management development. There is, admittedly, an overlap between the techniques used in both evaluation and auditing of management development, but the latter is more directly focused on business performance:

Auditing . . . is concerned with the gathering of information, analysing information, and then deciding what actions need to be taken to improve performance. (Storey and Sisson, 1993: p. 236).

Interest in auditing human resources has grown considerably in the 1990s, and has broadened from a focus on training and development to encompass the whole range of human resource activities. Already underway in the USA during the 1980s, human resource auditing was taken up in the UK in the 1990s. The lead did not just come from the corporate sector (although many of the big management consultancies developed refined human resource auditing techniques to assist clients refocus HR policies after organizational restructuring). Public-sector organizations who themselves were encountering radical change because of the introduction of internal markets, such as the NHS and local authorities, have also been enthusiasts for HR auditing. In the case of local authorities the move towards decentralized service provision and compulsory competitive tendering were the main stimuli. The reforms within the NHS after 1991 also devolved management away from district health authorities to trusts and even to clinical directorates and departments. As a result of these developments, a bewildering variety of audit frameworks have emerged. We shall now attempt to provide the tools for designing management development audit frameworks customized to the needs of the business.

AUDITING MANAGEMENT DEVELOPMENT: PURPOSES, SCOPE AND CRITERIA

There are three main issues that need to be addressed when designing any audit framework. First the underlying purpose should be clarified, as this will determine what information is required, and indicate how it should be collected. A decision on the scope of the audit follows on from this: should it just cover outcomes, or also take account of resource inputs and the process of implementation? Finally, the criteria against which the audit arrives at a judgement also need clarification – there are many different yardsticks.

Purpose The previously cited definition of auditing emphasizes the purpose of **improvement**. However, audits are not just used as a means to achieve improved performance. They can also be a means of providing feedback which will assist **learning**, or of **proving** that something has happened, or of **controlling** to check that it indeed has. This distinction is drawn from Easterby-Smith's (1986) work on the evaluation of management education, training and development, as outlined in exhibit 2.2. From this it can be seen that the process of auditing similar management development interventions will take on a different focus according to the purpose it is intended to serve: improving, learning, proving or controlling. It will necessitate asking different questions and searching for different indicators of measurement. In addition, it will enable a more precise definition of the boundaries or scope of auditing.

Scope As auditing is a systematic process, it makes sense to address the scope of a management development audit within a systems framework.

Inputs Inputs are quite easy to audit, and traditionally HR professionals have been more inclined to devote most of their attention to them to the exclusion of outcomes and processes. Measures of absolute or relative costs of staff and other resources are easy to construct as unit costs or ratios. However, as always, the direct costs of designing and delivering a management development programme are easier to identify than the indirect costs of activities related to management development – such as problem identification, internal consultancy, and *ad hoc* counselling. The problem with auditing inputs is that an exclusive focus on this can leave management development specialists very vulnerable to the accusation that they are ignoring organizational needs. Thus, auditing of inputs is usually more closely related to an audit of outcomes, as in the case of a 'value-added' approach, and occasionally to an audit of processes.

Processes Employing a systems framework for auditing management development, or indeed for monitoring any management processes, naturally leads to a focus on inputs and outcomes. The biggest drawback is that processes get overlooked in such a 'sausage-machine' model. Yet devoting attention to an audit of processes can often be the key to understanding why unexpected outcomes occur in contrast to what was assumed with a specified set of inputs. Thus attention to patterns of interaction of the participants and stakeholders in a management development programme, to their behaviours, roles and the procedures they follow, can all provide at least insight, and usually a basis for action. Of course, processes are the most difficult and time consuming to audit. They involve exploration of informal and often covert behaviour and values, which of course requires considerable political sensitivity on the part of whoever is doing the auditing. For this reason, process audits are seldom done which is regrettable. For example, how many times do organizations change their procedures for performance management in the hope that line managers will carry out more effective development reviews of their direct reports? Maybe if there were more detailed investigation of what actually happens during the development review process, then the urge to endless amendment of performance management processes would be less compulsive!

Outcomes Currently there is a great deal of interest in auditing outcomes. Perhaps this is because the purpose of many audits is 'proving', or comparison of actual performance with a required standard. Superficially this is appealingly simple, but in practice the definition of performance indicators for human resources in general, and management development in particular, is surrounded by both practical and political obstacles. Thus it is easy to calculate the average number of days of management training course attendance for each manager over a period of time. However, it is not so easy to identify the average volume and range of on-the-job development opportunities experienced by managers. To attempt to establish which of these made the greater contribution to improved organizational performance is contentious, not to say invidious. Perceptions may vary according to the different stakeholders whose identity is not always self-evident. Besides management development professionals and the participants in a management development programme, stakeholders could include line managers, and senior management at business unit, divisional or mainboard level. Outside providers of management development, the direct reports of participants and even business customers, may also have important contributions to make to the audit of management development outcomes.

Criteria Auditing is by definition an exercise of judgement. In arriving at a judgement, criteria are needed against which evidence can be assessed. While it is fashionable to claim that an audit of management development can demonstrate value added, this criterion is seldom defined with sufficient precision and it is often assumed that it is the only one that can be used as a basis for auditing the contribution of management development to business performance. Indeed, there are several (see exhibit 2.3 and table 2.2).

PROBLEMS WITH AUDITING MANAGEMENT DEVELOPMENT

The very terms 'audit' and 'value added' are derived from the world of management accounting and this is indicative of the source of pressure for an assessment of the management development capabilities of an organization. It is, however, more problematic to get a measure of the contribution in monetary terms, because improved performance can be due to a variety of intervening variables in addition to the impact of an intentional development intervention. We cannot stress too much the importance of unplanned, accidental processes, and the individual preference of learners in effective management development (see chapters 7 and 9). These are very difficult to record and audit in a way that is both valid and reliable, and demonstrating a link to business performance is even more tenuous. Even the outcome orientation of audits tends to over-focus on the tangible and ignore the subjective experience of participants, especially their assessment of the learning process involved in participating in a development activity.

The dilemmas encountered when auditing and evaluating any HR process also apply to management development and are:

- whether to use quantitative versus qualitative information;
- whether to use 'snapshot' (cross-sectional) data versus 'moving-picture' (longitudinal) data;
- whether to use absolute or relative and comparative measures;
- whether to focus on inputs, processes or outcomes – or a combination of all three (e.g. value added);
- how to isolate cause and effect when analysing audit data; e.g. it is easy to jump to illogical conclusions that the use of generic competencies leads to a better-prepared management team when in fact it may be the greater effort devoted to development reviews and coaching (associated with competence-based management development) that leads to improved management capability.

Finally, when auditing any human resource activity, it is important to proceed with caution, and to remember that there are no universally ideal methodologies, and that whichever approach is chosen it is as likely to exclude aspects of interest as much as to include them. This does not, however, mean that auditing should be rejected but that, it in the case of management development, it needs the additional perspective

Table 2.2 Overview of the Investors in People national standard

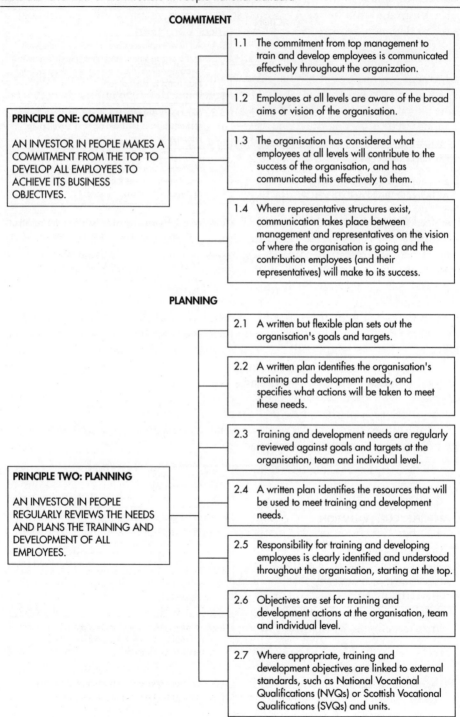

COMMITMENT

1.1 The commitment from top management to train and develop employees is communicated effectively throughout the organization.

1.2 Employees at all levels are aware of the broad aims or vision of the organisation.

1.3 The organisation has considered what employees at all levels will contribute to the success of the organisation, and has communicated this effectively to them.

1.4 Where representative structures exist, communication takes place between management and representatives on the vision of where the organisation is going and the contribution employees (and their representatives) will make to its success.

PRINCIPLE ONE: COMMITMENT

AN INVESTOR IN PEOPLE MAKES A COMMITMENT FROM THE TOP TO DEVELOP ALL EMPLOYEES TO ACHIEVE ITS BUSINESS OBJECTIVES.

PLANNING

2.1 A written but flexible plan sets out the organisation's goals and targets.

2.2 A written plan identifies the organisation's training and development needs, and specifies what actions will be taken to meet these needs.

2.3 Training and development needs are regularly reviewed against goals and targets at the organisation, team and individual level.

2.4 A written plan identifies the resources that will be used to meet training and development needs.

2.5 Responsibility for training and developing employees is clearly identified and understood throughout the organisation, starting at the top.

2.6 Objectives are set for training and development actions at the organisation, team and individual level.

2.7 Where appropriate, training and development objectives are linked to external standards, such as National Vocational Qualifications (NVQs) or Scottish Vocational Qualifications (SVQs) and units.

PRINCIPLE TWO: PLANNING

AN INVESTOR IN PEOPLE REGULARLY REVIEWS THE NEEDS AND PLANS THE TRAINING AND DEVELOPMENT OF ALL EMPLOYEES.

Table 2.2 Continued

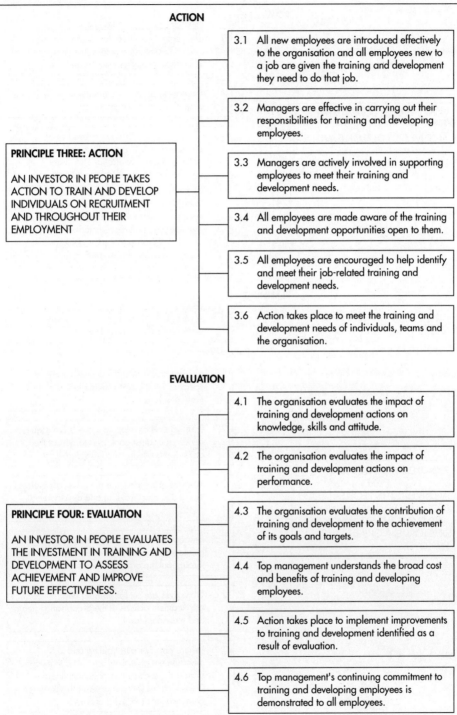

ACTION

PRINCIPLE THREE: ACTION

AN INVESTOR IN PEOPLE TAKES ACTION TO TRAIN AND DEVELOP INDIVIDUALS ON RECRUITMENT AND THROUGHOUT THEIR EMPLOYMENT

3.1 All new employees are introduced effectively to the organisation and all employees new to a job are given the training and development they need to do that job.

3.2 Managers are effective in carrying out their responsibilities for training and developing employees.

3.3 Managers are actively involved in supporting employees to meet their training and development needs.

3.4 All employees are made aware of the training and development opportunities open to them.

3.5 All employees are encouraged to help identify and meet their job-related training and development needs.

3.6 Action takes place to meet the training and development needs of individuals, teams and the organisation.

EVALUATION

PRINCIPLE FOUR: EVALUATION

AN INVESTOR IN PEOPLE EVALUATES THE INVESTMENT IN TRAINING AND DEVELOPMENT TO ASSESS ACHIEVEMENT AND IMPROVE FUTURE EFFECTIVENESS.

4.1 The organisation evaluates the impact of training and development actions on knowledge, skills and attitude.

4.2 The organisation evaluates the impact of training and development actions on performance.

4.3 The organisation evaluates the contribution of training and development to the achievement of its goals and targets.

4.4 Top management understands the broad cost and benefits of training and developing employees.

4.5 Action takes place to implement improvements to training and development identified as a result of evaluation.

4.6 Top management's continuing commitment to training and developing employees is demonstrated to all employees.

Source: ©Investors in People UK, 1996

•••• Exhibit 2.3 ••••
Criteria for Auditing Management Development

Economy This is a measure of whether costs and expenditure are as low as possible in real absolute terms, e.g. we may examine the management development budget and see whether the overall costs are being increased/reduced for one year as against another. However, by itself this information is not helpful unless it is compared to a standard level of service or output for the cost.

Efficiency This is the relationship between inputs (such as the resources used) and outcomes (such as number of managers trained or developed). Here we are looking at the maximization of positive outcomes using the minimization of expense, e.g. we could compare the efficiency of management training in project management techniques by means of short, externally run courses, or flexible self-managed learning, or experiential development projects and coaching.

Value added This is another measure of the relationship between inputs and outcomes, and where value added has occurred the outcomes must have a more positive value than the situation prior to the input stage. One of the UK's leading business schools uses value added as the criterion for evaluating its MBA programme. When recruited, course participants are asked to nominate a number of organizational stakeholders who complete a questionnaire relating to their perceptions of the course participants' initial competence. At the end of the programme the same stakeholders (ideally, or equivalent ones) are asked to score the course partici-pants' competence again. The results are compared with the original assessment, enabling a fairly precise identification of where the added value lies. Thus, like 'efficiency', value added is a relationship between inputs and outcomes, but one that focuses on the skills, abilities and competencies of individuals, rather than costs. However, beyond concrete knowledge and skills, or success in promotion, it is harder to measure value added.

Effectiveness This is another relationship involving outcomes, but in this case not in relation to resource inputs – but rather against the original objectives set for the activity, e.g. the purpose of training and developing line managers in project management techniques could be 'to enable them to take a leading role in managing a major project within x months of completion of training/commencement of development activity'. This could provide a comparative measure of the effectiveness of different development solutions.

Benchmarking This is another comparative measure often used between different organizations or business units, and even against a sector average. Often the benchmark chosen is a unit/organization that is perceived to be the 'excellent', e.g. a management development team could compare the services they deliver with those in another business unit or company. This is more useful for comparison of inputs or outcomes rather than processes, so per capita expenditure on management development, number of days of management training, number and level of managers sponsored for management education courses, etc. are examples of this.

Standards An alternative is to audit against some universally recognized standard such as ISO 9002 or Investors in People (the criteria for this are outlined in table 2.2). With the growth of contractual relationships between organizations, standards are also to be found in contract specifications or service-level agreements.

of identifying stakeholders and incorporating their subjective judgements. As Guest and Peccei (1994) have identified with relations auditing human resource management in general, ultimately it is stakeholder views which, although subjective, may count the most.

···· Summary ····

This chapter has emphasized a number of points. There is not a single approach to management development that suits all situations, and a number of contingent factors such as strategy, environmental context, organizational size and structure, etc. mean that management development has to be adapted to different situations. The importance of achieving an overall strategic fit between an individual organization's business and its management development policies and activities is recognized, but the difficulties of achieving this were noted, particularly outside the large corporate sector, and even in increasingly diverse multidivisional companies and small business. While these difficulties may not be easy to reconcile, they do need to be addressed rather than dismissed in favour of an *ad hoc*, informal approach to management development. The pressure to demonstrate that management development adds value to the business means that attention to evaluation and auditing is imperative. However, neither are simplistic and unproblematic activities, and although there are many complex issues that have to be resolved in conducting an evaluation or an audit, these should not be avoided in favour of an off-the-shelf solution. There are no bespoke auditing packages that can answer the needs of every organization, and this chapter has aimed to encourage those responsible for management development policy to develop their own skills of auditing and evaluation. However, in doing so, it is important not to lose sight of the fact that the target of management development is individual attitudes and behaviour and not just bottom-line financial considerations, and stakeholder approaches to auditing may be more useful than purely financial ones.

EXERCISE

Select an organization that you know well, and identify the approach to management development or a component of it. Devise a framework for carrying out a management development audit that will provide an assessment of how well activity in this area meets the business needs of the organization. Clarify the limitations as well as the advantages of the audit framework.

•••• References ••••

Abbott, B. 1995: Training strategies in small service sector firms: employer and employee perspectives. *Human Resource Management Journal*, 4, 2 pp. 70–87.

Barham, K., Fraser, J. and Heath, L. 1988: *Management for the Future*. Berkhamsted and London: Ashridge Management College and Foundation for Management Education.

Bramley, P. 1991: *Evaluating Training Effectiveness: translating theory into practice*. Maidenhead: McGraw-Hill.

Burgoyne, J. 1988: Management development for the individual and the organisation. *Personnel Management*, June, pp. 40–4.

Coopers and Lybrand Associates, 1985: *A Challenge to Complacency*. November. London: Manpower Services Commission/National Economic Development Office.

Constable, J. and McCormick, R. 1987: *The Making of British Managers*. London: British Institute of Management/Confederation of British Industry.

Department of Employment, 1993: Skills and training in small firms. *Skills and Enterprise Briefing*, 4, February, London: Department of Employment.

Drucker, P. 1988: The coming of the new organisation. *Harvard Business Review*, January–February, pp. 45–53.

Easterby-Smith, M., 1986: *Evaluation of Management Education, Training and Development*. Aldershot: Gower.

Guest, D. and Peccei, R. 1994: The nature and causes of effective human resource management. *British Journal of Industrial Relations*, 32, 2, pp. 219–42.

Hamel, G. and Prahalad, G. K. 1994: *Competing for the Future*. Boston, MA: Harvard Business School Press.

Hamel, G. and Pralahad, C. K. 1991: Corporate imagination and expeditionary marketing. *Harvard Business Review*, July–August, pp. 81–92.

Handy, C. 1984: The organisational revolution and how to harness it. *Personnel Management*, July, 16, 7, pp. 20–3.

Handy, C., Gow, I., Gordon, C., Randlesome, C. and Maloney, M. 1987: *The Making of Managers*. London: National Economic Development Office.

Handy, C. 1988: *Making Managers*. London: Pitman.

Handy, C. 1994: *The Empty Rain Coat: making sense of the future*. London: Hutchinson.

Institute of Management 1994: *Management Development to the Millenium. The Cannon and Taylor Working Party Reports*. Corby: Institute of Management.

Institute of Manpower Studies (now IES), 1984: *Competence and Competition*. London: National Economic Development Council (NEDC)/Manpower Services Commission (MSC).

Investors in People UK 1996: Overview of the Investors in People National Standard. London: Investors in People UK.

Mangham, I. and Silver, M. 1986: *Management Training: context and practice*. School of Management, University of Bath.

Miles, R. E. and Snow, C. C. 1984: Designing strategic human resource systems *Organizational Dynamics*, Summer, pp. 36–52.

Miller, P. 1987: Strategic industrial relations and human resource management – distinction, definition, and recognition. *Journal of Management Studies*, 24, 4, pp. 347–61.

Mintzberg, H. 1987: Crafting Strategy. *Harvard Business Review*, July–August, 65, 4, pp. 65–75.

Mumford, A. 1987: Book review. *Industrial and Commercial Training*. May/June, p. 27.

Porter, M. 1985: *The Competitive Advantage of Nations.* New York: Free Press.

Pralahad, C. K. and Hamel, G. 1990: The core competence of the corporation. *Harvard Business Review.* May–June, pp. 79–91.

Purcell, J. 1989: The impact of corporate strategy on human resource management in Storey, J. (ed)., *New Perspectives on Human Resource Management,* London: Routledge.

Purcell, J. 1995: Corporate strategy and its link with human resource management strategy. In Storey, J. (ed)., *Human Resource Management: a Critical Text,* London: Routledge.

Purcell, J. and Ahlstrand, B. 1994: *Human Resource Management in the Multi-Divisional Company.* Oxford: Oxford University Press.

Quinn, J. B. 1992: *Intelligent Enterprise.* New York: Free Press.

Robinson, D. G. and Robinson, J. C. 1989: *Training for Impact: how to link training to business needs and measure the results.* Oxford: Jossey Bass.

Sadler, P. and Barham, K. 1988: From Franks to the future, *Personnel Management,* May, pp. 48–51.

Schein, E. 1988: *Process Consultation Vol.1: its role in organization development.* 2nd edn, Reading, MA: Addison Wesley.

Storey, J. 1989: Management development: a literature review and implications for future research. Part I: conceptualisations and practices. *Personnel Review,* 18, 6, pp. 3–19.

Storey, J. and Sisson, K. 1993: *Managing Human Resources and Industrial Relations.* Milton Keynes: Open University Press.

Taylor, B. 1986: Corporate planning for the 1990s: the new frontiers. *Long Range Planning,* 19, 6, pp. 13–18.

Training Agency, and Deloitte, Haskins and Sells, 1989: *Management Challenge for the 1990s.* Sheffield: Training Agency.

Vickerstaff, S. 1991: The training needs of small firms. *Human Resource Management Journal,* 2, 2, pp. 1–15.

Whittington, R. 1993: *What is strategy and does it matter?* London: Routledge.

CHAPTER 3

Supporting Individual Managerial Careers

· · · · Introduction · · · ·

The examination of the purpose of management development undertaken so far in this book has been dominated by the organizational perspective. The subject of chapter 2 was relating management development directly to business needs, and the utility of management development as a tool for bringing about individual attitudinal and behavioural change. However, the individual manager also has a stake in determining the purpose of their own development. Indeed, our discussion of the nature of managerial work in chapter 4 suggests the importance of the individual manager input when defining the content, boundaries and style of their work, and would indicate that this stake is considerable.

The possibilities for conflict between organizational and individual aims are manifestly visible in the area of career development. Current issues of concern centre around who 'owns' a manager's career – the individual or the organization? Where should the responsibility for career development lie – with the individual or the organization? What should be the balance between an individual's development as a manager for the organization and their own professional development for an occupational career? Should career development be focused mainly on existing managers, or should it be available to the whole workforce? Above all, if organizations can no longer guarantee careers for life (although many never did), then how far can they and do they go to promote career development for employability? The literature on the changing nature of the psychological contract and the practice of delayering and downsizing has brought the notion of changing managerial careers to the fore.

Career development can be approached from two perspectives which reflect the tension over who owns careers; the individually focused or subjective career, and the organizationally focused or objective career. As we shall see, much career theory has centred around the individually focused subjective career, whereas most organizational career development activity has centred around career management. This is ironical, as current developments within organizations are challenging conventional assumptions about career management and impelling organizations to devote more attention to individual career planning.

This chapter begins by charting the changing models of managerial careers: first by examining subjective careers looking at the individual perspective, and then by examining the organizational perspective. It then examines the career challenges faced by employers and individuals in the light of changing organizational environments, advocates a focus for research and practice which takes into account the perspectives of the organization and the individual, and questions their changing needs by re-examining the mechanisms for delivering career paths which suit both groups.

•••• Learning Objectives ••••

After reading this chapter you should be able to:

- understand the basic psychological principles and techniques for analysing individual career self-concepts;
- identify the basic principles of traditional approaches to organizational succession planning and career management;
- critically evaluate the limitations of these approaches in a changing organizational context;
- critically assess the requirements for a new strategy of organizational–individual partnership to support development for employability, and assess whether the latter concept is indeed theoretically sound and practically possible;
- explore possible career development strategies for different organizational contexts.

•••• The Subjective Career and the Evolution of Models •••• of Managerial Careers

Beginning, then, with literature on career theory and the subjective career, there are two main foci of earlier research on individual careers: first, mapping career paths through life or through an organization and, second, exploration of the differing motivations and abilities underpinning different types of career.

CAREER PATH MAPPING

Mapping career paths can be either a very simple or highly complex activity. When asked to reflect on their career, most individuals will visualize it as a graph, charting the rise and fall of their personal career fortunes.

In order to assist our understanding of individual career paths, some occupational psychologists have attempted to map the changes in individual careers on to different life stages, each marked by distinctive individual needs, concerns, commitments, aspirations and interests. Super (1984) identified five life roles related to different life stages, and showed how they influenced career aspirations in his 'Life Career Rainbow'.

Others have provided similar classifications. For example Schein (1978, pp. 40–6) identified nine major stages: growth; entry into the world of work; basic training; full membership in early career (usually age 17–30); full membership mid-career (25–35); mid-career crisis (35–45); late career (40 to retirement); decline and disengagement (also from 40 until retirement); and retirement. But (with minor differences) all agree that there are one or two early stages of education/growth and exploration lasting up to age 25 during which the individual learns job-related skills and surveys career options before choosing a career. This is followed by the stage of identification and establishment up to age 40, and the subsequent phases of maintenance, stagnation and decline.

Much of this is based on the assumption that while the nature, duration and timing of an individual's career pattern may vary, certain pathways and tasks are predictable. Well, this may be so for white middle-class males, but we have evidence that it is not so for other groups, and for women in particular. Undaunted, these career theorists have revised their position to claim that the career patterns of men are essentially applicable to women if they are modified to take marriage and childbearing into account. Super's (1984) patterns for women's careers include: stable home making, conventional (work followed by marriage) stable working, double tracking, unstable, interrupted and multiple trial. Central to them all is the assumption that there is no difference in the self-concept of women and men – women's career paths were just the consequence of differing individual motivation, commitment and biological necessity!

However, studies of women's career life histories have revealed the above assumptions to be erroneous, and give force to the argument that women's careers not only tend to lag behind those of men but also may proceed in a different way – points which are developed further in chapter 11.

For this reason it could be argued that it is more meaningful to ask individuals to draw a career life-line recording the people, events and transitions in their lives that have been important. Only then is it possible to identify what the critical events were and who made the decisions, and subsequently look for underlying reasons. This can be done as one simple life-line with positive influences branching from one side and negative ones from the other. Alternatively, a more complex way of viewing this which incorporates more of the links and tensions between paid work, family and leisure, is the 'triple helix' model of Rapoport and Rapoport (1980) in which the three threads interweave and interact with each other, as outlined in figure 3.1. The model helps to illustrate why few careers turn out remotely as planned, particularly when related to the stereotypes of managerial career paths.

The dominant approach to the study of the subjective career focuses on the interrelation between age, work, family and leisure: the career life-cycle. This involves recognizing that not only can an individual's career change and pass through different stages or 'transitions', but that there is an interaction between these stages and an individual's experience and perceptions of their past, present and future life and aspirations.

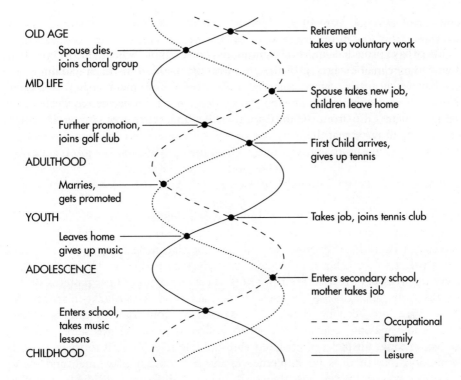

Figure 3.1 The Triple Helix Model with illustrative critical events
Source: Rapoport and Rapoport, 1980, p. 199

a career is an . . . individually perceived sequence of attitudes and behaviours associated with work-related experiences and activities over the span of a person's life. (Hall, 1976)

This approach places a great deal of emphasis upon an individual's self-concept which can both evolve and adapt through experience.

TYPOLOGIES OF CAREERS AND THEIR DRIVERS

Schein (1978) is one writer who develops the notion of career paths to examine differences and to link these to the abilities, motivations and values which an individual brings into working life and which he labels 'career anchors'. These three components, all of which arise out of individual self-perception, are identified in different ways:

(1) attitudes and values (evident from encounters with organizational norms);
(2) motives and needs (identified from self-diagnosis and feedback from others);
(3) skills and abilities (identified through success at work).

To uncover these self-perceptions Schein used questionnaire information within the context of guided one-to-one in-depth interviews, an approach which usefully can be incorporated into development programmes. For example, using a co-

counselling approach, pairs of students take turns to question each other and probe into these areas, (as in the exercise at the end of this chapter). However, until an individual has tested these in real-life situations, they will not necessarily be conscious of what their career anchor is. If they are incompatible with the form of work that is being undertaken, then there are direct implications for the psychological well-being of the individual. The main career anchors identified in his earlier work with male MBA graduates and later developed through further assessment with female MBAs are outlined in exhibit 3.1.

• • • • Exhibit 3.1 • • • •
Schein's Career Anchors

- *Technical/functional competence.* Career choice is based on the technical or functional content of work, and so self image relates to competence and skill in this area. Task accomplishment and getting the job done are highly valued. Such people avoid general management roles, seeing it as a 'jungle' or 'political arena'. They thus do not want to be promoted out of their area, require challenging work content, want pay commensurate with their expertise and experience, rather than their output, prefer a separate professional career stream and value the recognition of professional peers and opportunities for continued professional development.

- *General managerial competence.* Career choice is based on the key values and motives of organizational advancement, leadership, contribution to organizational success and high income. Thus they view specialization as a trap. However, to achieve success, their values and motivation need to be matched by skills and abilities in three key areas: analytical competence, interpersonal and intergroup competence, and emotional competence. They cannot function without some degree of each of these. Thus they are attracted to work that gives them organizational status, pay that reflects this and rewards their success, and recognition through frequent promotion to positions of higher responsibility, with accompanying financial rewards.

- *Autonomy/independence.* Career choice is determined by the need to avoid the restrictive, irrational, and intrusive nature of organizational life. Such people would prefer to stay in their current job if it permits autonomy, rather than move to a better job that involves giving this up. Very often this need stems from high levels of education or professionalism or childhood socialization. Such people want work with clear goals, but cannot stand close supervision. This often means that such people are employed on fixed-term contracts. They avoid 'golden handcuffs' and prefer flexible benefits, seek promotion only on the understanding that it leads to greater autonomy rather than greater responsibility, and respond more to public acknowledgment of their excellence than to changes in title, promotions or financial rewards.

- *Security/stability.* Career choice is guided and constrained by such concerns so that these people often seek jobs in organizations that provide tenure and good human resource practices, in exchange for which they are willing to be told what to do. While often giving an impression of a lack of ambition, they can include highly talented people, but ones who prefer jobs that require steady, predictable performance. Thus job enrichment and challenge are less important to them than good pay and working conditions, they prefer a seniority-based promotion system and want recognition for their loyalty and steady performance.

•••• Exhibit 3.1 continued ••••

- *Entrepreneurial creativity.* Career choice is determined by the need to create new organizations, products or services that can be identified closely with the entrepreneur's own efforts. Typically this need is developed early in life, and their high motivation is likely to be due to their family socialization. They differ from those who are 'autonomy' anchored in their drive to prove that they can create businesses, which often means sacrificing both autonomy and stability. They continually seek new challenges, and may lose interest in old ones. Individual ownership is much more important than levels or types of benefits. Power and freedom, public recognition and visibility are major drivers.

- *Sense of service/dedication to a cause.* Career choice is determined by central values that they want to be embodied in their work rather than the area of competence involved. Values such as working with people, serving humanity, environmental protection can be powerful anchors. Thus there is a need for work that permits them to influence their employing organization, they want fair pay, but money is not of central importance. They want promotion based on their contribution and recognition and support from both peers and superiors.

- *Challenge.* Some people anchor their careers in the perception that they can conquer anything or anybody. They define success as overcoming impossible obstacles and solving unsolvable problems. They define their careers as daily combat or a competition where winning is all. Thus the challenge overshadows concern with the area of work, the pay system and promotion and recognition. A career for such a person has meaning only if competitive skill can be exercised.

- *Lifestyle.* Here the motivation is towards a meaningful career on the condition that it is integrated with a total lifestyle in which there is integration with the needs of the individual, their family, leisure interests, etc. Requirements include flexibility of working hours, employer location and job mobility.

Source: Schein, 1988

Research to date has indicated that most people can be described in terms of the eight career anchors, although most individuals will not conform to the true type. What really matters is identifying the thing you would not give up if forced to make a choice. Most of the evidence would indicate that career anchors are relatively stable, although individual careers may not be. So, those who make dramatic mid-life career changes may just be coming to terms with their underlying career anchor or trying to actualize it in a different field.

A bigger issue is faced when we consider the opportunities to actualize these anchors. It does seem that some of the managerial strategies being advocated now may significantly clash and not match with subjective notions of career. For example, the balance between home, work and leisure and the life-style anchor may not fit with the culture and practice of long hours used in Japanese and US firms and being adopted widely in the UK. Those with the career anchors of 'security/stability', or 'sense of service' and even 'technical/functional competence' appear to have their expectations and needs dashed in certain sectors of the economy, such as banking and privatized public utilities, where there are moves away from job security and towards employability. The changes in managerial work that we have alluded to in chapter 1 and the debate concerning the changing psychological contract make these career anchors appear unobtainable. This begs the question of should organizational efforts for career management be aiming to employ those well matched to the organization, or should they aim to provide career and outplacement counselling for those who are not?

MANAGERIAL CAREER MODELS

There are other models which derive from an examination of different career paths and motivations pursued by managers, which begin to adapt the career models to organizational environments.

Driver (1982) distinguished between four career concepts which underlie a person's thinking about career:

(1) *Transitory.* Most in evidence where there is no pattern of movement from job to job and no permanent job set or field (at the time he felt that this would seldom apply to managers!).
(2) *Steady state.* Most common among professionals where individuals stay in one work role for life.
(3) *Linear.* The corporate manager model where a chosen field is followed from early in life and upward movements are planned and executed. This is also typical of those following the traditional 'functional chimney' route into management, less in evidence today.
(4) *Spiral.* An approach to managerial roles which is more compatible with contemporary prescriptions where managers move across functions, and lateral movement is as important as vertical.

The developments in organizational context outlined below suggest a movement away from steady state and linear career paths and towards transitory and spiral ones, as delayering reduces the number of vertical levels and job security is removed. Schein (1978) had also identified a career structure into management based on both linear and spiral movement, but also one which required movement towards the power centre of the organization. This three-dimensional view suggested movement along a functional or technical dimension (vertical promotion), across functional and technical dimensions (horizontal movement as people switch disciplines) and towards the inner circle of an occupation or function (a political movement).

Schein's three-dimensional view illustrates the importance for us to move away from the concept of a career ladder (one-dimensional functional chimney progression up through a number of management layers) and towards the notion of a 'climbing frame', a notion popularized in the literature by Gunz (1989a; 1989b). Thus it is possible to conceptualize both vertical and horizontal career tracks (Arthur et al., 1989), where vertical careers reflect movements up through the management layers of an organization and are based on formal authority, and horizontal careers may involve movement between different types of work and may be based on increments of prestige, expertise or experience. Using the climbing frame as a metaphor, people usually enter at its lower levels and move from rung to rung as vacancies arise, sometimes the rungs are higher, sometimes they are at the same level but in a different part of the frame, and sometimes they may be lower. Understanding the shapes of career climbing frames within organizations can help managers to make sense of the possible career patterns open to them and to others, and can thus provide a framework for career planning, career counselling and succession planning. Figure 3.2 provides an example of one career climbing frame for the NHS.

The extent to which this individual activity is translated into organizational support programmes for career development is a function of an organization's approach and commitment to career management, and it is to the organizational perspective we turn in the next section.

•••• Organizational Careers and the Evolution of •••• Career Management

ORGANIZATIONAL CAREER MANAGEMENT: THE TRADITIONAL APPROACH

Traditionally, when addressing the topic of careers, organizations have focused on the development of career management processes. Career management can be defined as:

> the design and implementation of organizational processes which enable the careers of individuals to be planned and managed in a way that optimizes both the needs of the organization and the preferences and capabilities of individuals. (Mayo, 1991, p. 69)

Organizations vary in how formal and explicit they choose to make their career management processes. Some will have highly structured career paths involving a complex system of career ladders, and provide careers guidance along with systematic assessment of potential, plus the career bridges and development positions necessary to ensure lateral cross-functional moves as well as vertical movement up the organizational hierarchy (Mayo, 1991, pp. 148–51). They will have decided whether to encourage separate dual career paths for functional specialists, or whether to encourage an upward spiral around the organization, which has traditionally been viewed as the most desirable career path for entry into senior management (Driver, 1982). A number of career management tools are available to assist this, as outlined in exhibit 3.2.

Recent research (Iles and Mabey, 1993) has shown that despite the proven high validity of some of the methods listed in exhibit 3.2, the least valid are those which are most commonly used: career reviews, information on job vacancies and career paths, informal mentors and fast track programmes. The current enthusiasm for 'competencies' (see chapters 4 and 5) has tempered this, as organizations are more inclined to use structured career development tools like assessment centres, career planning workshops and psychometric testing to assess and develop the competencies among their high flyers. Even so, these represent a costly investment, and in many

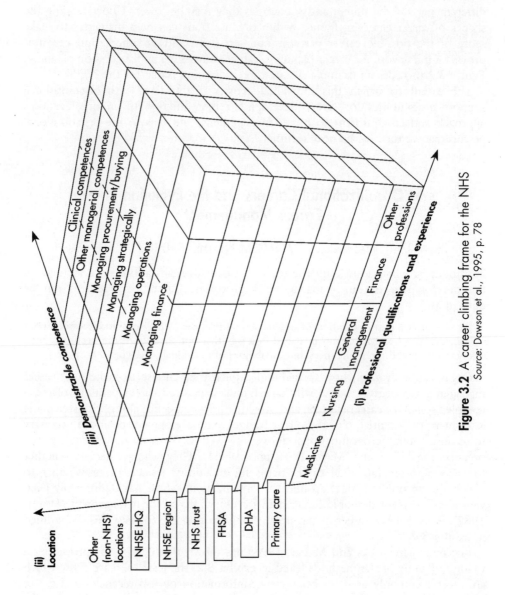

Figure 3.2 A career climbing frame for the NHS
Source: Dawson et al., 1995, p. 78

•••• Exhibit 3.2 ••••
Organizational career management tools

- *Information on career paths.* Written information on career paths within the organization providing a clear outline of available options and vacancies.
- *Career reviews or development appraisal.* With line manager involving a formal discussion of career progress and future aspirations.
- *Fast-track programmes.* Aimed at the early identification of managerial potential and the provision of training, development and job experiences to enable selected individuals to rise rapidly within the organization.
- *Assigned mentors.* People at a higher level who are formally assigned to an individual to provide information, coaching, counselling, support and help with career development.
- *Informal mentors.* People who are not formally assigned to carry out the mentoring role, but who have taken it on on an informal basis.
- *Developmental assessment centres.* A series of exercises in which a group of managers participate, are assessed by trained assessors, and given feedback and counselling on their developmental needs.
- *Psychometric testing and feedback.* Tests of ability, personality, values, interests or preferences followed by feedback to participants to improve self-awareness about where best to utilize their skills, aptitudes and interests (usually as part of a development centre, as well as independently).
- *Career planning workshops.* Off-the-job group activities run by a trainer or facilitator in self-assessment and planning in order to raise awareness of personal skills, goals and values to assist in devising appropriate career goals and strategies.
- *Personal development plan.* An action plan outlining individual development needs and career aims based on self-assessment of skills, goals and values.
- *Self-assessment materials.* Workbooks, videos or computer programmes on career planning to enable personal self-assessment and career planning.
- *Formal management development.* Formal off-the-job courses, seminars and workshops designed to enhance managerial skills, knowledge, and competence.
- *Work-related development opportunities.* Opportunities that arise in the course of everyday working life that can assist in the development of expertise and careers, these can take the form of job enrichment, job rotation, membership of an ad hoc task force or project team, delegation of responsibility, deputising, and developmental work-based projects (see chapter 10)

Source: Amended from Iles and Mabey, 1993 pp. 103–18.

organizations line managers still shoulder the burden of reviewing these competencies – a task for which many remain woefully unprepared. The move away from high-flyer routes is discussed below as we turn to the links between these formal career management programmes and succession planning and internal labour markets.

SUCCESSION PLANNING AND INTERNAL LABOUR MARKETS

The organizational perspective on careers is usually shaped by consideration of the internal labour market and the development of mechanisms for succession planning. Succession planning has been treated as a practical problem of either ensuring that all (or even just key) positions are mapped on to organizational succession plan charts or that a vertical slice of high flyers are identified within the organization and put on a fast track by means of devices such as graduate training schemes or executive development programmes.

High-flyer routes themselves are fast going out of fashion, particularly in the public sector, where a wider variety of entry routes is being opened up for senior positions, for example in the UK Civil Service. One reason for this is the negative effects these have had on the rest of the workforce. Another is the introduction of business values and structures and the break up of centrally run and managed services, towards more of a decentralized network of businesses, for example in the creation of Next Step Agencies. In general, high-flyer routes have been seen as a very British elitist phenomenon, particularly when compared with the Japanese approach (for an example of the comparison see Storey, 1991). Likewise the old-style promotion reviews are less in evidence, being replaced by newer-style performance appraisals linked to wider performance management processes. However, it is misleading to assume that there is no longer a bifurcation of managerial career paths in the organization. Increasingly the distinction is based around core and peripheral workforces, with those at the centre of the organization in core permanent work, having greater access to more interesting career paths. However, the notion of permanence is also being eroded, as we shall see below.

While on the surface succession planning would appear to be a simple task, it falls foul of the same difficulties encountered by the related activity of 'manpower planning'. Organizations seldom stand still, and new positions are created and old ones disappear. It is also a fact of life that influential organizational members may wish to exercise their own preferences in managerial appointments. Thus traditional succession planning is one of those managerial activities that is more honoured in the breach than the observance. It is for this reason that many organizations have shifted from a top-down 'planned development' approach (involving early identification of those with high potential and the creation of a fast track) to a bottom-up and more open-ended 'developing potential' policy (Hirsh, 1990) which is more heavily reliant on self-development and personal development planning (see chapter 7).

The limitations of succession planning could be partly caused by inadequate analysis of the organization's internal labour market. A simplistic illustration of the implications of internal labour market configurations for managerial careers is explained by Tyson and Fell (see Tyson and Fell, 1986, p. 93), with relation to the extent at different entry points at different managerial and organizational tiers. Further work has been carried out attempting to relate career systems and succession planning strategies to different corporate strategic contexts (Sonnenfeld et al., 1988;

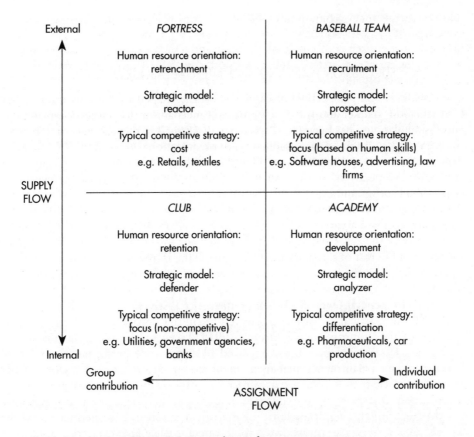

External · FORTRESS

Human resource orientation:
retrenchment

Strategic model:
reactor

Typical competitive strategy:
cost
e.g. Retails, textiles

BASEBALL TEAM

Human resource orientation:
recruitment

Strategic model:
prospector

Typical competitive strategy:
focus (based on human skills)
e.g. Software houses, advertising, law
firms

SUPPLY
FLOW

CLUB

Human resource orientation:
retention

Strategic model:
defender

Typical competitive strategy:
focus (non-competitive)
e.g. Utilities, government agencies,
banks

ACADEMY

Human resource orientation:
development

Strategic model:
analyzer

Typical competitive strategy:
differentiation
e.g. Pharmaceuticals, car
production

Internal

Group
contribution ← ASSIGNMENT FLOW → Individual
contribution

Figure 3.3 A typology of career systems
Source: Adapted from Sonnenfeld et al., 1988, pp. 369–88

Sonnenfeld, 1989; Gratton, 1990). In particular, the competitiveness of product markets and the openness of the organization to employment at all levels can be shown to have implications for the ways in which careers within that organization are structured. Using these two dimensions of competitiveness and openness, Sonnenfeld et al. identified at least four different types of organization as presented in the two-by-two matrix outlined in figure 3.3.

Thus the career system of the 'baseball team' relies on individual performance, and hence headhunting individuals with transferable skills. In contrast, the 'academy' is more stable and devotes effort to developing its highly committed members. The 'club' is a career system which is based on loyalty and promotion through seniority, while the 'fortress' is simply an organization under seige with low commitment from individuals and where the main goal is survival. This typology suggests that different career management processes will be required for each type and also that if product market and internal labour market conditions change, then companies can move from one part of the matrix to the other. Even so, the validity of such a model can be challenged today – few retailers feel they would be secure in the 'fortress', and utilities, government agencies and banks are gradually opening up the 'club' to outsiders. In any case, as shall see below, organizations are increasingly resorting to non-standard contracts of employment, indicating the need for more sophisticated models relating career systems and succession planning to corporate strategy.

It is not just organizational contexts and strategies which vary, but also the nature of managerial work (see chapter 4). Managers are not a homogenous group and may pose different career management demands according to the nature of their work and their life stage. For example, those at the start of their management career often need special attention. Graduates need close support and stimulus, and the new first-line managers with enhanced supervisory roles, often need a boost to their confidence and a broadening of their business awareness beyond their operational responsibilities. On the other hand, the mid-career 'plateaued' manager who is often demotivated, or the manager at the end of their career who is off the career ladder, also require special attention; as do the careers of dual-career families. Other specific groups with specific needs include professional or technical specialists and women managers, and are discussed more fully in chapters 10 and 11.

•••• Changing Organizational Contexts and •••• Career Development

The trends in organizational change, identified in chapter 1 and to be further elaborated in chapter 4, have a number of implications for career management:

- a smaller number of managers with a much wider span of control, and therefore a heavier workload and different role;
- fewer vertical career development opportunities with implications for individual advancement, regular pay rises and top-level succession planning;
- individuals need to be more self-reliant in shaping their own careers;
- technical and professional specialists (see chapter 10) may experience greater role conflict and a dramatic reduction in career options.

In particular, the implicit restructuring of managerial careers is evident in the literature on the changing psychological contract. A psychological contract can be defined as a:

> set of expectations held by the individual employee that specifies what the individual and the organization expect to give and receive in the working relationship. (Rousseau, 1990; p. 390 and in Rousseau, 1995)

Herriot and Pemberton (1995), Pemberton and Herriot (1995) and Sparrow (1996), among others, have outlined the differences between the old and the new psychological contract, for example see table 3.1. This clearly states that career paths are expected to have more of a horizontal focus, with less job security and the individual taking responsibility to improve employability. Although table 3.1 doesn't state this, the rhetoric usually states that organizations will support this process. We should not pass over such assumptions without comment. First, as is recognized by Pemberton and Herriot (1995) and Herriot and Pemberton (1995) there is not just

Table 3.1 Contrasts between the old and new psychological contracts, as espoused

	Old Contract	New Contract
Change environment	Stable, short-term focus	Continuous change
Culture	Paternalism, time served, exchange security for commitment	Those who perform get rewarded and have contract developed
Rewards	Paid on level, position and status	Paid on contribution
Motivational currency	Promotion	Job enrichment, competency development
Promotion basis	Expected, time served, technical competence	Less opportunity, new criteria, for those who deserve it
Mobility expectations	Infrequent and on employee's terms	Horizontal, used to rejuvenate organization, managed process
Redundancy tenure guarantee	Job for life if perform	Lucky to have a job, no guarantees
Responsibility	Instrumental employees, exchange promotion for more responsibility	To be encouraged, balanced with more accountability, linked to innovation
Status	Very important	To be earned by competence and credibility
Personal development	The organization's responsibility	Individual's responsibility to improve employability
Trust	High trust possible	Desirable, but expect employees' to be more committed to project or profession

Source: Sparrow, 1996, pp. 75–92

one new contract but a variety, for example relating to the core (a development contract), project staff (based on autonomy) and part-timers (the lifestyle contract), and different ones for graduates, middle management and clerical staff. In many cases there is evidence that the organization's rhetoric for supporting employability is more apparent than real, for example see Ebadan and Winstanley (1997). Also the features of these contracts do not reflect a true representation of organizations' and individuals' expectations. Clearly, many individuals still seek the old contract, and the expectations of the new contract are being unilaterally foisted on them by employers. This is hardly a contract if what we mean by this is that it is voluntarily entered into rather than imposed by force. Would the marriage contract still be upheld if one party was found to have been dragged to the altar and forcibly made to sign their name? Pemberton and Herriot (1995) demonstrate the gaps between what is offered and what is wanted by managers, and Herriot and Pemberton (1995) make it clear that there has to be a process of negotiation in the process.

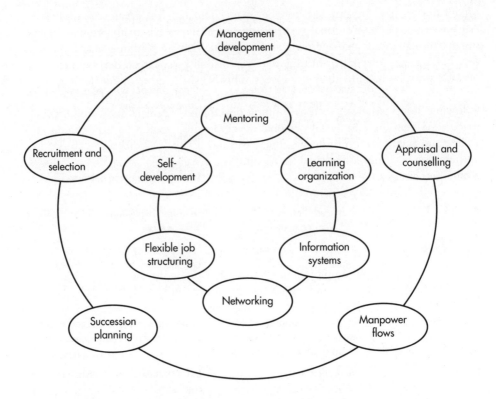

Figure 3.4 Career management systems in the old and the new organization
Source: Guest and Davey, 1996, pp. 22–5

Some (Herriot, 1992) have argued that the challenges of the new contracts make career paths and career ladders redundant as career management tools, and have raised the importance of help for individuals to pursue occupational careers involving moves between as opposed to within organizations. Davey and Guest (1995) and Guest and Davey (1996) contrast the old-style practices of career management structures with those of the new style (see figure 3.4). In this figure, traditional career management focused on those activities in the outer ring, namely recruitment and selection, management development, appraisal and counselling, manpower flows and succession planning. Those in the inner ring, namely, self-development, mentoring, the learning organization, information systems, networking and flexible job structuring, were used only in support. In the new organization, the roles are reversed. However, they found that efforts by the new organizations to encourage managers to support and develop these activities failed, mainly due to lack of individual employee and manager time. As a result, they found that the new approaches to career management which the organization had introduced were greeted with cynicism and a lack of commitment.

Thus we can begin to understand the way in which organizational restructuring presents a challenge to career management if we look at the way in which organizations have responded to the main demand for greater flexibility and responsiveness. Organizational restructuring of all types has major implications for organizational career management and individual career planning alike. Generally this has been resolved by shifting the responsibility of career development from organizations on to individual employees. This is usually done under the auspices of 'empowerment' and 'facilitation'. In some organizations this has involved recourse to following 'good practice', such as running development centres and career planning workshops, funding a range of personal development activities to maintain employ-ability, and the provision of development within the job (see chapter 9). Individuals in these organizations are warned to discount the possibility of their careers following a spiral, let alone a linear or steady-state, pathway through the organization, and are exhorted to be prepared for an almost continuous exercise of career choice across occupational fields, organizations and jobs. The spiral career path between organiza-tions has now become the most desirable for all managerial staff, and not just those destined for senior positions (Weick and Berlinguer, 1989). This may involve managing employment in a variety of different organizational contexts, including small business and self-employment – and even unemployment. This has drawn attention to the need for individuals to be more active in planning their own careers.

Many writers on career management continue to take the large business corporation or public bureaucracy as their focus. There is little that goes beyond rather general models relating career systems to business strategy (Gunz, 1989b) into a deeper analysis of the influence of organizational structure and culture. Thus the fragmentation of highly structured internal labour markets associated with the growth of the multidivisional firm or the introduction of an internal market, and the reduction in management layers are all seen as irritating deviations from the prescription of systematic career management. It is not surprising that one of the major texts on organizational career management (Mayo, 1991, p. 160) makes the observation that decentralization, delayering and cutting of central functional overheads is 'unhelpful to career management'. It is only disappointing that the opposite view was not addressed: namely that current career management practice may be unhelpful to ensuring the success of decentralization and also unhelpful to the individuals experiencing such changes.

Our discussion so far has focused on the processes of organizational career management and individual career planning outside individual specific organizational contexts. Beyond noting the challenge to both these processes presented by organizational restructuring, we have not explored how the mix of different career management tools and individual career planning activities might be different between organizations. However, we do know that 97 per cent of organizations employ less than 20 employees, and that by far the majority of managers work for small and medium-sized organizations which will not even have formal general HRM policies, let alone career management. In these circumstances it is likely that independent careers advice will need to be sought entirely outside the organization, along with access to professional and local business networks. Indeed, professional networking is essential to those who are self-employed (be it intentionally, or unintentionally following redundancy). Alternatively, returning to our earlier discussions about internal labour markets, we know that large organizations who previously 'grew' their own talent prior to downsizing and delayering will not over night move to sourcing this entirely on the external market. It may be more so the case for certain categories of managerial employees, but retention and development of many will still be necessary to meet business needs.

Thus we would agree with the conclusions of Davey and Guest (1995) that, due to pressure of work, innovations in career management are happening very much at the margins, and that career management change can succeed only if accompanied by a change in the culture of the organization, a point reinforced by Herriot and Pemberton (1995) and Mayo (1991). New career concepts will fail to become established if they are either introduced as adjuncts to existing procedures or given insufficient time to grow and mature.

•••• Bringing together the Individual and ••••
Organizational Perspectives

It is ironical that such a great deal of attention has been devoted to theorizing about individual careers but that so few individuals have the benefit of professional advice in career planning. Furthermore, the dominant discipline driving this research is occupational psychology, for which the individual is the unit of analysis. This often means that the organizational context is overlooked, at the expense of enquiry into the individual's self-concept, and how this evolves and is adjusted through experience. We find ourselves in agreement with Driver (1988, p. 248) that:

> Unfortunately, the individual and organizational focused research streams are not in close communication. A major need in the career area is for the psychological richness (in theory and method) of the individual theorists to connect better with the growing insights of organizational theorists as to how organizations operate and change in shaping careers.

Never was the need greater for this than at present. The organizational change alluded to earlier means that many organizations are embarrassed to admit that they can no longer guarantee a career for life, but at the best development for employability.

Unfortunately, recent research (Herriot et al., 1993; 1994) notes that managers still expect the same advancement and progression through the 'tournament' of opportunities as in the past. The result is that despite counselling, mid-career managers still expect to rebuild their past into the future. The inevitable disappointment is reflected in their commitment to organizations. These individual managers will all have to pass through a transition cycle, which (as we know from studies of organizational change) not all will find easy or will complete. This is illustrated in figure 3.5. The main point is that people need time to adjust, do so at different rates, and not all will pass through to the end of the cycle.

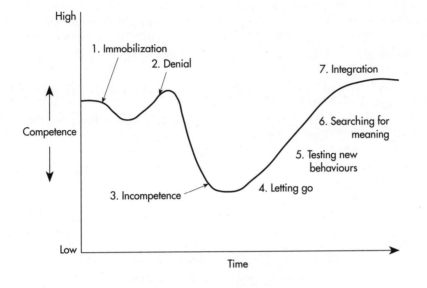

Figure 3.5 The transition curve
Source: Tyson and Jackson, 1992 p. 125

Thus it can be argued that organizations need to review the basis of their psychological contract with managers if they are to attract and retain employees, as these managers still aspire to upward career moves and expect equitable treatment. On the other hand, individual managers will need the space and support to explore their options. It is for this reason that many are now talking of the need for partnership in career development. One such example of how the responsibilities can be separated out between the individual and the organization is reproduced in table 3.2.

Table 3.2 Partnership in career development

What individuals can do	*What organizations can do*
Ask for independent counselling and support	Provide career counselling specialists
Self-market	Market services/jobs to staff
Actively network	Provide career development and planning workshops
Learn	Set up career resource centres
Develop new skills	Train managers in counselling skills
Ensure transferability	Encourage mentoring
Create career plans	Provide resources for self-development
Take personal charge	Facilitate and anticipate

There are no easy answers to establishing effective career management processes for a changing business environment, but perhaps the following activities could be useful.

- Identify the current strategic choice and potential strategic options of the organization.
- Identify which employees are affected by these, and which ones will be key to strategic success.
- Map the organization's internal labour market, identifying career paths and ladders, and mapping current career bridges and development positions. Establish whether any change is likely or required.
- Audit the current career management tools as outlined in exhibit 3.2, assessing their effectiveness.
- Survey samples of managers in terms of their 'subjective' careers (satisfaction, career anchors, aspirations, etc.).
- Design a career management process that meets both organizational and individual needs in a flexible fashion.

•••• Summary ••••

This chapter has emphasized the centrality of career considerations to management development. Besides introducing the main analytical frameworks and techniques of individual career planning and organizational career management, the main thrust of the argument has been to indicate how unprepared traditional approaches are to meet current organizational change. Succession planning has retreated to encompass only senior management positions, and organizational commitment of a career for life has been abandoned for, at best, development for employability. However, upholding this requires resources, and an approach that is more employee centred than previously. This is often difficult to incorporate into top-down approaches to management development, especially if a close fit is desired with business strategy. However, organizations wishing to retain and draw on the potential of high performers cannot afford the consequences of a hands-off approach to career development. It is inevitable that they will need to review their career development processes and invest resources.

EXERCISES

(1) Examine the career management processes in an organization that you know well. Are they mainly formal or informal? Which groups are covered, and how appropriate are the career management processes for different groups of management staff? If you were considering the development of a more strategically focused career management policy, what would it look like?

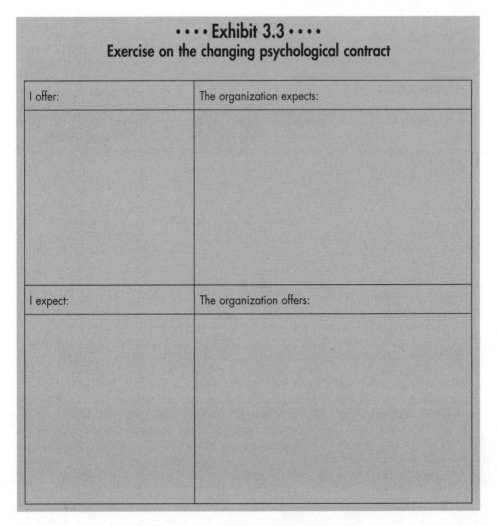

•••• **Exhibit 3.3** ••••
Exercise on the changing psychological contract

I offer:	The organization expects:
I expect:	The organization offers:

(2) Draw your own career life-line showing the major influences (people, events, experiences) that you think have shaped it. Find someone else who will do the same, and co-counsel one another.

(3) Using exhibit 3.3, identify what the basis of the psychological contract is which you have with your organization. Can you see any contradictions?

•••• **References** ••••

Arthur, M. B., Hall, D. T. and Lawrence, B. S. (eds) 1989: *Handbook of Career Theory* Cambridge: Cambridge University Press.

Davey, K. M. and Guest, D. 1995: *Managing the new career.* London: Careers Research Forum Ltd, October.

Dawson, S., Winstanley, D., Mole, V. and Sherval, J. 1995: *Managing in the NHS: a study of senior executives.* London: HMSO.

Driver, M. J. 1982: Career concepts: a new approach to career research. In R. Katz (ed.), *Career Issues in Human Resource Management,* Englewood Cliffs: Prentice-Hall.

Ebadan, G. and Winstanley, D. (1997): Downsizing, delayering and careers: the survivors perspective. *Human Resource Management Journal,* 7, 1., pp. 79–91.

Gratton, L. 1990: *Heirs Apparent: succession strategies for the 1990s* Oxford: Blackwell.

Guest, D. and Davey, K. 1996: Don't write off the traditional career. *People Management,* 22 February, pp. 22–5.

Gunz, H. 1989a: The dual meaning of managerial careers: organizational and individual levels of analysis. *Journal of Management Studies,* 26, 3, pp. 225–50.

Gunz, H. 1989b: *Careers and Corporate Cultures: managerial mobility in large corporations.* London: Blackwell.

Hall, D. T. 1976: *Careers in Organizations.* Pacific Palisades, CA: Goodyear.

Herriot, P. 1992: *The Career Management Challenge,* London: Sage.

Herriot, P. Gibbons, G. Pemberton, C. and Pinder, R. 1993: Dashed hopes: organisational determinants and personal perceptions of managerial careers. *Journal of Occupational and Organisational Psychology,* 66, pp. 115–23.

Herriot, P., Gibbons, P., Pemberton, C. and Jackson, P. R. 1994: An empirical model of managerial careers in organisations. *British Journal of Management,* 5, pp. 113–21.

Herriot, P. and Pemberton, C. 1995: *New Deals: the revolution in managerial careers.* Chichester: John Wiley.

Hirsh, W. 1990: Succession planning: current practice and future issues. *IMS Report* No. 184, Brighton: Institute of Manpower Studies (now Institute of Employment Studies).

Iles, P. and Mabey, C. 1993: Managerial career development programmes: effectiveness, availability and acceptability. *British Journal of Management* 4, 2, pp. 103–18.

Mayo, A. 1991: *Managing Careers: strategies for organisations.* London: Institute of Personnel Management (now Institute of Personnel and Development).

Pemberton, C. and Herriot P. 1995: Facilitating the deal. Paper presented at the 'New Deal' Conference, City University Business School, London, December.

Rapoport R. and Rapoport, R. N. 1980: Balancing work, family and leisure: a triple helix model. In Derr, C. B. (ed.), *Work, Family and the Career,* New York: Praeger.

Rousseau, D. 1990: New hire perceptions of their own and their employer's obligations. *Journal of Organizational Behaviour,* 11, pp. 389–400.

Rousseau, D. M. 1995: *Psychological Contracts in Organizations: understanding written and unwritten agreements.* London: Sage Publications.

Schein, E. 1978: *Career Dynamics: matching individual and organisational needs.* Reading, MA: Addison Wesley.

Schein, E. 1988: *Organizational Psychology.* 3rd edn., London: Prentice-Hall.

Sonnenfeld, J. A., Peiperl, M. A. and Kotter, J. P. 1988: Strategic determinants of managerial labour markets: a career systems view. *Human Resource Management,* 27, 4, pp. 369–88.

Sonnenfeld, J. A. 1989: Career system profiles and strategic staffing. In Arthur, M. B., Hall, D. T. and Lawrence, B.S. (eds), *Handbook of Career Theory* Cambridge: Cambridge University Press.

Sparrow, P. 1996: Transitions in the psychological contract: some evidence from the banking sector. In *Human Resource Management Journal* 6, 4, pp. 75–92.

Storey, J. 1991: Do the Japanese make better managers? *Personnel Management,* August, pp. 24–8.

Super, D. 1984: Career and life development. In Brown, D., Brooks, L. and Associates (eds), *Career Choice and Development*, London and San Francisco: Jossey-Bass.

Tyson, S. and Fell, A. 1986: *Evaluating the Personnel Function*. London: Hutchinson.

Tyson, S. and Jackson, T. 1992: *The Essence of Organizational Behavior*. London: Prentice-Hall.

Weick, K. E. and Berlinguer, L. R. 1989: Career improvisation in self-designing organisations. In Arthur, M. B., Hall D. T., and Lawrence, B. S. (eds), *Handbook of Career Theory*, Cambridge: Cambridge University Press.

White, B., Cox, C. and Cooper, C. 1992: *Women's Career Development: a study of high flyers*. Oxford: Blackwell.

PART II

Identifying Development Needs

••••CHAPTER 4••••

Understanding Managerial Work, Roles and Competencies

••••Introduction••••

In our Introduction, we have already indicated the nature of the growth in volume and range of managerial work. Not only are more people acquiring the title of 'manager', for example office manager, customer service manager, quality manager; but also more employees are being exhorted to incorporate 'management' into their everyday specialist and professional work; for example the clinical director of an NHS trust, the head teacher of a school, or geophysicists and biochemists managing an R&D project. Thus, while the function of managing is ever more pervasive, the challenge of designing management development activities that meet the specific needs and circumstances of an infinite range of individual managers becomes somewhat daunting. One way in which this task can be made easier is through the understanding and analysis of management work and the competencies required for its execution.

The chapter begins with an outline of the contradictions inherent in role theory, followed by an examination of its significance for the analysis of managerial roles and work. An alternative framework for examining the nature of managerial work is achieved through a review of the literature upon managerial competence and competency. The emphasis here is not on how their roles are described and prescribed, on what managers do and how they spend their time, but upon effective behaviour. Managerial competence and competency have received an enormous amount of attention in recent years, to the extent that managerial competence can be placed at the centre of an HR framework, driving human resource systems such as recruitment, reward, redundancy and notably training and development. We examine this burgeoning literature and try to make some sense of its key contributions as well as its internal inconsistencies. In particular we examine process and outcome approaches to defining competence or competency, and discuss particular and generic managerial competencies, individual, team, organization and core competencies.

Through identifying what we mean by managerial roles and managerial competencies in this chapter, it is then possible to examine how these are analysed and derived in the next chapter, and then examine methods for identifying individual development needs to enable managers to fulfil these roles and competencies in chapter 6. In this book we use the term competencies throughout, except with relation to the Managerial Charter Initiative, when we use the term competences.

•••• Learning Objectives ••••

After reading this chapter you should be able to:

- critically review the main arguments of role theory and its significance to the analysis of managerial roles;
- identify the main findings of earlier research on managerial roles;
- identify the impact of changes in the economy and employment on managerial roles;
- prepare a strategy for analysing managerial roles in an organization that you know well;
- explain the difference between input, process and outcome approaches to defining and using managerial competency;
- describe the strengths and weaknesses of at least one approach to competence led management development;
- define core competencies and explain their relation to business strategy and managerial development.

•••• Managerial Roles ••••

DEFINING ROLES

A role is the pattern of behaviour expected by others from a person occupying a certain position in an organizational hierarchy (Huczynski and Buchanan 1991, p. 413). The concept itself is open to ambiguity and can be challenged on many fronts.

A potential source of confusion is over whether the term is being used descriptively or prescriptively. One assumption is that roles can be defined descriptively in terms of the duties and activities of the person performing it. Yet in everyday practice management roles are more often referred to prescriptively. From managerial job descriptions (examined further in chapter 5) to behavioural competencies discussed below, there is an underlying assumption of what managers ought to do.

A key assumption of most role theory is that the role exists independently of the job incumbent. Thus the role of chairman of Sainsbury's is the same whether it is occupied by David Sainsbury or his successor; and likewise for the role of divisional human resource manager in a global company. The point here is that a role is a description of the job and not the attributes of the person, and yet in practice these are very interlinked, and become even more conflated if we utilize competency frameworks, where the competences used are anchored in descriptions of desirable behaviour for carrying out the role, which in turn defines both the job and the desired behaviour of the person. In the example given of the chairman of Sainsbury's the shared perception of the role is influenced by the characteristics and behaviour of the role holder.

Roles can also be instrumentally moulded, a position which does challenge the structurally determined analysis of role position within organizations. As we have noted, individual role incumbents do influence how the role is performed. Take for example a newly appointed senior manager who brings in their 'own' staff. Another example is the supervisor who previously had a very directive boss, and waited for instructions. A more empowering boss will initially cause them confusion, and role strain, but the supervisor might not fully adjust to this and might perform her or his role in a dysfunctional manner. Nonetheless it will be a role on which they firmly stamp their own identity! A symbolic interactionist frame of reference drawing on the work of authors such as Blumer (1969), Goffman (1956), Mead (1934) and Silverman (1970) would suggest that role is merely a construct that is not real in an objective sense. For them role expectations and behaviour are constantly adjusted in the course of interaction in an evolving, dynamic process of negotiation and mutual adjustment. Thus behaviour is only understandable, and therefore explicable, through the descriptions and terminology of those carrying it out.

Roles are also not in theory just 'given' by means of the nature of the tasks the role incumbent performs, what is often called the 'job description'. They are also the outcome of the expectations communicated by the 'role set' which is 'the set of roles with which a person interacts by virtue of occupying a particular position' (Huczynski and Buchanan, 1991, p. 413). The 'role perception' which is an individual's view of how he or she is supposed to act in a given situation, and 'role expectations', which are how others believe a person should act in a given situation, can thus influence role behaviour and interpersonal interactions, and must therefore be considered alongside observable designated tasks and behaviours. For example the role of the divisional human resource manager will be influenced by their role set which could include: corporate human resource director; the divisional management team; divisional line managers/project managers; and human resource assistants. Peers, superiors, subordinates and even customers are usually the most important members of a role set.

Organizations consist of multiple roles which overlap in some way with one another, and are often not easy for an individual to manage, giving rise to role conflict and role ambiguity. In theory it is a shared perception of both role holders and others. In practice these expectations may clash. One inference is that conflict and ambiguity have negative consequences for organizational and individual performance, and should be removed as far as possible by means of appropriate job design and allocation of authority. However, the dysfunctional nature of role conflict and ambiguity may be something that is inherent in the nature of work within organizations, and might even be sought by job incumbents themselves.

So, in discussing managerial roles it is dangerous to adopt an overly deterministic concept of role behaviour in which the manager faces an environment of 'role senders' who hold expectations about appropriate behaviour, send signals to communicate these expectations and react to the manager's behaviour with rewards and punishments:

(Not all managers are) puppet(s) in the puppet-show with hundreds of people pulling the strings and forcing (them) to act in one way or another. (Fondas and Stewart, 1994 quoting Carlson, 1951, p. 52).

THE SIGNIFICANCE OF ROLE THEORY FOR THE ANALYSIS OF MANAGERIAL ROLES

The ambiguity surrounding role theory in general is vastly magnified when we come to analyse managerial roles. Prescription needs to be disentangled from description, which in turn needs to be separated from an evaluation of how a job incumbent performs their role and their own style. Moving from description to explanation and generalization is made difficult because of the different approaches.

Approaches to describing managerial roles have examined *inter alia* 'managers' work patterns, interpersonal contacts, job characteristics, behavioural roles, social networks, influence strategies and other aspects of managerial life (Fondas and Stewart, 1994, p. 83). It is customary to dismiss the work of Fayol (1949), and others in the school of scientific management, in their reduction of management to five major activities: planning, organizing, commanding, co-ordinating, controlling. Yet the durability of this model is surprising. As we shall show below, the Management Charter Initiative's definition of occupational competence owes much to this.

Chapter 5 examines the different ways the members of what has become called the 'work activity school' (Kotter, 1982; Stewart, 1967, 1982, 1986, 1991; Mintzberg, 1973, 1990), have employed different approaches to studying what managers actually do, and which types of manager they studied. Key findings from this school included Kotter (1982) for whom agenda setting, network building and task execution were the most significant aspects of senior managerial roles. Similarly, Mintzberg (1973, 1990) identified his now famous ten managerial roles which could be grouped into three categories: interpersonal, informational and decisional (see exhibit 4.1). He also highlighted three crucial aspects of managerial work:

(1) brevity, variety, and fragmentation;
(2) emphasis upon verbal as opposed to written communication;
(3) emphasis upon a network of contacts.

Finally, Stewart (1967) anticipated several of Mintzberg's findings in her study of 160 British managers at middle and senior levels where she analysed her data in terms of the demands, constraints and choices they faced. In later work (Stewart 1982, 1986, 1991) she made an important contribution in showing that in practice, managerial work was very ill defined, and managers exercised considerable choice over **what** they do and **when** they do it: thus managerial work actually involved defining the content and boundaries of the role.

Kotter's, Mintzberg's and Stewart's work is the most well known, but there are several other studies, which add to the confusion. A valiant attempt to clarify what managers do was made by Hales (1986, pp. 88–115) when he classified the methodologies and findings of a large number of studies and attempted to find some common observations about managerial roles, very similar to the list provided by Mintzberg (exhibit 4.1). He also found that managers perform both specialist–

···· **Exhibit 4.1** ····
Mintzberg's ten managerial roles

Interpersonal roles
(1) Figurehead
(2) Leader
(3) Liaison

Informational Roles
(4) Monitor
(5) Disseminator
(6) Spokesperson

Decisional Roles
(7) Entrepreneur
(8) Disturbance handler
(9) Resource allocator
(10) Negotiator

Source: Mintzberg, 1973

technical and general–administrative work; and the latter is so ill defined that an essential component of managerial work is the drawing of its own boundaries. While this is not surprising, Hales (1986) does add several qualifications. His overview revealed that at least two-thirds of managerial time is spent on receiving information (although this varies between jobs) with most communication being lateral rather than vertical (i.e. with managers of the same status), and informal in nature. Above all, what managers do has different durations, rhythms, degrees of certainty and origins. This led him to four main conclusions, that:

(1) managerial work is contingent upon, *inter alia*, function, level, organization (type, structure and size) and environment;
(2) managerial jobs are in general so loosely defined that they are negotiable with considerable choice in terms of style and content;
(3) managerial work is not a neat, coherent and unproblematic set of activities – they are competing and contradictory, and require the continual exercise of negotiation and compromise;
(4) much managerial work is an unreflective response to circumstances.

The main message therefore, is that a search for uniformity and consistency in managerial work roles in misplaced, and hence attempts to design management development activities to meet generic or prescribed role sets may end up meeting neither individual nor organizational needs.

THE DIVERSITY OF MANAGERIAL ROLES

Thus the urge to identify common aspects of managerial roles has drawn attention away from the considerable diversity in the nature of managerial work. The elaboration of a framework may help to illustrate this. In large organizations managers can be classified by the **scope** of the activities they perform. They can be 'functional managers' supervising specialist employees in a particular operational area (for example human resource management, marketing or production) or 'general managers' responsible for the overall operations of a more complex unit such as a division, strategic business unit or profit centre. In addition, the pressure to innovate and bring products and services more speedily to market has resulted in an increase in the number of 'project managers' who co-ordinate several people across several departments to accomplish a specific project. Outside large organizations, many managers in small and medium enterprises may be occupying a multifunctional role, especially if they are owner–managers.

Another way of classifying managers is by the level that they occupy within the organization. In large organizations a loose distinction is made between senior, middle and first-line (supervisory) management. Senior management is responsible for the overall direction and operation of an organization, developing appropriate policies and strategy and setting objectives for the rest of the organization. They do not interact so much with subordinates as with one another and people outside the organization. This is particularly the case with those at board level. Middle managers are generally found only in medium to large organizations, responsible for business units and departments where they are also responsible for implementing the overall strategies and policies defined by top managers. To do this they rely on encouraging teamwork, resolving conflicts and establishing a good network of contacts around the organization. Finally, the first-line managers' responsibility for the production of goods and services makes them the point of interface with non-managerial employees. For example, Daft (1994, p. 19) identifies the differing extent of conceptual, human and technical skills required at the different levels of management.

Yet, this is a very hierarchical view of the organization and, as we noted in chapter 1, organizations are delayering and reducing their number of managerial layers so some of these distinctions may not apply. It is as a result of the merging of management layers in some organizations that there has been interest in defining the meaning of managerial roles as a driver to steering development. In any case the hierarchical view does not really apply to small or professionally-based organizations.

These formal distinctions in themselves are only tools for classification. Reality, as always, is much more complex. In particular, the boundaries between different levels of management are very fluid and mean that a specific managerial status and job title may have different job-role content across different organizations. In addition, changes in economic structure and employment affect the demands, constraints and choices inherent in different managerial roles.

Economic factors and changes in the structure of employment are affecting managerial roles at all levels. In particular, the two major recessions that hit Western economies during the early 1980s and early 1990s, increasing exposure to competition, and the impact of information technology, affected the demand for managerial work. In the early 1990s this was associated with a 'shakeout' of unskilled and skilled manual labour in manufacturing, while at the same time drawing attention to growing skills shortages in respect of technical, professional and managerial level employees. In contrast, the early 1990s has witnessed considerable organizational restructuring involving drastic cuts in corporate headquarters staff; delayering of management and reorganizing work between a reduced number of grades; and downsizing which has meant a substantial reduction in the middle-management workforce. This has had a drastic effect on managerial work roles at different levels and in different sectors. We will now explore what this means for four types of manager: middle manager, first-line managers/supervisors, and small business managers.

There are also huge changes affecting the roles played by technical specialists and professionals in organizations, including an expansion of numbers, a proliferation of new professions described as 'know-how' and 'knowledge work', a growth in the extent to which professionals are involved in management, and a decline in the security of employment. The changes to roles in this area and its implications for management development are discussed in chapter 10.

MIDDLE MANAGEMENT ROLES

We start with middle management, largely because there has been considerable debate over whether middle management work was disappearing, or had changed considerably. This is admirably summarized in Dopson and Stewart (1990, p. 3):

> Most writers portray the middle manager as a frustrated, disillusioned individual caught in the middle of a hierarchy, impotent and with no real hope of career progression. The work is dreary, the careers are frustrating, and information technology, some writers argue, will make the role yet more routine, uninteresting, and unimportant. The numbers and role of middle managers will, therefore, decline.

Dopson, and Stewart (1990) give a different perspective, based on a small number of case studies, from which they drew the following general tendencies.

- Middle management jobs are becoming more generalist, with greater responsibility for a wider range of tasks.
- Middle managers are acquiring a wider span of control and responsibility for a wider mix of staff.
- The increasing use of information technology has made middle management performance more visible, and therefore more accountable.
- Middle managers are requiring new skills and attitudes in order to cope with their wider responsibilities (such as greater flexibility, adaptability financial knowledge, people management).
- Middle managers are occupying a more strategic role requiring a growing awareness of what goes on in other parts of their organization, as well as the external environment.

Their conclusions that 'a smaller number of middle managers had a greater responsibility for a wider range of duties for which they are now clearly accountable' has been confirmed by more recent case study findings on the impact of organizational restructuring (Woodall et al., 1995), as is their enhanced role in both business strategy development and implementation (Nonaka, 1988). While it is important to avoid overstating the general trend, this appears to be a phenomenon common to both public and private sector services. Formerly bureaucratic 'role culture' organizations from local authorities, the police service, health authorities through to private sector organizations in financial services, telecommunications and pharmaceuticals are all exhibiting the same requirements of their middle managers. This has tremendous implications for management development, both in terms of what is required to bring about appropriate behavioural and attitudinal change and the scale of their requirement. Project management, finance for non-financial managers, situational leadership, performance management and coaching all need to be instilled and, given the attitudinal change required, may not always be best achieved through formal off-the-job development activities but by means of work-related development opportunities (see chapters 7, 8 and 9).

FIRST-LINE MANAGERS AND SUPERVISORY ROLES

A simultaneous change is taking place at the level of first-line management. Always particularly vulnerable to role ambiguity and even conflict, supervisors have been variously categorized as the 'man in the middle', 'marginal man' or 'man on the way out' (see Lowe, 1992); supervisory work is now acquiring a firmer role, becoming incorporated into management and increasingly likely to be carried out by females. Much of this can be explained by the demands of structural change in the economy. With over 75 per cent of UK employees now working in services, and the 20 per cent in manufacturing increasingly involved in 'new wave manufacturing systems' (Storey, 1994), competitive pressure and the demands of customer responsiveness place much emphasis upon the supervisor/first-line manager at the focal point of service or product delivery.

In the rhetoric of the 'new' supervisory role (such as discussed in Lowe, 1992; Storey 1995, p. 7), much has been made of the devolution of activities which would traditionally have been conducted by HR specialists, to line managers, as the HR role becomes more of an in-house consultant, or strategist. Typically, line managers would be taking a greater role in recruitment, appraisal, target setting, the allocation of rewards and performance-related pay, controlling absenteeism, dealing with disciplinary situations and conducting team briefings.

While research has called attention to the low level of technical expertise and qualifications of UK supervisors in comparison with their German counterparts (Partridge, 1989; NEDO, 1992), the demands of their new work in high performance work systems or new wave manufacturing are pulling them increasingly into a managerial role which emphasizes the importance not only of hard process skills, such as ordering, prioritizing, planning, diagnosing, analysing and problem solving, checking and assessing; but increasingly the soft people-management skills such as team leadership, coaching, conflict management, motivation. For example, the work of Buchanan and McCalman (1989), on the experience of Digital at Ayr in Scotland, and Garavan and Morley (1992) found high-performance work teams required greater support for self-management, multiskilling, peer selection and review, open communications and high levels of commitment.

There is thus a debate about whether supervisors require further development in their technical area of expertise, or management development. To this end, we shall see that much of the focus of the Management Charter Initiative's emphasis on the development of competence has been directed at the first-line manager/supervisory level. Nonetheless, it is unwise to be too sanguine about the direction of change in supervisory roles. It is still worth asking what supervisors have in common (if at all) in a food processing business such as United Biscuits, retail multiples like Marks & Spencer, Rail Track station management, or nurse ward management within an NHS trust.

SMALL BUSINESS MANAGERS AND THEIR ROLES

Most discussion of managerial work tacitly assumes that managers are employed in large, or at the very least medium-size organizations. Indeed, research into small business management is a separate field of study with a separate agenda of interest. Yet it is important to have some discussion of the context of managerial roles in small business. For a start small business is the biggest employer in the UK, 97 per cent of all businesses employ fewer than 20 people, and this accounts for about one-third of total employment. There is also evidence that there has been a steady growth in both self-employment and small business start-ups since the early 1980s (Department of Employment, 1993). The explanation for this lies partly with the outcome of the two major recessions since then, partly with changes in the supply of expert services to large business, and partly with changes in the labour force participation of women. Many who lost their jobs in larger companies moved into self-employment or started small businesses. Also, the spin off from large organizations of small firms such as specialist research and development organizations and consultancies, and the growth in outsourcing of specialist expertise, also boosted the growth of small business. Finally, the experience of many women managers trying to combine home and work life, or also hitting a glass ceiling in terms of career opportunities, has made them turn to setting up small businesses, and they now account for the fastest-growing groups of owner–managers.

However, the rate of increase of small business start-up is matched only by the rate of increase of business failure. It would appear that over 90 per cent of small businesses fail within six years of start up (Storey, 1994). This provides both a tremendous constraint upon management development activity and simultaneously a demand for it. However, the role of the small business manager is extremely varied (Curran, 1990). The biggest problem in this respect is a tendency to assume that this is a homogeneous role. Given that managers come into small business for very different reasons and with very different backgrounds, and into very different sectors, it is likely that there will be differences in their roles. Take for example the manager of a kitchen design consultancy who relies on suppliers of a product and a network of self-employed building contactors to assemble the product. This is different from being the manager of a franchised health food store, or the manager of a design consultancy where the franchisee will receive detailed training, or where a business employs highly qualified professionals. The key point is that it is unwise to make too many assumptions about the nature of the managerial role without analyzing the context and role set (see above). Thus universal prescriptions about the managerial role requirements of small business managers are to be avoided at all costs. This obviously has tremendous implications for management development in small firms. A reluctance to contemplate external formal training, a low priority for management skills relative to technical issues such as health and safety, product knowledge and IT, and a focus on the immediate short term, are among the biggest obstacles to be overcome, (Curran et al., 1996).

STRATEGIES FOR MANAGERIAL ROLE ANALYSIS

Thus we would argue that despite the insights provided by academic studies of managerial roles, it is important to see how specific roles are carried out in their organizational and business environment context. This is what we understand by a 'strategic' analysis of managerial roles. We do not presume to advocate a foolproof method of ensuring a fit between managerial role analysis and strategic concerns. What we would propose is the following checklist of questions that should be answered prior to selection of any strategy.

(1) How long established are managerial job roles?
(2) Is there any reason to expect that changes in business strategy are imminent, and what is their potential impact on managerial job roles?
(3) How many different categories of managerial job roles need to be analysed?
(4) Who is in the managerial role set(s), and who is(are) the focal manager(s)?
(5) What are the resource constraints applying to managerial role analysis in terms of expertise, time, money and access to respondents?
(6) What are the political constraints in terms of senior management policy, employee relations, the organizational climate and deadlines?

•••• Managerial Competency Frameworks and Managerial ••••
Role Analysis

An alternative framework has been developing alongside work on role analysis is that based around managerial competencies. However, before we embark on a detailed discussion of the origins and utility of the competency approach we need to sound a note of caution. It bears many of the potential problems that have dogged the managerial role analysis approach, such as the fact that management is not a sequential exercise of discrete skills, it is changing, complex and paradoxical, with the role highly impacted by the person performing it.

Competency is a current buzz word and is used widely in new human resource management across a range of industries. Because it is used very loosely, and is used to denote different things in different contexts, this leads to confusion. For example, four different definitions have been identified.

(1) Characteristics that are causally related to effective and/or superior performance in a job. This means that there is evidence that indicates that possession of the characteristic precedes and leads to effective and/or superior performance on the job. (Boyatzis, 1982, p. 23)

(2) A high performance or H-competency is a relatively stable set of behaviours which produces significantly superior workgroup performance in more complex organizational environments. (Schroder, 1989, p. 22)

(3) Occupational competence (is) . . . the ability to perform the activities within an occupational area to the level of performance expected in management. (Management Charter Initiative)

(4) The skills, knowledge and understanding, qualities and attributes, sets of values beliefs and attitudes which lead to effective managerial performance in a given context, situation or role. (used by one of the authors)

What these definitions have in common is the view that competency is concerned with behaviours which lead to effectiveness within a context. Although managerial competency is more commonly associated with behavioural processes and outcomes, as we shall see below, personal competencies are still predominantly linked to inputs. Even with relation to behavioural definitions there is little common agreement. Generally the characteristics leading to the behaviours are defined differently within different contexts. Table 4.1 identifies the way competency-based management development has moved away from traditional approaches.

Table 4.1 Two paradigms for management development (MD)

	Pre-competency	Competency-based MD
View of management development	Managers born not made or MD as discrete training in management functions	Management a skill and behaviour which can be developed
Focus for MD content/evaluation	Formal knowledge and skills, personal qualitites, attributes and attitudes	Work-related knowledge, demonstrated skill, practised in real work
Who has access?	Elite or At most ad hoc and by chance	Open access
How delivered	Formal courses	Variety of ways Open and distance learning Learning on the job
Evaluation processes	Examination	Portfolios Practical demonstrations Accreditation of prior learning

We will attempt to unravel the meaning of competence or competency by first turning to its origins in the US, the UK and elsewhere to explain how it has been influenced by a variety of movements.

THE US APPROACH

At this point it is relevent to point out that in the US it is more common to use the spelling 'competencies', unlike in the UK where 'competences' is as common. In this book we generally use 'competencies' unless we are referring to a specific context where the alternative spelling is used such as with relation to the MCI.

In the US, competencies have been around since the 1970s. At this time the American Management Association decided to sponsor investigation into what made a manager competent, and to design a programme where managers could learn these competencies. McBer and Company were commissioned to do this and adopted a Job Competency model, drawing on their work with the Florida Council on Education Management and the work of Boyatzis (1982).

Boyatzis (1982) was one of the most influential writers who made a link between competency and effectiveness. The Boyatzis research was based on a study of over 2,000 practising managers in 41 different types of jobs in 12 different organizations in both private and public sectors. Boyatzis put forward the thesis that various competencies differentiated between the managers of average and high performing workgroups. He thus distinguished between two different levels of competency, threshold competency (satisfactory performance) and superior competency (excellence). The research resulted in 18 generic management competencies consisting of 'a mix of motives, traits, skills, aspects of self-image or social role, or body of knowledge used by an individual' (Boyatzis, 1982). These cluster into five groups: goal and action management, leadership, human resource management, and focus on others and directing subordinates. These are listed more fully in exhibit 4.2.

THE UK APPROACH

In the UK failing industrial competitiveness led to a number of reports identifying the causes of the UK's lack of international competitiveness (see chapter 2). The formation of the Charter Group and the Management Charter Initiative (MCI) in 1988 by a large number of companies such as Shell, who were worried about the findings of these reports and were committed to improving the quality of management, confirmed the desire for a competence approach. Their approach has been to develop agreed classifications of managerial competences based on 'what managers do' rather than 'what management is', represented by the skills, knowledge and understanding needed by managers. Advocates of this approach include the CBI, the Foundation for Management Education, the British Institute of Management, their offspring of the Council for Management Education and Development, and the Association of Management and Business Education. As a result of these efforts, level 1 junior/supervisory, level 2 middle management and now senior management level competences have been drawn up at the national level as a basis for education and

•••• **Exhibit 4.2** ••••
Boyatzis' Competencies

The *goal and action management* cluster

Concern with impact: being concerned with symbols of power to have impact on others, concerned about status and reputation

Diagnostic use of concepts: identifying and recognising patterns from an assortment of information, by bringing a concept to the situation and attempting to interpret events through that concept

Efficiency orientation: being concerned to do something better

Proactivity: being a disposition toward taking action to achieve something

The *leadership* cluster

Conceptualization: developing a concept that describes a pattern or structure perceived in a set of facts: the concept emerges from the information

Self-confidence: having decisiveness or presence; knowing what you are doing and feeling you are doing it well

Use of oral presentations: making effective verbal presentations in situations ranging from one-to-one to several hundred people (plus threshold competency of logical thought)

The *human resource management* cluster

Use of socialized power: using forms of influence to build alliances, networks, coalitions and teams

Managing group process: stimulating others to work effectively in group settings (plus threshold competencies of accurate self-assessment and positive regard)

The *focus on others* cluster

Perceptual objectivity: being able to be relatively objective, avoiding bias or prejudice

Self-control: being able to inhibit personal needs or desires in service of organizational needs

Stamina and adaptability: being able to sustain long hours of work and have the flexibility and orientation to adapt to changes in life and the organizational environment

The *directing subordinates* cluster

(Threshold competencies of developing others, spontaneity and use of unilateral power)

Source: Boyatzis, 1982

an outline of their categories for these managerial standards are reproduced in exhibit 4.3.

Because of the MCI concern with minimum standards and raising the status of management as a profession, the emphasis has been upon job performance in specific functions and is much more geared to certification and accreditation than is the AMA

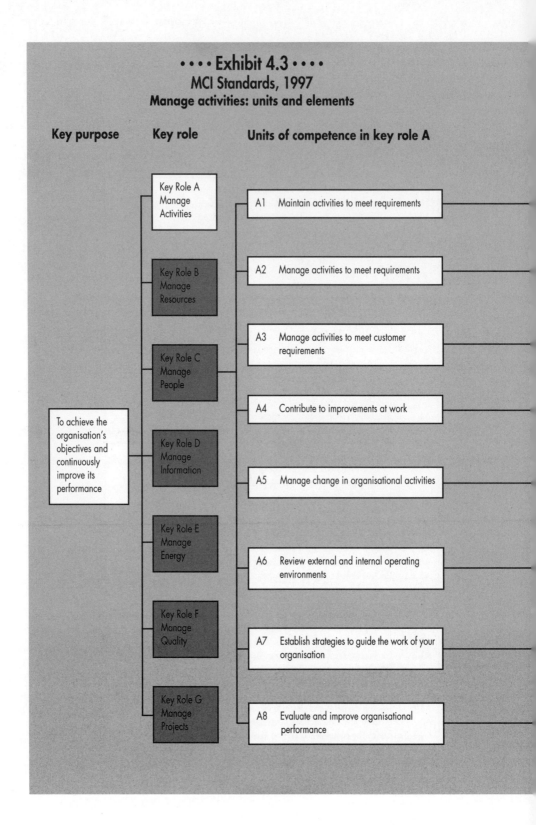

···· Exhibit 4.3 ····
MCI Standards, 1997
Manage activities: units and elements

Key purpose   **Key role**   **Units of competence in key role A**

Key Role A
Manage
Activities

A1   Maintain activities to meet requirements

Key Role B
Manage
Resources

A2   Manage activities to meet requirements

Key Role C
Manage
People

A3   Manage activities to meet customer
       requirements

A4   Contribute to improvements at work

To achieve the
organisation's
objectives and
continuously
improve its
performance

Key Role D
Manage
Information

A5   Manage change in organisational activities

Key Role E
Manage
Energy

A6   Review external and internal operating
       environments

Key Role F
Manage
Quality

A7   Establish strategies to guide the work of your
       organisation

Key Role G
Manage
Projects

A8   Evaluate and improve organisational
       performance

Elements of competence in key role A

A1.1	Maintain work activities to meet requirements
A1.2	Maintain healthy, safe and productive working conditions
A1.3	Make recommendations for improvements to work activities

A2.1	Implement plans to meet customer requirements
A2.2	Maintain a healthy, safe and productive work environment
A2.3	Ensure products and services meet quality requirements

A3.1	Agree customer requirements
A3.2	Plan activities to meet customer requirements
A3.3	Maintain a healthy, safe and productive work environment
A3.4	Ensure products and services meet customer requirements

A4.1	Improve work activities
A4.2	Recommend improvements to organisational plans

A5.1	Identify opportunities for improvements in activities
A5.2	Evaluate proposed changes for benefits and disadvantages
A5.3	Plan the implementaion of change in activities
A5.4	Agree the introduction of change
A5.5	Implement changes in activities

A6.1	Analyse your organisation's external operating environment
A6.2	Evaluate competitors and collaborators
A6.3	Develop effective relationships with stakeholders
A6.4	Review your organisation's structures and systems

A7.1	Create a shared vision and mission to give purpose to your organisation
A7.2	Define values and policies to guide the work of your organisation
A7.3	Formulate objectives and strategies to guide your organisation
A7.4	Gain suport for organisational strategies

A8.1	Develop measures and criteria to evaluate your organisation's performance
A8.2	Evaluate your organisation's performance
A8.3	Explain the causes of success and failure in organisational strategies

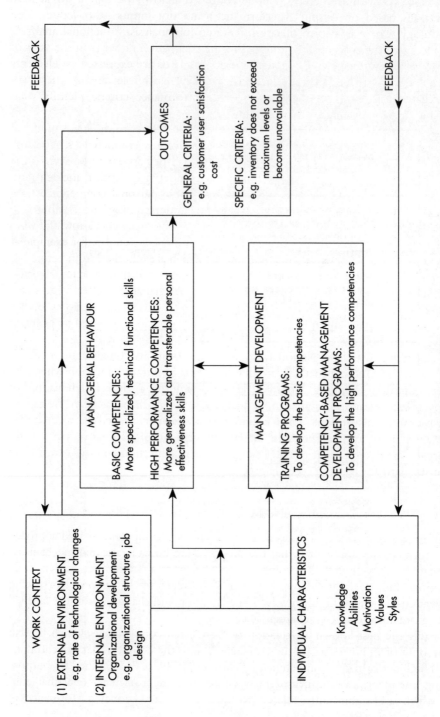

Figure 4.1 Schroder's model of managerial effectiveness
Source: Schroder, 1989

McBer case. As with the NCVQ model outlined below, the aim is to achieve qualifications based on outputs (performance) and not inputs (knowledge). The methodology used was a form of task-orientated job analysis, 'functional analysis', which identified the roles, tasks and duties of the occupation rather than the skills of successful job incumbents (see chapter 5). The standards are expressed as 'elements of competence', within major functional or key work-role areas. These are disaggregated into units of competence, and performance criteria identify what acceptable performance against these might be.

However, the MCI have adopted a different approach closer to the AMA model of behavioural competency to identify personal effectiveness competences. The link between these and functional competences is unclear; they appear to be seen as the inputs that influence the outputs of functional competence. Critical incident and repertory grid methodologies are used to derive these personal competences (see chapter 5). Inputs, such as knowledge, skills and understanding, are attributes of individuals (Mansfield, 1989). Inputs concentrate on what managers know and what managers are, and those things a manager brings with them to a job, for example at the point of recruitment, and these are the topics which are inherited from before the competence movement and, generally, are not on their own used as competencies. For example Schroder (1989, p. 10), in his model of managerial effectiveness (see figure 4.1) defines these individual variables as entry-level characteristics of the workforce, which have an impact on the managerial behaviour required to generate effective outcomes.

Developments with the National Council for Vocational Qualifications are in parallel with the MCI approach as are developments in higher education where the Higher Education Funding Council (HEFC) requires a clearer delineation of learning objectives and outcomes in its quality assessment than has been the case in the past for many institutions. The Government has also encouraged the specification and evaluation of competencies in its encouragement of national curricula and support for the development of national standards in education and the Investors in People standard for training (see chapter 2).

BEYOND STATIC AND MECHANISTIC COMPETENCIES

One of the biggest criticisms directed at those taking a competency-based approach to management development is that the processes are bureaucratic and mechanistic, and that once outlined the competencies become a straitjacket which stifle innovation and flexibility. This is particularly seen to be a problem facing organizations which are highly involved in adaptation and change, and those labelled 'learning organizations' (see chapter 14).

Probably the best-known articulation of managerial competencies which tries to take account of and incorporate these objections into the design is that of Schroder's (1989) high performance competencies. Schroder (1989, p. 7) identified his purpose as being 'the identification, measurement and development of managerial character-istics which are significantly related to superior organizational performance in particular organizational contexts'.

Schroder (1989) drew heavily on the work of Boyatzis (1982) and the work of Huff et al. (1982) as well as his own research to derive a set of 11 high-performance competencies.

- *Cognitive competencies:*
    (1) Information search
    (2) Concept formulation
    (3) Conceptual flexibility

- *Motivation competencies:*
    (4) Interpersonal search
    (5) Managing interaction
    (6) Developmental orientation

- *Directional competencies:*
    (7) Self-confidence
    (8) Presentation
    (9) Impact

- *Achievement competencies:*
    (10) Proactive orientation
    (11) Achievement orientation

Note: the reader is advised to consult Schroder (1989, table 4) for further details.

He validated these competencies using a sample of middle-level managers selected by their vice-presidents and directors of human resources in one organization. The selection was based on their potential to take more responsibility in the changing organization. The competencies identified are applicable for managers operating in dynamic, high-change, unknown and turbulent environments and thus highlight the cognitive and interpersonal dimensions of adaptability.

For Schroder, management development 'is a process of expanding the range of contributions based on competency strengths that a manager makes to workgroups' (Schroder, 1982, pp. 31–2). As well as rounding out an individual's strengths and developing limitations into strengths, development can focus on expanding contributions based on existing strong competencies. The experience of participating in a competency assessment programme gives managers awareness of their strengths and enables them to design a developmental plan to practice making new contributions, and by taking these contributions into new situations. Also, according to Schroder (1982), management development is a matter of capitalizing on the complementary strengths of other workgroup members. Thus if development is largely on-the-job or expanding the job, it is by use of the understanding provided by competency assessment of oneself and others.

Sparrow (1992) also contributes to the literature at this level by proposing a life-cycle perspective which takes account of some of the criticisms addressing the static nature of competencies. For example, he suggests three categories of competencies, emerging, maturing and transitional. Emerging competencies are those which may not be so relevant now but may be key to an organization's future; maturing competencies are those which have played an important part in organizational life in the past, but are becoming less relevant for the future; and transitional competencies are those which represent an integral part of the change process, for example as illustrated by Cadbury Schweppes, National Westminster Bank and Shell.

Sparrow (1992) also makes another important distinction for those interested in studying competencies: that of identifying competencies for change (such as is embodied in the transitional concept, and of analysing changing competencies (for example where organizations are moving from maturing to emerging competencies (see Sparrow and Boam, 1992). These are both particularly important as drivers for development, given the changes taking place in the workplace mentioned in chapter 1. Both being capable to manage change and an understanding of the changing core competences of the organization must be seen to be vital in organizations today. This can be seen in the way BT have reprofiled their human resource competencies.

SPECIFIC AND GENERIC COMPETENCIES

We can whether management competencies should be defined for an individual, for a particular job, for an occupation, for an organizational context, for a managerial level or even for management in general. In reality all these things have been done. Thus, for example, the MCI Managerial Standards are an attempt at defining generic standards for a specific levels of management (see exhibit 4.3).

In general, most organizations find they have to adapt a generic description of competency to their own needs. Even some of the MCI founding organizations assume there is something in their specific business situation which needs to be taken into account when identifying managerial competences. Thus for example Shell Canada (see Sparrow 1994) have focused on a series of characteristics or competencies at the organizational level which facilitate the comprehension and management of complexity and uncertainty. The competencies they identified included:

- building bridges and alliances;
- reframing problems;
- scanning;
- forecasting;
- identifying fracture lines;
- visioning;
- empowering;
- skills of remote management;
- creativity;
- learning;
- motivation.

Cadbury Schweppes (see Sparrow, 1994) concentrates on the skills and behaviours associated with strategic planning and thinking, and their competencies highlight the need to sustain a competitive advantage through the importance of adaptability, decisiveness, innovation, leadership, risk taking and strategic vision.

However, most organizations are still at the more basic level of sifting through a mass of literature and determining what is going to work for them. Early innovators such as BP, who developed highly complex systems which were well publicized (for example, see Greatrex and Phillips, 1989), have now learnt the lessons of over-complexity and have now reined in their systems, making them more simple and intelligible. Another common mistake is for organizations to rely too heavily on consultants in their development, so that once the consultants have left the competencies begin to wither. It seems that those organizations in which competencies are believed to be working well are those which have tailored them to the organization, involved staff through the process, used the organization's own language in defining them, and ensured that their ownership continues to be internal. The competencies then need to be quickly demonstrated as worthwhile for those involved in recruitment, development and reward. At one such organization a manager was heard by the author to say, 'I could not possibly recruit now without competencies, my whole thinking revolves around competencies, it is instinctive, I would not know how not to use them' and another, 'We are now breaking into coaching using the competencies, it is very exciting'.

It is important to not get carried away by the activity and lose sight of its effects. There are still many managers and organizations for whom the competency approach has gone down like a lead balloon. For example one manager in a chain of jewellers was heard to comment, 'Nobody can ever persuade me it will ever be worthwhile. No one has ever demonstrated that it adds value at all to the business. As far as I'm concerned it's a waste of time.'

MAXIMUM AND MINIMUM COMPETENCIES

One problem facing organizations using the output competency approach is whether they are stipulating the minimum requirements for effective performance which all managers should achieve, or the maximum criteria for performance, i.e. those which only a small percentage of the managers, and those really excellent and outstanding, will achieve. Some forms of training and development focus on the first, for example courses in psychometric testing usually finish with assessments where people are awarded the certificate of competency or are not, there are no distinctions made within this. On the other hand, some formal courses, for example MBA courses, distinguish between excellent performance (in provisions for a distinction) and satisfactory performance (a pass). Thus the assessment of development and training programmes is beset by this distinction in general, not just with relation to training for competency. However it is generally viewed that competency when assessed in training is viewed as satisfactory rather than excellent behaviour, and a person is either competent or they are not, they pass or fail, there are no graduations.

ORGANIZATIONAL AND CORE COMPETENCIES

Sparrow (1994) provides a distinction between management, behavioural and organizational competencies (see table 4.2). Organizational and core competencies are very different to managerial and behavioural competencies, and have developed from a totally separate management arena, from within the realm of strategy and competitive advantage (see the discussion in chapter 2). As we pointed out in chapter

Table 4.2 Three concepts of individual and organizational competencies

Element of definition	What are management competencies?	What are behavioural competencies?	What are organizational competencies?
Describe . . .	Knowledge, skills and attitudes (and a few personal behaviours)	Behavioural repertoires which people input to a job, role or organization context	Resources and capabilities of the organization linked with business performance
Identified through	Functional analysis of job roles and responsibilities	Behavioural event investigation techniques	Market analysis methods. Strategic and business planning evaluation
Which focus on	Task-centred analysis of jobs which reflect expectations of workplace performance	Person-centred analysis of jobs that reflects effectiveness	Internal resources (such as tangible technical or capital assets as well as strategic management skills)
And indicate	Areas of competency (fields of knowledge) which a person must demonstrate effectively	What people need to bring to a role to perform to the required level	What makes the organization more successful than others, i.e. long-term and fixed sources of competitive advantage
Performance criterion based on	Entry (threshold) standard, i.e. wide reach into broad range of management jobs	Characteristics of superior (excellent) individual performance, i.e. more senior management levels	Superior records of innovation, learning, quality and other long-term business criteria
Applied to	Generic vocational education and training standards across organizations and occupations, i.e. common denominators	Tailored excellent behaviours to integrate all areas of HRM, i.e. reinforce distinguishing characteristics	Marketing and product strategies, selection of best economic rent-generating activities, underlying business processes
Level of analysis	Occupation and sector based on sample of key jobs	Job level, or across the management hierarchy	Organization level and underlying business process
Ownership	Competency owned by national institutions and organizations and granted to individuals	Competency held by the individual and brought to the organization	Competency held by the organization and jointly developed by individuals
Assessment onus	Accreditation of past activities to grant professional status	Identification of potential to ensure best internal resourcing decisions	Articulation of key success factors and unique proprietary know how
Individual motivation	Externally transferable achievement and qualification	Internally rewardable achievement and recognition	Organizationally sustainable employment and security

Source: Sparrow, 1994

2, there is some conceptual stretching to call the 'strategic resources' (Pralahad and Hamel, 1990), core competencies (Hamel and Prahalad, 1994). However, there are two ways in which management development can be linked to the notion of core competencies as developed in the strategic literature.

It can act as an enabler, where management development activities underpin, develop and sustain an organization's core competencies by making them more visible and by developing managers in ways which enable them to put the core competencies into practice. Thus a management development programme could even be based around an organization's core competencies in terms of its content, who is recruited on to the programme and how they then put their learning into practice.

Management development could also play a second role with respect to core competencies. Management development itself could constitute and create and make up part of a core competency itself, being one of the strategic resources which could feasibly sustain competitive advantage.

•••• Utilizing Competencies to Drive Management •••• Development – Designing a Competency-Led Management Development Programme

To recap some of the major problems that beset those intent on taking a competency-based approach to management development, there are four main sets of questions and decisions which face an organization when embarking on this path:

(1) What is the purpose of defining competency? To what use will it be put? Although the answer here may be 'to drive management development', what other questions need to be asked? Is this to steer management development on its own, or is it intended for use as an integrated approach to human resource management where competencies are used to bring together recruitment, development, remuneration and mobility? Also at this stage we need to ask why is an organization choosing a competency approach, what are the alternatives, what are the strengths and weaknesses of the different approaches? One ray of light here is that in general, organizations seem to be more successful at using competencies if they begin with the objective of communication and development rather than that of reward. The benefits are more easily recognized by managers if they see tangible improvements in their own development and feel better equipped to develop their own careers than if they see it as something used for payment purposes.

(2) How will we identify the competencies? Will these be generic or particular competencies and be related to the organization or specific to roles, levels and occupations within it? Will they be input, process or outcome based? What is the organization's definition of competency? Will we take some off-the-shelf or develop

our own? Who will be involved in developing these competencies? How will the managers themselves be involved? Examples of methods used for this are described in chapter 5.

(3) How should we involve consultants in developing a competency approach? At this stage it is salutary to note the experience of those organizations who have failed in their use of competency for the very reason that ownership was not with the organization, but left with consultants. It is not possible to stress enough the importance of involving staff in the process of identifying competencies in order to develop ownership and commitment. The language must be that used by managers in every day usage, and this is something that needs to be addressed from within the organization. Thus for competencies to become embedded in the everyday practice, it is important that consultants are used only in an advisory capacity and not given the role of pioneering competencies. Otherwise the competencies will become associated with something being foisted on an unwelcome organization by outsiders.

(4) How will we use these competencies in management development? Will there be assessment of managers against the competencies, and how will this be conducted, for example will assessment centres be used, or questionnaires? Once a manager's competencies have been assessed how will those demonstrated by the manager and those required by the manager be compared? Where a competency gap or learning need is identified how will development take place to bridge this gap? Will the manager be given support and how – for example through self-learning modules or short courses, or through mentoring and counselling?

•••• Summary ••••

This chapter began with outlining the evolution of managerial role analysis and explained that role analysis involves more than just examining the tasks contained within managerial jobs. The different expectations and evaluations of different members of the managerial role set are equally valid. We then moved on to consider the findings of academic research on generic managerial roles, and concluded that this was an elusive quest and that managerial roles were indeed contingent upon a variety of other organizational factors. This was illustrated by a brief overview of how the changes in the structure of the UK economy and employment patterns have modified what is required of different groups of managers, and in particular middle managers, first-line managers/supervisors and small-business managers. The practical implication of this is that nothing can be taken for granted, that managerial roles must be analysed in their ever-changing context, and that individual management development solutions must take this into account.

The chapter went on to discuss the use of competencies as an alternative approach to managerial role analysis and thus a driver for identifying development needs. We explained the evolution of competencies and how this has resulted in a plethora of different approaches all masquerading as 'competence or competency frameworks'. We distinguished between input, process and outcome approaches, static and changing competencies, and behavioural and organizational. We argued that for a competency framework to be successful it needs to be developed and owned by the organization and its staff, it needs to be complementary with the context and in the language used, and be simple enough to be communicated easily throughout the organization. We suggest that a competency approach is more likely to succeed if it is development rather than evaluation led, but strike a note of caution that many organizations using the competency approach have failed in the process, and suggest that for this course to be embarked on, its benefits must be clearly defined. In the next chapter we will explore in more detail how an organization can go about defining managerial roles and competencies if they are to use them for development.

EXERCISES

(1) Select an organization that you know well, and assuming you had decided to conduct a managerial role analysis, answer the questions on page 74.

(2) If your own organization has not introduced a competency framework, suggest whether or not you think they should have one. Justify your case using the points raised in the section above on utilizing competencies to drive management development.

(3) Identify one organization which uses a competency framework for identifying and defining managerial roles. Ask yourself the following questions.

- What are the nature of these competencies – are they generic or specific, and are they individual, team, organization, occupation, or management level based?
- How are the competencies used – are they used for recruitment, development, reward and appraisal, for promotion and outplacement?
- What core competencies does this organization exhibit and foster?

•••• References ••••

Blumer, H. 1969: *Symbolic Interactionism: perspectives and method*. Englewood Cliffs, NJ: Prentice-Hall.

Boyatzis, R. E. 1982: *The Competent Manager: a model for effective performance*, Chichester: John Wiley and Sons.

Buchanan, D. and McCalman, J. 1989: *High Performance Work Systems: the digital experience* London: Routledge.

Carlson, S. 1951: *Executive Behaviour: a study of the workload and working methods of managing directors*. Stockholm: Strombergs.

Curran, J. 1990: Rethinking economic structure: exploring the role of the small firm and self-employment in the British economy. *Work, Employment and Society*, special issue, May, pp. 125–46.

Curran, J., Blackburn, R. A., Kitching, J., and North, J. 1996: *Establishing Small Firms' Training Practices, Needs, Difficulties and Use of Industry Training Organisations*. London: HMSO.

Daft, R. 1994: *Management*. 3rd edn, international edition, Orlando: The Dryden Press.

Department of Employment, 1993: Skills and training in small firms. *Skills and Enterprise Briefing*. No. 4, February, London: Department of Employment.

Dopson, S. and Stewart, R. 1990: What is happening to middle management? *British Journal of Management*, 1, pp. 3–16.

Fayol, H. 1949: *General and Industrial Management*. London: Pitman.

Fondas, N. and Stewart, R. 1994: Enactment in managerial jobs: a role analysis. *Journal of Management Studies*, 31, pp. 83–103.

Garavan, T. and Morley, M. 1992: Organizational development and change: introducing flexible working groups in a high tech environment. In Winstanley, D. and Woodall, J. (eds), *Case Studies in Personnel*, London: IPM (now Institute of Personnel and Development).

Goffman, E. 1956: *The Presentation of Self in Everyday Life*. Edinburgh University of Edinburgh Social Science Research Centre.

Greatrex, J. and Phillips, P. 1989: Oiling the wheels of competence. *Personnel Management*, August, pp. 36–9.

Hales, C. P. 1986: What do managers do? A critical review of the evidence. *Journal of Management Studies*, 23, pp. 89–115.

Hamel, G. and Prahalad, G. K. 1994: *Competing for the Future*. Boston, MA: Harvard Business School Press.

Huczynski, A. and Buchanan, D. 1991: *Organizational Behaviour: an introductory text*, 2nd edn, London: Prentice-Hall.

Huff, S., Lake, D. and Schaalman, M. 1982: *Principal Differences*, report to the Florida Council on Educational Management, Department of Education, Tallahassee.

Kotter, J. 1982: *The General Managers*. New York: Free Press.

Lowe, J. 1992: Locating the line: the front-line supervisor and human resource management. In Blyton, P. and Turnbull, P. (eds), *Reassessing Human Resource Management*. London: Sage.

Mansfield, B. 1989: Competence and standards. In Burke, J. (ed.), *Competency Based Education and Training*, Lewes: Falmer Press.

Mead, G. 1934: *Mind, Self and Society*. Chicago: University of Chicago Press.

Mintzberg, H. 1973: *The Nature of Managerial Work*. New York: Harper and Row.

Mintzberg, H. 1990: The manager's job: folklore and fact. *Harvard Business Review Classic*, March–April, pp. 163–76.

National Economic Development Office (NEDO) 1992: *What makes a supervisor world class?* London: NEDO.

Nonaka, I. 1988: Towards middle up/down management: accelerating information creation. *Sloan Management Review*, 29, pp. 9–18.

Partridge, B. 1989: The problem of supervision. In Sisson, K. (ed.), *Personnel Management in Britain*. Oxford: Blackwell.

Prahalad, G. K. and Hamel, G. 1990: The core competence of the corporation. *Harvard Business Review*, 68, 3, pp. 79–91.

Schroder, M. 1989: *Managerial Competence: the key to excellence*. Dubuque, IA: Kendall and Hunt.

Silverman, D. 1970: *The Theory of Organization*. London: Heinemann.

Sparrow, P. 1992: Building human resource strategies around competencies: a life-cycle model. Manchester: Manchester Business School, Working Paper No. 235.

Sparrow, P. 1994: Organizational competencies. In Anderson, N. and Herriot, P., *Assessment and Selection in Organizations*, Chichester: John Wiley and Sons.

Sparrow, P. and Boam, R. (1992): Strengths and weaknesses of existing competency based approaches: where do we go from here? In Boam, R. and Sparrow, P. (eds), *Designing and Achieving Competency: a competency-based approach to managing people and organisations*, London: McGraw-Hill.

Stewart, R. 1967: *Managers and their Jobs: a study of the similarities and differences in the ways managers spend their time*. London: Macmillan.

Stewart, R. 1982: *Choices for the Manager*. London: McGraw-Hill.

Stewart, R. 1986: *The Reality of Management*. 3rd edn. London: Pan Books.

Stewart, R., 1991: *Managing Today and Tomorrow*. London: Macmillan.

Storey, D. 1994: *Understanding the Small Business Sector*. London: Routledge.

Storey, J. (ed.) 1994: *New Wave Manufacturing Strategies: organizational and human resource management dimensions*. London: Paul Chapman Publishing.

Storey, J. (ed.) 1995: *Human Resource Management: A Critical Text*. London: Routledge.

Torrington, D. and Hall, L. 1995: *Personnel Management: HRM in Action*. 3rd edn, Hemel Hampstead: Prentice-Hall.

Torrington, D. and Weightman, J. 1989: *Effective Management: people and organisation*. Hemel Hempstead: Prentice-Hall.

Woodall J., Edwards, C., and Welchman, R. 1995: Winning the lottery? Organisational restructuring and women's managerial career development. *Women in Management Review*, 10, 3, pp. 32–9.

CHAPTER 5

Methodologies for Analysing Managerial Roles and Competencies

• • • • Introduction • • • •

In the last chapter we looked at the development of theory and research on managerial roles and competencies as a potential basis for defining the content of management development programmes. In this chapter we explain the methodologies used to identify these job and role requirements and the competencies needed by managers to fulfil these roles. In the next chapter we move on to focus more on those methodologies used to identify learning needs in the individual as a driver for development. Inevitably some of the tools examined in this and chapter 6 are interchangeable, in that tools to uncover skills required in the job are also used to uncover learning needs of the individual to do that job. Many such tools are used in this way, as a basis for matching roles and individuals to identify learning gaps between the needs of the job and capabilities of the person which can in part be addressed by development.

We begin by overviewing the main processes for role and job analysis including more widely used techniques such as observation, diaries, job analysis interviews and questionnaires; and more specialist and less familiar methodologies such as critical incident analysis and repertory grid analysis. We discuss how the use of competency frameworks has broked down the more traditional distinction in job analysis between the job description and specification, and the separate delineation of a person specification, the distinction between the tasks and duties required in the job and the skills and attributes needed to carry it out. To some extent, competencies, in anchoring the person-centred definition in behaviour in the role, blurs this distinction.

It is argued that it is easier to identify programmes based on current roles and harder to identify those which relate to changing and future needs. Also role analysis is harder to do for those jobs which have higher levels of conceptual activity and discretion. It is suggested that where development is primarily for preparation for future managerial roles within an organization, approaches which incorporate the views and perspectives of a wider stakeholder constituency, although producing difficulties in reconciling different views, may be more robust than those which solicit information from role holders only, and using only one method in so doing.

•••• Learning Objectives ••••

As a result of reading this chapter you should be able to:

- describe the main techniques used in job and role analysis;
- appreciate how some of the major studies into managerial roles have generated their data;
- explain the difference between a job description and a person specification, and why the competency frameworks blur this distinction;
- identify an appropriate technique to use to analyse the requirements of a job in a specific situation.

•••• Techniques for Role and Job Analysis ••••

Here we begin by summarizing some of the major techniques for job and role analysis as a starting point in identifying what the content of development programmes should be. Most methods of role analysis can be linked to the wider repertoire of job analysis techniques. Many of these have a long history, and can be traced back to the Scientific Management interest in work study (Pearn and Kandola, 1993). These techniques include checklists and inventories to be completed by an observer or interviewer and, occasionally, the job incumbent. For example see Pearn and Kandola's (1993) list of methods for job analysis in exhibit 5.1, and exhibit 5.2 for a comparison of the main ones in terms of their focus, strengths and weaknesses.

•••• Exhibit 5.1 ••••
Pearn and Kandola's list of methods for job analysis

Observation	Participant observation
Self-description/diaries/logs	Content analysis
Job analysis interviews	Expert conferences
Critical incident technique	Work performance survey system
Repertory grid technique	Combination job analysis method
Checklists/inventories	Functional job analysis
Job-learning analysis	Job element method
Job components inventory	Ability requirement scales
Position analysis questionnaire	

Source: Pearn and Kandola, 1993
This list is reproduced with the permission of the publishers, the Institute of Personnel and Development, IPD House, 35 Camp Road, Wimbledon, London, SW19 4UX.

•••• Exhibit 5.2 ••••
Techniques for job and role analysis compared

Method	Advantages	Disadvantages	Focus/output	Who gives data?
(1) Self-report diary method	Easy to administer Good for existing jobs	Low reliability Overly task focused Time consuming data collection Time consuming analysis Poor for new jobs	Job/role Current only Performance data possible through comparison of diaries of high and low performers	Job holder
(2) Job analysis role/job interview	High face validity Accessible and flexible Goes beyond tasks Some ability to capture stakeholder perceptions re. changing and future role	Requires skilled interviewers Requires skilled analysis	Predominantly job role May include performance data Current/future	Job holder usually Can include others e.g. boss, subordinate, peers potentially all stakeholders
(3) Critical incident technique	Goes beyond tasks to context and style Flexible Data on effective and ineffective performance	Low reliability (relies on memory) Requires skilled interviewers Time consuming to collect data Time consuming to analyse Poor for new jobs	Job performance and behaviours May include role Current only	Job holder usually Can also include others e.g. boss, subordinate, peers potentially all stakeholders
(4) Repertory grid technique	Systematic Efficient	Requires expertise for conduct and analysis Complex Takes time to gather and analyse data Poor for new jobs	Person or job/role Non-comparative between person/ role Performance data/ behaviours/ attributes Current	Job holders Bosses, subordinates, peers, customers, all stakeholders
(5) Job/role analysis questionnaire or skill inventory	Statistical analysis for validity and reliability possible Highly systematic Universal applicability Ready made off-the-shelf	Unwieldy (due to high number of questions needed) Requires skilled interviewers and expert analysts Possible but not easy for new jobs	Person and job/ role Comparative person/role data possibleCurrent (future possible)	Job holders Potential job holders (re. selves)

Four issues face the management-development programme designer when faced with approaches which focus on analysis of job requirements as a basis for management development. First, because of their task-centred nature they are more suited to operative and technical jobs in manufacturing, particularly at the manual and semi-skilled levels, rather than management or service-sector work. It is much harder to conduct job analysis on jobs with significant management content.

Second, where such tools exist, and in particular the questionnaires and inventories, an organization may need outside help from the consultancies in designing such tools, (a problem which exists for individual tools also as explained in chapter 6).

Third, these tools are better at identifying and analysing jobs which already exist, rather than future changes to jobs or roles which have not yet been conducted. Harder still is the identification of roles and tasks and capabilities when the tasks themselves are unclear and uncertain and subject to change. Obviously, methods based on rigid task definition are of little use if helping identify managerial role content. Job analysis is less successful for those very jobs at which management development activity is aimed, as managerial roles are often uncertain, intangible and constantly changing, and require considerable discretion and innovation, as outlined in chapter 4.

Fourth, the lack of consistency in managerial roles, and the importance of taking into account the expectations and demands of the managerial role set (i.e. those managers whose jobs are included in a particular role set, or have similar job content and titles) present a tough challenge for the management development professional. On the one hand they face political pressure from the organization prescribing how managers should behave, and on the other they are faced with a variety of managerial work situations occupied by incumbents whose own personal attributes and experience is equally variable.

However, in many development situations there is a need to consider not just the development needs of an individual *or* the development needs for a task, but the development needs of a person in relation to a new task or role, and thus a need for tools which will assess both the person and the task and involve some matching process between the two as a vehicle for identifying development needs. Some tools are used to assess the task or work role which needs to be performed as a focus for development. For example, where an organization has made significant changes or entered a new business area or environment, it may recruit consultants to identify development which needs to take place. Most of the questionnaires, inventories, profiles and techniques have been adapted to allow for a matching process between the two, where the questionnaire or the technique is applied to both the task and the individual. Computerization has enabled such analysis and a matching of the two to be more cost effective and less time consuming.

SELF-REPORT DIARIES

Here managers are asked to keep a diary over a specific work period and record their activities (actions, decisions, encounters, etc.) at regular intervals (anything from half an hour to half a day). These are then scrutinized and analysis of both individuals and groups can take place. One of the most famous writers on managerial roles, Stewart (1967), utilized the diary approach when she asked 160 British managers to complete diaries for one month, which she went on to analyse in terms of demands, constraints and choices. An example of a self-report diary is provided in exhibit 5.3.

Advantages This is very useful when it is impossible to observe actions and decisions because, for example, the managers are moving around between locations, or are meeting other managers, employees and clients on a confidential basis. It can also achieve a high degree of validity in respect of what an individual manager does.

Disadvantages Unfortunately, the practical disadvantages are substantial. The most obvious is that, even when appropriately coached, managers may not complete the diary in an authentic manner. Omissions, and even deliberate fabrication, are possible. Also, this is still a task-oriented method, and may not get at other behavioural or attitudinal aspects of managerial work such as management style. Furthermore, managers may only record that which they perceive to be important which, as we have seen above, may not be the same as that perceived by other members of the role set, i.e. other managers with similar jobs and roles.

JOB ANALYSIS INTERVIEWS

This is probably the most frequently encountered method, and usually takes the form of structured interviews preceded by careful preparation and briefing of the respondent. The interviews can be with a sample of job or role holders, previous job holders, or with the incumbent's manager or subordinate, or even can include a wider constituency, depending on whose perceptions of the role are considered important. Confident interviewers may prefer to adopt a free-flowing unstructured interview style, but this is a high-risk strategy. Even more ambitious is co-counselling (Pearn and Kandola, 1993, p. 23), where two job holders are brought together to interview one another about the work they carry out, without the involvement of the interviewer.

Where there are a large number of incumbents or stakeholders to be interviewed, some prefer to utilize focus groups rather than one-to-one interviews. The focus group technique broadly uses a semistructured group session, moderated by a facilitator, held in an informal setting, with the purpose of collecting information on a designated topic, in this case the nature and content of a managerial role. For further information on the focus group technique see Carey (1994), Krueger (1988), Merton et al. (1990), Morgan (1988), Stewart and Shamdsani (1990).

Advantages Job analysis interviews are an accessible and flexible technique, that comes very easily to HR professionals, and can generate a lot of very valid data about aspects of the job that are not amenable to observation, such as thoughts and feelings.

• • • • Exhibit 5.3 • • • •
Extract from a self-report diary

Role: University lecturer
Day: Monday   Date:

	Teaching	Course administration	Project supervision	Marking	Research	General administration	Personal	Other	For comments
8.00									
8.30									
9.00									
9.30									
10.00									
10.30									
11.00									
etc									
13.00									
13.30									
etc.									

Please fill this out at the end of each day in the week allocated, and return it at the end of the week to be analysed

Disadvantages The success of this method is highly dependent upon the skills and experience of the interviewer, especially in the case of unstructured interviews, and the willingness of the respondent to be interviewed. In the case of the co-counselling method, the managers involved may be poorly skilled interviewers, or may be reluctant to play the game or share all their findings with the analyst. Where focus groups are used for interviewing, there are the pitfalls that are present in any group interaction, for example problems relating to 'groupthink' (Janis 1982, 1988), including the potential impact of censoring and conforming and members' attempts at consensus building (see Carey, 1994), all of which can bias the data received. Furthermore, job analysis interviews are mainly useful where the job already exists, but cannot be used to identify the components of a new managerial role. Like the diary method, it generates a great deal of narrative data, and where there has been a departure from a structured interview, this can be time consuming to analyse and may require a more grounded approach which creates categories (for example of job content areas) from the data rather than relying on precoded categorizations.

The grounded approach which, is a tradition within research methodology and analysis, is also transferable to job analysis interview applications, although it is unlikely that a totally qualitative and unstructured interview approach will be used. The grounded approach to interpreting qualitative data can be found in Glaser and Strauss (1967) and also is explained in Strauss and Corbin (1994). Although computer packages to aid quantitative data analysis have long been available (e.g. SPSS) there are now computer packages which help with qualitative data analysis, for example Ethnograph and NUDIST (see Fielding and Lee, 1991 or Weitzman and Miles, 1995 for a discussion of their merits).

OBSERVATION

An alternative to interviewing a manager about their role is to observe them in it. Rather than getting the manager's rather self-conscious rationale of how they spend their time, as in the diary or interview approach, this enables a third party to assess the activities. Mintzberg (1973, 1990) for example, in his well-known study reported in chapter 4, observed five managers, each over a one-week period in order to distill out his ten managerial roles (see exhibit 4.1, p. 69).

Advantages There are advantages in using a third party to collect the data. They may be more expert than the manager at so doing, and may benefit from more detailed training in what to look for. The depth of information is likely to be greater than that gained from an interview, and has the advantage in that it does not suffer from *post hoc* rationalization which can contaminate job analysis interviews. It is an immediate approach which can increase the validity of the data, as there is no time lag between the activity and data capture, a problem for critical incident approaches.

Disadvantages This can be one of the most time-consuming methods in terms of data collection, and a strain for both the manager being observed and the observer. It can be very tiring collecting data over such a long period (such as a week), and an obvious disadvantage is in being left with a huge amount of information to digest.

More importantly, much managerial work is occurring internally, or cognitively, and thus cannot be observed easily in their behaviour. Therefore the observer may have to engage the manager in a conversation about what he or she is doing, thinking and feeling at any particular time.

CRITICAL INCIDENT TECHNIQUE

The critical incident method is used to elicit scenarios or incidents in a job or role which are critical to success or failure, to find out what behaviours are critical to good or poor job performance (see Flanagan, 1954). Essentially the method requires the respondent to identify an example of good job performance and/or an example of poor job performance and talk through their perspective of what was going on in that incident, what were the defining characteristics, why were they successful or unsuccessful in their performance, what led to the good or poor performance, etc. Through inductive coding from the narratives of these critical incidents it is then possible to draw up characteristics which contributed to the good or poor performance. These characteristics can then be incorporated into management development programmes in terms of behaviour and skills to learn or avoid for a given task or role or, alternatively, skills and behaviour for an individual to learn or avoid.

Unlike the preceding methods the emphasis is not on the task content, but on *how* key tasks are performed. Respondents have to be clearly briefed about the task, especially about the type of incidents being sought (they must be sufficiently observable for logical inferences to be made about how they were performed, and also critical in the sense that their purpose and consequences are clear). The procedure for carrying out this method is normally as follows.

(1) The respondent is asked to describe an incident which did or did not meet the objective of a managerial process, or in which he or she was particularly effective or ineffective as a manager.
(2) The respondent is asked to describe the background to the incident.
(3) The respondent is asked to explain what they actually did which was so effective/ineffective.
(4) The respondent is asked for an indication as to when the incident occurred; usually the incident is required to be within a certain time period, for example the previous 12 months.

The information can be collected in a variety of ways. Individual interviews, group interviews and self-completion questionnaires can all be used. The process can either use one-off critical incidents (as in Dawson et al., 1995), or can be continued until respondents have produced many critical incidents and even exhausted the number of incidents they can recall. It is recommended that observations are obtained from more than one group involved in the work area, in this case various members of the managerial role set. Indeed, it is often considered necessary to have a large number of respondents. Dawson et al. (1995) considered critical incidents raised by 173 respondents in managerial positions in the NHS where each respondent was asked to recall an incident where they believed they had been effective as a manager over the previous year, as described in further detail in exhibit 5.4.

•••• Exhibit 5.4 ••••
Example of a critical incident technique used to identify senior managerial competence in the NHS

Dawson et al. (1995) used the critical incident method to elicit information about successful job performance in order to identify senior managerial competences and management development and learning needs of senior managers in the NHS. They asked 173 managers to 'describe an incident in which you were particularly effective in your job, for whatever reasons'. The answers were then sorted according to:

- the type of incident and activity involved;
- how people achieved success in their critical incident.

Those items which were commonly mentioned by many respondents were then identified as important areas for management development activity. Despite the variety of types of critical incident mentioned, such as the reorganization of services, human resource and staffing issues, improving IT and getting trust status, there was much greater convergence of opinion over why they thought that they had been particularly effective. The three most commonly cited forms of behaviour which led to effectiveness were:

(1) working with and through others, networking, collaboration and consultation;
(2) the use of pursuasion, influence and negotiation;
(3) an openness of communication and the provision of relevent information to others.

Interestingly, these were all to do with working with and through others. These findings were then cross-referenced with other data from other research methods, including descriptions in their own words of their job content and roles, inventories identifying level of importance of various behaviours and skills in their job, allocation of managerial time across a number of activities, and an identification of the three attributes considered most important for doing their job. It was found that there was considerable agreement with the findings reported above. For example, the most common attribute identified by respondents when asked an open-ended question on managerial attributes ('In your opinion what are the three most important attributes you personally possess which lead you to being an effective executive') was interpersonal and communication skills, scored by 68 per cent of respondents. Likewise when respondents were given a list of categories and asked the attributes to be rated in terms of their importance for their job, the highest-scored category was communication skills, which was scored as being highly important to 82 per cent of respondents.

Source: Dawson et al., 1995

Pearn and Kandola (1993, p. 29) state that thousands of incidents may need to be analysed for job analysis for professional and managerial jobs, which could involve hundreds of repondents each recalling ten incidents. However, they also indicate a more cost-effective way of using critical incident technique by identifying up to five behaviours from each incident to generate a behavioural classification of a job.

For example, Herzberg et al. (1959) used this technique in interview with accountants and engineers in one company to identify the characteristics of job incidents which were critical to high motivation and job satisfaction, or alternatively demotivation and job dissatisfaction. It is from this that he evolved his dual theory of motivation identifying job content factors as critical to motivation and job context factors as critical to dissatisfaction.

Advantages   This is a flexible technique which can be used for a variety of managerial job situations as well as a whole range of activities outside management development. The anecdotes and stories generated can bring contextual flavour and freshness to the managerial role under analysis.

Disadvantages   Despite its flexibility, this technique is demanding, both technically and practically. In terms of practicality, it relies on memory, and is therefore of most use in recalling recent events. Also, the better the recall possessed by an individual, then it follows that the description of the event will be better. This may well be possible with respect to airforce pilot training (for which the technique was originally developed in the US), when respondents are asked to identify critical incidents relatively recently after the event. However, the timespans for recall of critical incidents could well be much longer, thus leading to greater selectivity on the part of the respondents. Other practical problems include the time needed to generate the volume of incidents required to provide a comprehensive description of a managerial job role; the stamina of respondents; and care in ensuring that all procedures are followed. As to the technical problems, they are centred around the analysis of data. As with the analysis of personal diaries and job analysis interviews, the data generated by critical incident technique require qualitative analysis and inductive reasoning. The incidents need to be sorted and categorized through an iterative process so that incidents that describe the same behaviour are placed together. It goes without saying that this is time consuming. Finally, like all the job analysis techniques examined to date, critical incident technique is of benefit for examining established job roles but, because it focuses on the observable, it has no place in contributing to the design of a job role that does not exist.

A common problem with using a large quantity of qualitative data is in demonstrating the validity of the findings. This can in part be countered by 'triangulation', which can involve cross-checking answers by using different types of questioning technique and different methods to uncover and compare responses, and this approach is taken in the vignette in exhibit 5.4. This is one of the widest used techniques in qualitative research to check and improve data validity (Denzin, 1978; Jick, 1983; Smith, 1975; Van Maanen 1983), and is discussed further in chapter 6. This a particularly useful technique to use when critical incidents are employed, as it limits some of the negative consequences of utilizing a wide range of examples from which to deduce generalizations on skills and management development needs.

REPERTORY GRID TECHNIQUE

Repertory grid technique provides a very systematic way to get at the personal constructs which determine the way we behave or view one another's behaviour. One way it is used in management development is as a means of distinguishing the attributes of good from poor managers in relation to a particular managerial role.

The repertory grid technique is based on Kelly's (1955) Personal Construct Theory which evolved from his work in clinical psychology as a result of his finding existing theoretical models unhelpful. Kelly suggested that people develop their own representation of the world so that they can predict and control events, and each individual builds up a unique repertoire of 'constructs' based on their experience.

The repertory grid technique is the method devised for identifying and illustrating the structure of an individual's repertoire of constructs. Commonly, a number of cards are prepared which contain the elements about which the respondent's constructs are sought. For example, if it is being used to identify behaviour which leads to effective performance in a job, or another form of job analysis, one way would be to list out the names of current job holders, each name on a separate card. Managers may be asked this of those who report to them, or those to whom they report, or their peers with whom they interact. These individuals would constitute the elements. The manager would then be asked to sort these into two piles of good and bad performers. Each pile is shuffled, and the respondent would be asked to take two cards from one pile and compare them to a third from the other, and these are used as a basis for questioning about the basis of similarity between two good elements that distinguished them from the one bad element. This should generate a clear construct, for which an 'emergent pole' would be identified for the construct, i.e. describing how two are similar, and an 'implict pole' of how the two are different from the third. The next stage is 'laddering' in which the denotation of the construct is further defined by means of probing questions. For example, if they say that the good performers were 'verbally fluent' as opposed to being 'muddled speakers' they can be asked why this is preferable. If they say because verbally fluent people are able to get ideas across whereas muddled speakers only confuse people, then get their ideas across' versus confuse people' is another construct, subordinate to the first. Thus use of the 'why' technique in laddering, if used repeatedly, can ladder down through a number of other constructs (see Bannister and Fransella, 1986, p. 51). This should generate specific behaviours.

When this stage has been exhausted, the cards are replaced in their piles and reshuffled, and another three are selected in order to repeat the process. If some or all of the same cards are selected again, it does not matter, as the respondent is asked to identify a different construct to differentiate the good and bad performers. The whole process continues until the respondent has exhausted their constructs. This 'triadic' technique produces a list of bipolar constructs. Having elicited constructs, an examination of the relationships between them can be undertaken by asking respondents to complete a grid of the elements generated, and the relationship between the elements and the constructs can then be quantified. Visual inspection or more complex statistical methods such as cluster or factoral analysis can be utilized to analyse the data (Fransella and Bannister, 1977), and there is now computer software available to assist the process.

Stewart and Stewart (1981) illustrate the wide number of applications to which the repertory grid can be put, for example in market research, quality control, selection, motivation, organizational climate and managerial effectiveness, the evaluation of training, conflict resolution, team building, coaching and counselling. In terms of identifying and assessing management development needs, some relevent applications involve job and role analysis, and performance assessment of individual managers, as methods for identifying what the content of management development programmes should be. It could be used for example to elicit service staff's perceptions of customers as a way of designing development to increase customer awareness skills. One use is in evaluating training or management development, and an illustration of an example grid in its construction is given in table 5.1.

In this particular grid, the first stage would be to ask members of a group being trained to identify six management trainers whom they knew quite well, covering a range from effective to ineffective trainers. The names of the people would be written on cards as the elements. Three cards would be selected and the respondent asked how two were different from the third. The repetition of this process would create the constructs listed in table 5.1. The respondent could then score each element according to their level of fit to the description for the construct given ranging from 1 (total agreement with the description on the left-hand side), to 5 (total agreement with the opposite pole on the right-hand side). This needs to be repeated with different selections of cards to create new constructs against which to score the elements. At the end of generating a grid with each respondent they could be asked to give a single rating for each element on a scale of effective and ineffective, as shown at the bottom of table 5.1. The scoring for overall effectiveness can then be compared with individual aspects to highlight differences and provide effectiveness indicators. In order to check scoring the overall effectiveness scores can be reversed as shown. Then, the scorings for each construct line would be obtained by producing and noting the difference for each element against the overall effectiveness figures and reversed effectiveness figures. From this information it would be possible to identify the aspects which go towards the behavioural skills of a management trainer, and also rate each trainer.

Advantages This is a very systematic and efficient way to identify a range of both individual and inter-personal behaviours associated with effective and ineffective performance in a range of similar jobs. As long as more than one respondent is used and other participants in the role set are involved, it can generate a great deal of information in a short time. Also, compared with the critical incident technique, this information emerges in a systematic fashion, and causes fewer problems in analysis and classification.

Disadvantages Repertory grid technique requires interviewers who are highly trained and, above all, who are able to avoid leading the respondent to a construct,

Table 5.1 An example of a repertory grid being constructed in the evaluation of training

	JOE	FRED	MARY	HARRY	JEAN	EDDIE				
	1	2	3	4	5	6	7	8	9	
Runs courses with many activities	x 1	x 1	2	4	3	x 5				Most of course consists of lectures
Uses a wide range of aids in lectures	3	2	x 1	x 2	x 5	3				Just talks in lectures
Has an empathy with students	x 1	2	x 2	5	3	x 5				Has a stand-offish approach
Is a swashbuckler in arrangements	3	x 1	4	x 2	x 5	5				Has careful approach to training arrangements
Prefers learner-centred training	x 1	4	x 5	x 2	3	5				Prefers tutor-centred training
Is knowledgeable over a wide range of methods	2	x 1	3	3	x 5	x 2				Limited knowledge of methods
Has an easy articulation	x 1	x 2	3	x 5	4	3				Explanations are unclear
Always presents a good professional appearance	x 1	x 5	x 2	3	1	5				Can often be over-casually dressed
Prefers to work unaided	1	3	2	x 1	x 3	x 5				Always wants tutor support
Activist	x 2	x 1	3	4	x 5	3				Reflector
Effective	1	1	2	3	4	5				Ineffective
(Reversed scores)	5	5	4	3	2	1				

Source: Rae, 1986, p. 49

injecting bias and imprecision into the laddering process. The limitations of this approach are largely to do with the complexity of the method and the requirement for training in its application. A number of researchers have commented on its abuse by people who have no background in using it or no understanding of its statistical limitations (for example see the comments of Phillips, 1989, p. 194). However, for those who are willing to make the investment in training, there are now computer packages available which make it much easier to operationalize.

SKILLS INVENTORIES AND QUESTIONNAIRES

All of the techniques so far have relied on the generation of qualitative information, and with the exception of repertory grid technique, this is acquired through an inductive process of analysis. All of this requires time and expertise. Thus it is not surprising that many HR professionals have welcomed ready-made systems with proven validity and reliability, from which findings can be subject to statistical analysis through data input into a computer package.

The best known of these was the position analysis questionnaire (PAQ) originally launched in 1969 as a universal job analysis tool containing 187 job elements. The questionnaire is delivered by means of an interview and responses to each element are scaled according to importance, extent of use, amount of time and applicability, etc. The completed results are then sent to PAQ Inc. (or their partner in the UK), where the results are entered into a computer, factor analysed and normative comparisons are made between the job being analysed and other jobs. Because it was gradually recognized that the PAQ paid insufficient attention to decision making, planning, prioratizing and other managerial activities it has been modified for professional and managerial jobs, and this version is known as the 'Professional and managerial position questionnaire'. It is a highly complex system, and users need to be trained in understanding its use and the range of options available.

The unwieldy nature of the PAQ, its lack of user-friendliness, and its visible weakness in analysing managerial jobs, led to the launching of the work profiling system (WPS) by Saville and Holdsworth in 1988. Like the PAQ the WPS was designed as a universal, structured system. It starts with three separate questionnaires, one of which is for managerial–professional staff. The questionnaire is in two parts. The first involves the candidate identifying the main job activities and associated tasks through a process of sorting and resorting cards, and then rating them in terms of time spent and importance. The second part of the questionnaire requests information on the context in which the job is performed; the education and training required; the level of reporting, responsibility, travel involved, the physical environment, hours worked, remuneration, etc. The completion of the questionnaire is followed up by a validation interview with an analyst before the completed questionnaire is returned to Saville and Holdsworth for computer analysis.

The highly structured nature of the questionnaire enables it to be easily coded and analysed by computer. Not only can the main work activities and tasks be analysed in detail, but this can be used for identifying the personal attributes (skills and personality characteristics) required in the job and the most relevant assessment

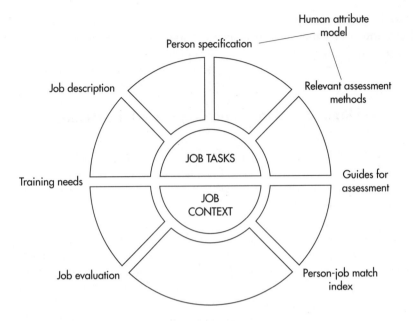

Figure 5.1 Saville and Holdsworth's work profiling system
Source: Saville and Holdsworth

methods for identifying candidates for particular positions. The WPS has a myriad uses, among which are the construction of job descriptions, individual development or performance review, candidate selection and succession planning. Pearn and Kandola (1993, p. 56) are correct when they describe it as an expert system rather than just a job analysis instrument.

An example of Saville and Holdsworth's work profiling system is provided in figure 5.1, which demonstrates that skills inventories can be used to assess a person's skills, or the skills required in a task, or indeed a comparison between the two.

Advantages Both the PAQ and the WPS offer a systematic and rigorous method, and can generate a lot of data that can be analysed relatively quickly. Both also offer a wide range of options for uses, including the ability to assess a person, assess a role, and compare the two for identifying possible development needs.

Disadvantages Although possessing considerable psychological rigour, both systems take the responsibility for analysis away from the organization into expert hands. In both cases specially trained staff are required for administration, interviewing and analysis. Although detailed written feedback is provided, care is needed to ensure that the analysis is used correctly and the results are interpreted properly. There is always the danger that the client organization can select this approach as a 'quick fix' and be seduced by the mystique.

These systems use standardized questionnaires which have advantages for analysis but meet problems when faced with unusual jobs which do not have activities and tasks commonly found in managerial work. Such questionnaires can never be as flexible as interviews and the critical incident approach in capturing atypical tasks and activities.

•••• Role Mapping: Analysing the Whole Picture ••••

The analysis so far has concentrated on ways to identify development needs for individual roles or for an individual career. However, in reality, management development is often a collective activity, and the process of identifying managerial roles requires not just consideration of roles in isolation but also a consideration of all the roles, an exploration of overlaps and gaps, a discussion over the tensions between different and competing roles. This activity may then be one driver for change, for example to eliminate overlap or develop new roles. This requires us to take more of a 'system' viewpoint, where an individual role can only be seen in the light of how it interacts with the rest of the system. A role map would not just show us a description of various roles in isolation, but would show the relationship between roles in an organization, much in the same way that a good road map would not just show you one road, but would show it in relation to the town it was in, or the country.

One way of doing this is to turn the activity of job analysis into information for job descriptions, using a standardized format, which can then be compared and contrasted in terms of roles and responsibilities and key tasks and performance targets. **A job description** is defined as a broad statement of the purpose, scope, duties and responsibilities of a particular job or position. It can be distinguished from **a person specification** which, rather than describing the job, describes the qualities required in the person who would best perform the job. It is a match between these two that are commonly used for recruitment, and also to identify the management development needed to plug any gaps.

Many of the techniques in the toolkit outlined above can be used to identify the totality of managerial roles, and many managerial competencies methodologies take this approach, and role or competence map the whole organization. However, as a result of the increasing prevalence of the competency approaches described in chapter 4, many descriptions of jobs and people are fused together so that a person is described not so much in terms of their qualities as in relation to the necessary behaviours to carry out a role successfully. Increasingly job descriptions and person specifications are both written in terms of behavioural competencies which underpin recruitment, training and development, appraisal and even reward and promotion.

These days, as well as assessing individuals along with performance in role, rather than just the role itself, job analysts and researchers tend to build on multiple methodologies, and nowhere more so than in the generation of management competencies. Boyatzis (1982) collected data using the behavioural event interview (similar to the critical incident), through a picture story exercise and a learning style inventory, to assess the competencies of samples of low, average and high performing

managers. Schroder (1989) used complex experimental simulations of team performance and assessment centre experiences to derive his set of 11 high-performance
competencies, which he validated against a sample of managers chosen by senior
managers as having potential for thriving on and driving through organizational
change. Another approach is that of the Training Agency, reported by Mitchell
(1989), who recommends functional analysis as an appropriate method for identifying standards. This method involves breaking the work role for a particular
occupational area into purposes and functions, and requires employees to think
about the key purpose of their organization or their particular place within it, and to
consider what they do in terms of the outcomes which are to be met. In this way the
outcomes provide the focus of the standards. However, a problem here is that
functional analysis is still in its infancy and requires expertise to implement. It is clear
therefore that there is no one way for identifying roles, but approaches need to take
into account the context and the type of role to be studied, and then utilize a range
of methods which capture the information required, preferably in the context of the
managerial environment and role set. All methods have their own advantages and
disadvantages.

•••• Summary ••••

In this chapter we have identified a range of methods for uncovering development
needs, and in particular have highlighted those which arise from study of the
individual and their attributes, and those which arise from the study of managerial
roles and job analysis. We have discussed a number of tools which are now designed
to match the individual in terms of their attributes and abilities with measurements
of the prospective managerial role, and their demands, data which through
comparison can be used for managerial selection and also to dictate management
development needs where role requirements are not currently met by individual
capabilities.

Some approaches have utilized highly structured approaches such as questionnaires, whereas others have not begun with pre-set categories but taken a more
semi- or unstructured and grounded approach to collecting the data on which
development decisions can be taken, for example the repertory grid or critical
incident approach. Although there is no one best way, we have attempted to
highlight in this chapter the benefits and disadvantages of each approach and to
provide some advice on the pitfalls and ways to make the best use of the tools
available.

The main limitation of the current tools available is that none of the methods
appears to be strong in analysing what would be required for a newly created
managerial job role. If we take into account the rate of organizational change
currently taking place, management development does not just serve the purpose of
preparing people for existing, well-established job roles, but also of preparing people
to fill future, imprecisely defined positions. We have seen earlier in chapter 2 how
business strategy is dependent on ensuring that the organization has the core

capability to meet future challenges, and also how organizations are much more prone to restructure themselves in response to strategic outcomes. It thus follows that if management development is to support changing job/role requirements, in these circumstances, then managerial role analysis will need to be cost effective, quick to deliver, and forward looking.

Unfortunately, none of the above methods could fulfil all of these criteria over a range of different circumstances. However, it is not appropriate to approach the process of selecting methods for identifying management development needs or for role analysis as one would in choosing the supreme champion of Crufts Dog Show. Rather, we would recommend a strategic contingency approach in which the selection of methods is related to strategic concerns. It may be that some or none of the above methods are desirable or feasible.

EXERCISES

(1) In pairs, using the critical incident technique:
  - Taking turns, and taking about ten minutes per incident, making notes as you go, ask the other to 'describe an incident in which you were particularly effective in your job, for whatever reasons, in the last year'. Then probe about the type of activity and why they were effective. If there is time, you could repeat this until the number of critical incidents is exhausted. You can also ask the same question with relation to ineffective behaviour. Then swap over.
  - Now review your notes and see if it is possible to identify the codes you could generate from this data to identify managerial competency with relation to your role.
  - How useful do you think are the data you have generated, and what are the difficulties of using the data?
(2) Taking an organization known to you:,
  - Identify which of the above methods for assessing development needs are currently used in the organization to identify management development needs.
  - Identify which of the above methods you believe are not currently used but could be used to identify and assess management development needs, giving reasons why. Alternatively identify other ways in which management development needs could be identified and assessed in your organization.

  Where necessary re-read part of this chapter and other reading identified in the chapter, for example Pearn and Kandola (1993)

•••• References ••••

Bannister, D. and Fransella, F. 1986: *Inquiring Man: the psychology of personal constructs*. 3rd edn, London: Routledge.

Boyatzis, R. E. 1982: *The Competent Manager: a model for effective performance* Chichester: John Wiley and Sons.

Carey, M. A. 1994: 'The group effect in focus groups: planning, implementing, and interpreting focus group research. In Morse, J. M. (ed.), *Critical Issues in Qualitative Research Methods*, London: Sage.

Dawson, S., Winstanley, D., Mole, V. and Sherval, J. 1995: *Managing in the NHS: a study of senior executives*. London: HMSO.

Denzin, N. K. 1978: *The Research Act*. 2nd edn, New York: McGraw-Hill.

Fielding, N. and Lee, R. 1991: *Using Computers in Qualitative Research*. London: Sage.

Flanagan, J. C. 1954: The critical incidents technique. *Psychological Bulletin* 51, pp. 327–58.

Fransella, F. and Bannister D. 1977: *A Manual for the Repertory Grid Technique*, London: Academic Press.

Glaser, B. G. and Strauss, A. L. 1967: *The Discovery of Grounded Theory: strategies for qualitative research*. Chicago: Aldine.

Herzberg F., Mausner, B. and Synderman, B. B. 1959: *The Motivation to Work*. 2nd edn, London: Chapman and Hall.

Janis, I. 1982: *Victims of Group Think: a psychological study of foreign policy decisions and fiascos*. 2nd edn, Boston, MA: Houghton Mifflin.

Janis, I. 1988: Groupthink. In Katz, R. (ed.), *Managing Professionals in Innovative Organizations*, Cambridge, MA: Ballinger.

Jick, T. 1983: Mixing qualitative and quantitative methods: triangulation in action. In Van Maanen, J. (ed.), 1983: *Qualitative Methodology*, London: Sage.

Kelly, G. A. 1955: *The Psychology of Personal Constructs*. Vols 1 and 2, New York: Norton.

Krueger, R. 1988: *Focus Groups: a practical guide for applied research*. Newbury Park; CA: Sage.

Merton, R., Fiske, M. and Kendall, P. 1990: *The Focused Interview: a manual of problems and procedures*, 2nd edn, New York: Free Press.

Mintzberg, H. 1973: *The Nature of Managerial Work*. New York: Harper and Row.

Mintzberg, H. 1990: The manager's job: folklore and fact' *Harvard Business Review Classic*, March–April, pp. 163–76.

Mitchell, L. 1989: The definition of standards and their assessment. In Burke, J. (ed.), *Competence Based Education and Training*. Lewes: The Falmer Press.

Morgan, D. 1988: *Focus Groups as Qualitative Research*. Newbury Park, CA: Sage.

Pearn, M. and Kandola, R. 1993: *Job Analysis*. 2nd edn, London: IPM (now Institute of Personnel and Development).

Phillips, E. 1989: Use and abuse of the repertory grid: a PLP approach. *The Psychologist*, 5, pp. 194–8.

Rae, L. 1986: *How to Measure Training Effectiveness*. Aldershot: Gower.

Saville and Holdsworth

Schroder, M. 1989: *Managerial Competence: the key to excellence*. Dubuque, IO: Kendall and Hunt.

Smith, H. W. 1975: *Strategies of Social Research: the methodological imagination*, Engleword Cliffs, NJ: Prentice-Hall.

Stewart, R. 1967: *Managers and their Jobs: a study of the similarities and differences in the ways managers spend their time*. London: Macmillan.

Stewart, D. and Shamdsani, P. 1990: *Focus Groups: theory and practice*. Newbury Park, CA: Sage.

Stewart, V. and Stewart, A. 1981: *Business Applications of the Repertory Grid*. Maidenhead: McGraw-Hill.

Strauss, A. and Corbin, J. 1994: Grounded theory methodology: an overview. In Denzin, N. K. and Lincoln, Y. S. (eds), *Handbook of Qualitative Research*, London: Sage.

Van Maanen, J. (ed.) 1983: *Qualitative Methodology*. London: Sage.

Weitzman, E. and Miles, M. 1995: *Computer Programs for Data Analysis*. Thousand Oaks, CA: Sage.

CHAPTER 6

Analysing Individual Development Needs

•••• **Introduction** ••••

In this chapter we examine how the content and delivery of development programmes can be tailored to suit specific individual needs. Such customization requires tools for assessing individuals, their attitudes, capabilities and competencies in respect of organizational needs and their own career objectives, as outlined in chapter 3. There is a range of techniques used to assess individual managers' development needs. Some are used to identify development needs in the context of redundancy and career counselling, others to deal with the loss of hierarchical promotion associated with delayering strategies and the need for more lateral development, and others to maintain employability. Many of the changing contextual factors which were identified in chapter 1 and discussed in chapter 3 with relation to changing individual careers have meant that tools for assessing individual development needs have become a central part of any development programme. In particular there has been a shift of responsibility onto the individual for managing their own development within the context of a supportive organizational framework.

Two opposing forces in particular can be identified. One is the recognition that the informal 'British' way of identifying managerial talent may not be foolproof. While belonging to the club may still be an important criterion for entry into middle and senior management, it is no longer enough. We have already examined how this has been expressed in the pursuit of management competencies. However, using competencies also involves assessing individual managerial performance and behaviour against them. This requires more than a casual reflection on whether someone is a 'good chap'.

The other is the recognition that overly centralized, highly complex management development programmes which assess and develop a manager's capabilities from cradle to grave may no longer be appropriate. Many such organizations have been fragmenting and decentralizing, such as the NHS and the Civil Service, and are using a more localized approach which requires the individual to be more responsible for managing their development process, with the organization playing a supportive role, such as in the area of helping the manager assess their own development needs.

The first stage of the process of assessing individual development needs is to help an individual to clarify their capabilities and interests and produce a realistic appraisal of their current situation and alternatives for the future. The chapter begins by outlining the main techniques for so doing. Issues of reliability and validity are then discussed, as the search for greater rigour in the processes used has placed these issues at centre stage, with heated debate over the use of some methods at all. The complexity of implementing and validating some processes raises questions as to the role of line managers and generalist human resource personnel compared to that of external specialists and consultants, and these changing roles will be examined.

•••• Learning Objectives ••••

As a result of reading this chapter you should be able to:

- describe various tools and methods for identifying individual management development needs, including personality instruments and ability tests, assessment centres and performance appraisals, and explain their utility and limitations;
- identify appropriate tools for determining management development needs for a range of different managers and different organizations;
- explain the need to separate assessment for development from assessment for selection both in using assessment centres and in performance appraisals;
- Present a methodology for designing a development centre;
- explain various ways in which the reliability and validity of information collected by the various techniques can be determined.

•••• Appraisal Interviews ••••

For many organizations, the performance review process, utilizing the appraisal interview is the mainstay of their approach to identifying individual development needs. This is particularly true for small and medium companies who do not have the facilities to run more complex assessment centres, although they may have a more informal approach to the review process than the one outlined here.

Performance review processes have been consolidated in practice by a more general trend in human resource management towards assessment and evaluation at the organizational, team and individual level. In the public sector, the Audit Commission encourage performance management based on a cascading of organizational objectives down to the individual level with processes for measuring and reviewing performance at each level (for example, see Audit Commission, 1995). There has been a gradual extension of performance review processes across the public and private sectors, and through different tiers of management. Despite this upward trend, the coverage is still patchy, and fewer utilize these processes in a fully fledged performance management system. The IPD have monitored these changes in the UK in a series of longtitudinal studies conducted by Gill et al. (1973) and Gill (1977), followed by Long (1986) and more recently a broader study of performance management in the UK by Bevan and Thompson (1992a) and Fletcher and Williams (1992). Bevan and Thompson (1992a) found from their survey of just under 20 per cent of the UK workforce that although under 20 per cent of organizations operated a formal performance management system, 66 per cent of employers were operating other policies to manage employee performance, and only 14 per cent had no policies to manage employee performance. Appraisal, which they define as the conduct of 'a formal review of progress towards these targets' is in practice a key component of the performance management system. For many organizations, the review included issues to do with potential and promotability.

For organizations with performance management or related policies, between 60 and 70 per cent used the performance reviews to identify training needs for current positions, and between 41 and 52 per cent for future career positions. In addition some organizations used them for career counselling, for formal career mentoring, for career workshops, developmental centres, identification of potential, and succession planning.

One trend in the use of performance review is greater discussion and mention of upward appraisal and 360-degree appraisal (Redman and Snape; 1992 Tornow, 1993), but it may take some time for these processes to get consolidated into practice. The most common form of review is a joint discussion, usually called an 'appraisal interview' between the employee and the line manager, with less than 10 per cent of organizations making reference to jobholder's subordinates, and less than 16 per cent of performance reviews taking place with the employee's peers, and less than 25 per cent utilizing self-assessment (Bevan and Thompson, 1992a). Thus, the main formal commentator on a manager's development needs in the performance review context continues to be their line manager.

While much of the earlier debate over appraisal centred around the design of the appraisal form and whether it would record behaviour or achievement against objectives, and how different levels of performance would be rated and scaled, time and again this has proved to be of little avail because those who are carrying out the review are ill-informed about how to do it, or lack the commitment to the process. The techniques of appraisal interviewing are mid-way between interviewing for selection and counselling. Not everyone is naturally predisposed to such an approach, nor is trained for it, and less than 22 per cent of line managers are trained in career counselling (Bevan and Thompson, 1992a), nor do they have time. Organizational restructuring, especially involving cuts at middle management level, increase pressure on managers to find the time and motivation to conduct a development appraisal. Human resource management entrusts line and project managers with greater responsibility in this respect, but in practice does not always deliver the resources and support to ensure that this is effective or equitable. The reality is therefore that many appraisals can degenerate into character assassinations which leave the individual feeling bruised and unappreciated. Other problems have been identified with respect to line manager bias and subjectivity, probably linked to their lack of training, and in

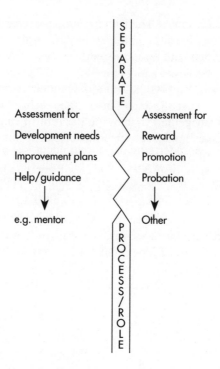

Figure 6.1 The separation of performance review processes: development and reward

particular this has a negative effect on women (Alimo-Metcalfe, 1993; Bevan and Thompson, 1992b; Townley 1990). Even if the individual is expected to take more responsibility for managing their development in the light of these dicussions, there is thus still a strong role for the line manager who needs training in the skills of positive and constructive feedback and joint problem solving.

A number of writers have commented that the bringing together of issues of development and issues of reward into one unitary review process can have disastrous consequences for development (for example, Woodruffe, 1993). In particular the difficulties for the appraiser are in dealing with the conflicting roles of being judge and coach. For the appraisee, there is the problem that revealing learning and developmental needs may expose weaknesses, when for performance reward discussions the main aim is to present personal strengths to achieve the best rating for performance-related pay. This may be why Bevan and Thompson (1992a) found that just under 50 per cent of organizations separated the discussion of individual promotion and potential from performance. In this case, the discussions may be separated in time, for example by having one review for development in January and the other for reward in June. Alternatively they may utilize a separate person to review performance for development (such as a mentor) from the individual responsible for reviewing it for reward (such as a line manager). The separation of these processes is illustrated in figure 6.1.

Advantages   Appraisal can link assessment for future development in with current performance. It provides a stronger role for line management in development. It gives the individual the opportunity to discuss his or her career intentions, concerns and views with somebody else. It can become a vehicle for mentoring where the manager is supported and provided with developmental opportunities.

Disadvantages   When conducted by untrained, uninterested appraisers, the process can become highly destructive and demotivating to the individual concerned. Assessments for reward can undermine the development benefits, and lack of follow-up can make it irrelevant. There is also the problem that the changing way in which managerial work is carried out, makes it very difficult for appraiser and appraisee to communicate. Broad spans of control and remote location make it difficult for the appraiser to be well informed about the appraisee. This is the reason underlying the growing interest in peer appraisal and 360-degree review. However, there are implementation problems relating to their acceptability within the prevailing organizational culture and politics, and the process of record keeping and analysis, not to mention the time involved.

Thus as well as the requirement for more time and resources to be put into training for and implementing appraisal processes, there needs to be a consolidation within the culture and norms of the organization. One way to achieve this is through assessment of a manager's ability to appraise, coach and develop others within their own appraisal processes, particularly those which are related to rewards, and this also requires a move towards a wider constituency involved in evaluating performance.

•••• Interest Inventories ••••

Interest inventories seek to measure, not what a person is good at, their abilities, but what a person is interested in, for the purpose of identifying in which direction that individual may want to go in terms of their career or occupation. They typically contain a wide sample of questions which might cover hobbies, school work and general life experiences. These are commonly used by those at the point of giving careers advice to those uncertain of what direction they intend to move, for example those placed in university or college careers advisory services. For example Saville and Holdsworth's Management Interest Inventory includes the management functions of production operations, technical services, research and development, distribution, purchasing, sales, marketing support, personnel and training, computer systems, finance, legal and secretarial and administration. It also includes the management skills of information collecting and processing, problem solving, decision making, modelling, communicating orally, communicating in writing, organizing things, organizing people, persuading, developing people and representing.

Advantages   Interest inventories are particularly useful at the start of a management career, or during a career transition. They can be fairly simplistic and really only give broad indications of potential careers.

Disadvantages They are less useful when an individual is aware of the broad direction of his or her career path.

•••• Psychometric Instruments for Personality Profiling ••••

Psychometrics, a word derived from the Greek, *psychometria*, literally means soul or mind measuring. There are thousands of instruments available for assessing different aspects of people's minds and personalities. We have broadly classified these according to whether they are ipsative or normative, although increasingly there are tools and instruments which have a normative and an ipsative version. We will deal with questionnaires assessing ability and team roles separately. The aim of these personality assessment instruments is to match an individual's personality with that required for a current or future management task or role.

IPSATIVE INSTRUMENTS

Ipsative instruments compare a person to themself by an assessment, usually, but not always, conducted through self-assessment questionnaires, which require them to compare and trade off personality dimensions within themself. For example, a questionnaire might give five different adjectives to describe aspects of personality and ask the individual to say which they are most like and which they are least like. As a result, the profile achieved is relative only to the person's own qualities and to nobody else. For example a person may be more extrovert than stable, but this does not mean that they are better or worse than other individuals. Although these assessments are usually quick and easy to do and produce quick results, there is considerable controversy about their utility at all (Fletcher 1989, 1993; Johnson et al. 1988). The main limitation of these instruments is that standard approaches to checking validity (see below) cannot be conducted on them, and that the profiles cannot be compared between people; for example, just because one person scores higher on compliance than another, it doesn't mean they are more compliant than the other person, it only means that in comparison to their other personality characteristics (such as influence and dominance) they are more compliant. Another crucial point is that it is impossible to score high or low on all the scales, and for this reason the scores on the scales cannot be treated as ordinary numbers. It can also be gaulling to a respondent that they are forced to choose between statements where they may feel they all apply to them or none of them do, and being forced to opt for one can falsely skew the findings. As Johnson dramatically points out (Fletcher, 1989), using an extreme hypothetical example, you could be asked to opt for one of (1) I regularly torture my children, or (2) I often steal from pensioners, and thus by rejecting one statement, you are implying you are either a sadist or a thief.

One example of a commonly used ipsative personality profile is called Personal Profile Analysis (PPA) by Thomas International, and the Personality Survey by Success Dynamics. These are drawn from research conducted by Cleaver into Marsden's personality types and identify the four dimensions of:

(1)   dominance;
(2)   influence;
(3)   stability;
(4)   compliance.

Other examples of ipsative instruments are the Gordon Personal Profile (GPP), the Gordon Personal Inventory (GPI), Kostick Perception and Preference Inventory (PAPI), the PAL Personality Profile System (PPS), Performax Personal Profile System Personality. Also, tools more associated with normative use now frequently have an ipsative variant, such as Octagon Two of the Occupational Personality Questionnaire (OPQ) and the Concept Four of the Occupational Personality Questionnaire (OPQ) discussed below.

NORMATIVE TESTS

Normative instruments and tests compare a score for each dimension of personality or ability against a relevant population of people – 'a norm group'. For example, middle managers in an engineering organization would need to be compared to a relevant population, namely other middle managers in engineering organizations. Scores are often reported in percentiles; thus, for example, if a score is on the 90th percentile for extroversion, it means that the person is more extrovert than 90 per cent of the norm group with which they are being compared.

Confusingly, not all tests which use a forced-choice format are ipsative. The Myers-Briggs is an example of a normative forced-choice test – to be ipsative, the instrument must require the forced choice to be made between descriptions which score on different scales. The Myers-Briggs Type Indicator (MBTI) is one of the world's most popular ipsative personality questionnaires for use in management development, and particularly with relation to team building, career planning, time management, communication and organizational development (Myers and McCaulley, 1985). Based on Carl Jung's theory of psychological types (Jung, 1966), and developed by Isobel Myers and her mother Katherine Briggs, in its original form it identified four pairs of preferences as outlined in exhibit 6.1.

The MBTI asks the person completing it to choose one from each of four pairs of preferences. Each preference interacts with the others to form 16 different combinations. For example, ISTJ is one of the most frequently occurring types in top management in many countries. Although psychological type is complicated, there are several other ways the information can be broken down. It is possible to identify pairs of preferences which can be related to various temperaments. For example an NT reacts to stress by overwork, fight, intolerance, conform rebelliously and through pedantic debate (Bayne, 1990; Keirsey and Bates, 1978). More recently, the MBTI has been extended – the new Extended Analysis Report version (EAR) with a longer questionnaire of 136 items, and a new scoring system to expand through factor analysis the original four scales to 20 scales. Thus the original Sensing-Intuition scale can now be read as an individual's tendency to vary on five bi-polar scales (McHenry, 1994):

···· Exhibit 6.1 ····
The Myers-Briggs Type Indicator: the original four preferences

1 Four pairs of preferences

The descriptions are of behaviour associated with each preference when it is sufficiently developed

Extraversion (E)
Prefer the 'outer world' of people and things
   to reflection
Active
Gain energy from others
Want to experience things in order to understand them
Work by trial and error
Like variety

Introversion (I)
Prefer reflection and the 'inner world' to
   action
Prefer writing to talking
May enjoy social contact but need to recover
   from it
Want to understand something before trying it
Like a quiet space to work in

Sensing (S)
Like facts
Realistic and practical
Observant about what is actually happening
Work steadily and step by step
Enjoy owning things and making them work
Patient, good with detail

Intuition (N)
See possibilities and patterns
Imaginative, speculative
Like to see the overall picture
Work in bursts of energy with quiet periods in
   between (need inspiration)
Like variety
Impatient with routine

Thinking (T)
Fair, firm-minded, sceptical
Analytical and logical
Brief and businesslike
Critical
Clear and consistent principles

Feeling (F)
Warm, sympathetic, aware how others feel
Trusting
Enjoy pleasing others
Need harmony
Clear and consistent values

Judging (J)
Decisive
Industrious and determined
Organized and systematic
Take deadlines seriously
Like to have things decided and settled

Perceiving (P)
Curious
Flexible and tolerant
Leave things open
Pull things together well at last minute
Sample many more experiences than can be
   digested or used

Source: Bayne, 1990

Concrete	Abstract
Realistic	Imaginative
Pragmatic	Intellectual
Experiential	Theoretical
Traditional	Original

The MBTI needs to be analysed by trained assessors, and is most commonly used as a part of a development centre programme.

Another example of a norm-referenced personality instrument is Saville and Holdsworth's Occupational Personality Questionnaire (OPQ) Concept 5, 1984. This questionnaire has 186 questions where people are asked questions such as 'I tend to be assertive in groups' and are given a 5-point Likert scale to answer ranging from strongly disagree to strongly agree.

Unlike the ipsative instrument, each question relates to only one personality category at a time which can then be scored; personality categories are not compared and traded off against each other, as in the case of 'least like most like' ipsative questions. In the OPQ 30 personality categories relate to the nine sub-dimensions of three broader personality dimensions, as shown in exhibit 6.2.

Thus, for example, the sub-dimension of 'assertive', breaks down into 'persuasive', 'controlling' and 'independent'. This instrument is also available in other formats which take a more ipsative form, and which are considerably quicker to complete. For example IMAGES is one version of the OPQ which breaks down personality into six areas: imaginative; methodical; achieving; gregarious; emotional; and sympathetic.

Ipsative tools utilize fewer questions, as more than one dimension can be identified in each question in an ipsative tool. However, the ipsative variants are harder to use in comparing people and with reference to norm groups.

Management competence or competency questionnaires which go beyond the specification of personality attributes to identify skills and competence as well, are increasingly popular. These are hybrids of personality questionnaires and ability tests, as they ask respondents to assess themselves using a behaviourally defined but psychometrically based performance measure. For example Saville and Holdsworth's Inventory of Management Competencies identifies 16 competencies divided up into four main areas: relationships with people; thinking skills; feelings and energies; and business/technical.

This instrument can generate an individual profile that is either norm referenced against a norm group of other managers, or that is ipsative as it derives from a set of forced choices, and thus can be used to help identify an individual's relative strengths and weaknesses.

There are many other alternatives, for example the 16 PF (personality factors) based on the work of Cattell et al. (1988), and produced by ASE (Assessment and Selection for Employment); PRISM – the Profile Report Individual Style and Motivation, available from DSA Ltd (Development Strategy and Assessment), and highlighting motivation; and the CPI-309 (California Personality Inventory 309) available from the Oxford Psychologists Press, and which is particularly useful for measuring personal integrity, individual initiative and leadership potential. The Insight Inventory, based on the field theory of Kurt Lewin (1951), is particularly

•••• Exhibit 6.2 ••••
The OPQ's personality dimensions

Relationships with people

Persuasive – Enjoys selling, changes opinions of others, convincing with arguments, negotiates

Controlling – Takes charge, directs, manages, organizes, supervises others

Independent – Has strong views on things, difficult to manage, speaks up, argues, dislikes ties

Outgoing – Fun loving, humorous, sociable, vibrant, talkative, jovial

Affiliative – Has many friends, enjoys being in groups, likes companionship, shares things with friends

Socially confident – Puts people at ease, knows what to say, good with words

Modest – Reserved about achievements, avoids talking about self, accepts others, avoids trappings of status

Democratic – Encourages others to contribute, consults, listens and refers to others

Caring – Considerate to others, helps those in need, sympathetic, tolerant

Thinking style

Practical – Down-to-earth, likes repairing and mending things, better with the concrete

Data rational – Good with data, operates on facts, enjoys assessing and measuring

Artistic – Appreciates culture, shows artistic flair, sensitive to visual arts and music

Behavioural – Analyses thoughts and behaviour, psychologically minded, likes to understand people

Traditional – Preserves well-proven methods, prefers the orthodox, disciplined, conventional

Change orientated – Enjoys doing new things, seeks variety, prefers novelty to routine, accepts changes

Conceptual – Theoretical, intellectually curious, enjoys the complex and abstract

Innovative – Generates ideas, shows ingenuity, thinks up solutions

Assertive · _Gregarious_ · _Empathy_ · _Fields of use_ · _Abstract_

•••• Exhibit 6.2 continued ••••

Forward planning – Prepares well in advance, enjoys target setting, forecasts trends, plans projects

Detail conscious – Methodical, keeps things neat and tidy, precise, accurate

Conscientious – Sticks to deadlines, completes jobs, perseveres with routine, likes fixed schedules

Structure

Feelings and emotions

Relaxed – Calm, relaxed, cool under pressure, free from anxiety, can switch off

Worrying – Worries when things go wrong, keyed-up before important events, anxious to do well

Anxieties

Tough minded – Difficult to hurt or upset, can brush off insults, unaffected by unfair remarks

Emotional control – Restrained in showing emotions, keeps feelings back, avoids outbursts

Optimistic – Cheerful, happy, keeps spirits up despite setbacks

Critical – Good at probing the facts, sees the disadvantages, challenges assumptions

Controls

Active – Has energy, moves quickly, enjoys physical exercise, doesn't sit still

Competitive – Plays to win, determined to beat others, poor loser

Achieving – Ambitious, sets sights high, career centred, results orientated

Decisive – Quick at conclusions, weighs things up rapidly, may be hasty, takes risks

Energies

Social desirability response – Has tended to respond in a socially desirable way

Source: Saville and Holdsworth

oriented for companies wanting an easy-to-use insight into behaviour, and to empower managers to do their own selection, training and team building without over-reliance on consultants and experts. This is distributed by the Test Agency.

The use of psychometric instruments is not without its critics and caveats. First, as with assessment centres, there are well-designed and validated tools, but that does not mean to say that they all are. There are many poorly designed and tested ones on the market. Second, even when a test has been well proven, that does not automatically confer on it a universal validity. It is easy to take a well-designed instrument and use it in an inappropriate way (see Fletcher, 1993, p. 46). Many organizations will require outside help, either in terms of designing the instruments or in training their assessors to use them.

Advantages   These are difficult to talk about in general, as they vary so much. For example ipsative tests have the benefit of speed whereas normative tests have the benefit of allowing for comparison between individuals. Their main benefit is to provide an additional source of information for use in discussions over one's suitability for an existing role or for future development within a wider context, such as in an assessment centre.

Disadvantages   Validity data is generally not as good as data drawn from assessment centres, or when using multiple measures, and generally they are best used alongside other forms of assessments to get other views of personality, but also to receive information on other aspects of an individual, such as their skills and abilities. Although most instruments have anti-faking devices and checks for social desirability scores, there is always the possibility that subjects answer them either as they would like to be or as they think the organization would like them to be, rather than as they actually are. Also people's own perceptions of themselves can be unrealistic (except to them). It is possible to correct for this by means of comparison's between self-assessment and assessment by others such as peers. In addition, some individuals may find such instruments intrusive, and there are a host of ethical questions surrounding the use and keeping of the results (see Baker and Cooper, 1995).

•••• Ability Tests ••••

Ability tests are used in management development to identify potential through testing the abilities of the person, and these are usually broken down into a number of distinct and relevant categories, for example verbal, numerical, spatial, mechanical and so on. Generally ability tests are norm referenced and the validity of the information produced is highly dependent on the choice of appropriate norm groups. An example of a battery of ability tests, appropriate at the managerial level, is the Advanced Managerial Tests (AMTs) produced by Saville and Holdsworth: which include four tests, verbal application, numerical reasoning, verbal analysis and numerical analysis.

Advantages   These tests go beyond an individual's perceptions of their abilities, to test their abilities in pencil-and-paper contexts. However, they do not generally go beyond this to test abilities in action in a real work situation itself. These tests also have the advantage of allowing for comparison against norm groups.

Disadvantages   The categories can be quite limiting, and usually need to be linked to other aspects of assessment, for example personality. Also the test of ability is usually synthetic, and not based within a real situation.

•••• Team-Building Instruments ••••

There are also tools to assess individuals in relation to teams. Most personality instruments and ability tests can examine the strengths and weaknesses of teams by looking at the feedback collectively, for example the Myers-Briggs indicator may be used for this. However there are also other instruments which are more explicitly designed for team building. For example the Belbin (1981 and 1993) instrument for management teams. This takes as its starting-point the view that although it may be impossible to find a perfect individual, it is possible to bring together high-quality teams, and can help those teams overcome their weaknesses and build on their strengths. Belbin (1981) identifies people in terms of their team roles, and originally identified eight roles, but since has developed a ninth role with the addition of 'specialist' (Belbin, 1993). These roles are outlined in table 6.1.

As well as helping the subject to gain self-awareness, such tools can also identify appropriate learning methods and opportunities to fit in with each preferred team role in order to build on strengths or improve areas of weakness. Alternatively the development can be consodilated through team-building discussions aimed at identifying ways of dealing with role gaps in teams and and exploring ways of using team members most effectively. A way of developing the use of such tools further is to go beyond merely taking an individual's perception of themselves through the questionnaire and to get teams to fill in the questionnaires with relation to each other. The discrepancies which arise between one's own perception and those of others with relation to preferred team roles can be the topic of interesting team discussion and debate.

A similar model has been developed by Margerison and McCann (1989) in their team management profile, and is seen as helpful in providing managers with feedback on their preferred way of working, using a wheel to distinguish between explorers, organizers, controllers and advisers, which can be related to job demands and types of work.

Advantages   These models provide assessment for people in relation to each other within real organizational settings. They tend to have higher acceptability than individually orientated psychometric instruments which may be used for less positive forms of development such as identifying people for redundancy. They provide a vehicle for teams to discuss in a non-threatening way how they can work together more effectively. It is possibly the suspicion that many instruments assume we are trying to assemble an identikit of a perfect manager which causes such mistrust and ill-feeling towards them. To some extent, the team-based tools assume that each personality has its own associated strengths and weaknesses and that teams can be trained to perform well despite individual limitations.

Disadvantages   As with all self-perception questionnaires, team-building instruments examine people's perceptions of their preferences abilities and behaviours, rather

Table 6.1 Belbin's nine team roles

Roles and descriptions – team-role contribution	Allowable weaknesses
Plant: Creative, imaginative, unorthodox. Solves difficult problems	Ignores details. Too pre-occupied to communicate effectively.
Resource investigator: Extrovert, enthusiastic, communicative. Explores opportunities. Develops contacts.	Overoptimistic. Loses interest once initial enthusiasm has passed.
Co-ordinator: Mature, confident, a good chairperson. Clarifies goals, promotes decision-making, delegates well.	Can be seen as manipulative. Delegates personal work.
Shaper: Challenging, dynamic, thrives on pressure. Has the drive and courage to overcome obstacles.	Can provoke others. Hurts people's feelings.
Monitor evaluator: Sober, strategic and discerning. Sees all options. Judges accurately.	Lacks drive and ability to inspire others. Overly critical.
Teamworker: Co-operative, mild, perceptive and diplomatic. Listens, builds, averts friction, calms the waters.	Indecisive in crunch situations. Can be easily influenced.
Implementer: Disciplined, reliable, conservative and efficient. Turns ideas into practical actions.	Somewhat inflexible. Slow to respond to new possibilities.
Completer: Painstaking, conscientious, anxious. Searches out errors and omissions. Delivers on time.	Inclined to worry unduly. Reluctant to delegate. Can be a nit-picker.
Specialist: Single-minded, self-starting, dedicated. Provides knowledge and skills in rare supply.	Contributes on only a narrow front. Dwells on technicalities. Overlooks the 'big picture'.

Strength of contribution in any one of the roles is commonly associated with particular weaknesses. These are called allowable weaknesses. Executives are seldom strong in all nine team roles.
Source: Belbin, 1993

than scoring these objectively. They are not so useful when people do not work in a team environment, nor where individuals are not used to working with each other.

•••• Developmental Assessment Centres ••••

Assessment centres, which are designed and grounded in systematic job analysis using the methods mentioned in chapter five are a vehicle for assessing the person in relation to the competencies or qualities deemed relevant to performance of the job. They are more usually used for identifying management potential and for selection. With some adjustment, mainly in terms of involving the candidates and providing more detailed feedback and follow-up, they can be used as a method for identifying development needs. Although traditionally they were used developmentally for reviewing promotion potential or for identifying high flyers, now they are just as likely to be used to help a manager identify their own strengths and weaknesses through providing self-knowledge in relation to their competence in role and in relation to future development paths. Thus they are increasingly used for coaching and identifying suitable development activities. Woodruffe (1993) provides clear guidance on assessment-centre use and design, as do Lee and Beard (1994) on development centres. All assessment centres aim to 'obtain the best possible indication of people's actual or potential competence to perform at the target job or job level . . . They focus squarely on behaviour and include a set of exercises to capture and simulate the major aspects of the job' (Woodruffe, 1993, p. 2).

In the UK assessment centres date back to the War Office Selection Boards which were introduced in 1942 to select officers, and were developed subsequently by the Civil Service and other parts of the public sector. In the United States, the history was similar, with their use being instigated in wartime, but with subsequent movement in peacetime into the private sector such as into the American Telephone and Telegraph Company. By the mid 1980s over 2,000 American organizations were using some type of assessment-centre programme (Gaugler et al., 1987), and Mabey (1989) reported in a survey that over a third of companies employing more than 1,000 people had used them in the past year in the UK. The latter statistic has been capped more recently by Boyle et al. (1993) who claim that nearly half the organizations (45 per cent) responding to their survey used assessment centres. Although their use is widespread, it is patchy, and is dominated by large organizations and those in the private sector, and even here it may only be for certain types of role, for example for selecting graduates, (Boyle et al., 1993; Robertson and Makin, 1986).

Woodruffe (1993) points out that it is advisable to separate assessment centres for development from those for selection, as otherwise the selection process will undermine the development process, and the role of judge will inhibit the role of facilitator and coach for the assessor; a similar point was made earlier with regard to using appraisal interviews for both development and reward. For example a candidate will be reluctant to explore their weaknesses and potential development areas if, in so doing, they may injure their chances in the selection process. Woodruffe (1993) places these two extremes on a continuum to explain the differences (figure 6.2). Despite these differences, Woodruffe (1993) shows how assessment centres can be linked to management development and a coherent integrated system for HR

	Development centre ←	→ Selection centre	
Purpose	Development/career planning	Promotion/development	Selection
Label	Development centre		Selection centre
Philosophy	Done by the participant	Done with the participant	Done to the candidate
Method	Self-assessment/peer assessment plus assessor's view	Assessment with feedback	Testing/no feedback
Assessor's role	Facilitator		Judge
Includes	Self-insight materials		Cognitive test
Output	Personal development plan	Report	Selection decision
Information on exercises	Open		Secret
Feedback given	After each exercise	After centre	Not given
Owner of information	Participant	Participant and organization	Organization
Duration	One week		One day

Figure 6.2 The continuum of assessment and development centres

Source: Woodruffe, 1993, Assessment Centres: Identifying and Developing Competence. 2nd ed. London: IPM (now IPD) and reproduced with the kind permission of the publishers, The Institute of Personnel and Development, IPD House, 35 Camp Road, Wimbledon, London, SW19 4UX

management. However, in this latter example, the centres are used for assessing potential with management development activity coming after promotion. An alternative approach would be for the development assessment centre to form the basis for recommending and agreeing appropriate management development activity.

One reason for the higher validity coefficients quoted (cited below) for development centres as a tool for assessing development need, is the careful construction of multiple exercises which are able to sample multiple competencies from various different points of view. Although the exact choice of exercises requires careful diagnosis there are a number of commonly utilized exercises.

First, there are those methods which are used widely outside assessment centres as well as within them, both for selection and development. For example:

- *one to one interviews*   both for information collecting and giving feedback;
- *psychometric instruments*   (discussed above);
- *ability tests*   often including assessments of verbal and critical reasoning (discussed above);
- *verbal presentations*   where participants may give a verbal presentation on a pre-prepared subject or one given immediately prior to the presentation. The subject may be self-chosen or dictated by the assessors.

In addition there are a number of methods which are less widely used elsewhere but are central to assessment-centre approaches.

- *In-tray exercises*   These simulate the typical pile of papers that might confront a job holder, for example on return from a holiday. Participants are usually required to conduct a written exercise outlining the action they would take in response to each of the items. They may be assessed on their organization skills, their ability to set priorities, on their speed and quality of decision taking, such as incisiveness, and even on qualities such as delegation, interpersonal skills and imagination.
- *Analytical exercises*   A participant may be asked to conduct a piece of written analytical work, or be asked to resolve a business problem or a case study. For example, a market research company may ask someone to write a report based on some market research data presented to them.
- *Group role playing exercises*   A group of participants is commonly given a brief about an organization and given individual roles to play within it, with individual views and priorities set for each individual. The group is then often asked to have a meeting which is drawn together to solve a problem or take a decision on a particular issue. For example the group may be asked to role play directors at a board meeting convened to consider how to make budget savings of £1 million. Participants are often given conflicting and differing perspectives, enabling the exercise to be used to examine, for example, their assertiveness, their interpersonal skills such as in negotiation, communication or persuasiveness, their group role and behaviour. These exercises require considerable skill and training for assessment, as participant behaviour may be influenced heavily by group dynamics (thus reducing reliability of data), and it may not always be clear why someone is behaving the way they are, for example is someone mute because of

lack of self-confidence or lack of cognitive skills? Some group exercises may be chaired by a non-assessee to tease out some of these ambiguities. Often several assessors observe the exercise, and sometimes even one assessor per participant. Worryingly, there is a great deal of evidence that women can be disadvantaged by these role plays (Alimo-Metcalfe, 1995).

- *One-to-one role play exercises* Generally one participant and one assessor may conduct a role play, possibly with an assessing observer. For example, for customer-focused jobs, the assessor may role play an angry customer with a complaint or a reluctant customer. This process is, however, resource intensive.

There are many different types of exercises which can be designed, the important point is that they are developed to elicit a knowledge of relevant skills and competencies, and that they are well tested prior to use. An example of how these different exercises can be compared to a grid of competencies is outlined in table 6.2.

Advantages Some of the reasons why organizations may consider having development centres are highlighted in Woodruffe (1993) in his discussion of the achievements of well-designed centres (pp. 26–27).

- The emphasis on development is motivating, and particularly when compared to the demotivating effect of selection centres.
- They are compatible with a move towards continuous development.
- They are compatible for use with competency based approaches to development.
- They give a clear and energized starting-point and impetus to the development process.
- They help people to buy in and take responsibility for their own development plan.
- Where exercises are tailored to the organization, the feedback on strengths and weaknesses is particularly persuasive.
- They facilitate self-assessment and enable participants to consider their career aspirations and possibilities.
- They enable assessment and feedback from peers, and are a forum for the instigation of networks of support which continue long after the centre itself.
- They provide good PR, and in a sense are their own 'ambassadors'.
- They are perceived by assessors and participants to be fair.
- They have face validity, and are seen to be relevant to the organization's needs.
- They generate greater acceptance of their findings among participants than other methods.
- They have better validity coefficients than other methods in general (see below).

Disadvantages 'Assessment centres are complex to design. They are also time-consuming and resource-intensive to administer. There will clearly be many situations where no one other than a complete zealot would claim they are warranted' (Woodruffe, 1993, p. 47). For example they may not be appropriate for lower-level trainees, where tests of aptitude or ability or a structured interview may be more appropriate (Wright et al., 1989). We have already mentioned that use of development centres is dominated by larger companies and organizations. There are logistical problems of using centres for smaller organizations. For example, a centre generally needs at least six participants for it to run, and it may be difficult to get this number from within one small organization at one time. The investment in time and resources in setting up and running a centre may just not be worth it for such organizations, unless they can obtain suitable off-the-shelf variants, and focus on generic competency dimensions across a range of jobs rather than emphasizing the specifics of each job. There is also a problem in relation to obsolescence. Woodruffe (1993) suggests that the centre should be checked for any updating needed at least every couple of years. For fast-changing organizations the continual updating needed may be difficult to achieve.

•••• Validity and Reliability ••••

A whole industry has developed which provides tools which allow for assessment of people and tasks, and provides flexibility and customization to different needs in different environments. It is difficult for those embarking on this journey to assess the reliability and validity of these different toolkits to select the appropriate ones to use. Some key questions need to be asked in order to help with the search for reliability and validity.

- Where off-the-peg questionnaires and inventories are available, what evidence is there that this can be used for a context and need such as mine?
- Are the categories being assessed of interest in my situation?
- What professional qualifications and accreditation do the providers of the instruments have?
- What training and support will we get in using these tools?
- What data do the suppliers have on reliability and validity for this tool? Where validity data is provided, in what context is it given?

An instrument cannot be valid in general, only with a view to a given purpose, and thus it may be useful to know that it has been used many times to assess the development needs of computer programmers and shows good validity data on this if you are using it for this purpose, but not if you are using it to assess the ability to deal with customer complaints in local government.

There are a number of different ways of assessing validity and reliability.

RELIABILITY

Reliability is the consistency of measurement, irrespective of time or circumstances. For example a test or method must give the same results on different occasions and so produce trustworthy and stable results. Reliability data can be produced in a number of different ways, but most usually is reported as a co-efficient ranging from

Table 6.2 Example of assessment techniques applied to a grid of competencies

	Group neg'n problem	Group problem	In tray	Analysis	Sub 1 to 1	Interview
Breadth of awareness to be well-informed Develops and maintains networks and formal channels of communication, within the organization and with the outside world; keeps abreast of relevant local, national and international political and economic developments; monitors competitor activity; has a general awareness of what should be happening and what progress is being made		X	X	X		X
Incisiveness to have a clear understanding Gets a clear overview of an issue; grasps information accurately; relates pieces of information; identifies causal relationships; gets to the heart of a problem; identifies the most productive lines of enquiry; appreciates all the variables affecting an issue; identifies limitations to information; adapts thinking in the light of new information; tolerates and handles conflicting/ambiguous information and ideas	X	X	X	X		
Imagination to find ways forward Generates options; evaluates options by examining the positive and negative results if they were put into effect; anticipates effects of options on others; foresees others' reactions; demonstrates initiative and common sense	X		X	X	X	
Organization to work productively Identifies priorities; thinks back from deadline; identifies elements of tasks; schedules elements; anticipates resource needs; allocates resources to tasks; sets objectives for staff; manages own and others' time		X	X	X	X	

Drive to achieve results
Prepared to compromise to achieve a result; installs solution within timeframe; innovates or adapts existing procedures to ensure a result; takes on problems; suffers personal inconvenience to ensure problems are solved; comes forward with ideas; sets challenging targets; sets out to win new business; sets own objectives; recognizes areas for self-development; acquires new skills and capabilities; accepts new challenges — X X X

Self-confidence to lead the way
Expresses and conveys a belief in own ability; prepared to take and support decisions; stands up to seniors; willing to take calculated risks; admits to areas of inexpertise — X X X

Sensitivity to identify others' viewpoints
Listens to others' viewpoints; adapts to other people; takes account of others' needs; sees situation from others' viewpoints; emphasizes; aware of others expectations — X X X X

Co-operativeness to work with other people
Involves others in own area and ideas; keeps others informed; makes use of available support services; utilizes skills of team members; open to others' ideas and suggestions — X X X

Patience to win in the long term
Sticks to a strategic plan; does not get side-tracked; sacrifices the present for the future; bides time when conditions are not favourable — X X X X

Source: Woodruffe, 1993
Reproduced with the kind permission of the publishers, The Institute of Personnel and Development, IPD House, 35, Camp Road, Wimbledon, London, SW19 4UX

1 which is totally reliable to 0 which has no reliability. The main methods for assessing the reliability of instruments such as tests involve one of the following.

- *Test-retest reliability* For example where an individual takes a test on two separate occasions, without differences in training and development in the meantime, the extent to which the two results correlate (are the same).
- *Alternate form reliability* On two different versions of the same test, the extent of correlation between an individual's two scores.
- *Split half reliability* Where the questions in a test are split into two halves, and a correlation is conducted on the similarity of individual scores on both halves.

VALIDITY

Validity is the ability of a tool to provide useful and relevant information. Thus for example a test should measure the quality it is supposed to measure, and differences identified between individuals should reflect differences on the criterion being measured. There are a number of different tests for validity, and often the validity coefficient is reported as either ranging from -1 (which means there is a negative correlation between the test score and the quality being measured) to 0 (which means that there is largely a random or neutral correlation) to $+1$ which is rarely achieved and suggests that all the information is accurate and measures what it purports to measure). Some report validity in terms of percentages, for example 83 per cent could mean by some suppliers that 83 per cent of the information you get about an individual or task is accurate. The following are common indicators of validity.

- *Face* Does the tool or instrument look right, is it acceptable to the candidate as well as the company, does it look as though it produces relevant information?
- *Faith* What relevant qualifications do the suppliers of the tool have? What do the experts say about the tool? For example are they members of the British Psychological Society (BPS) and is the tool certificated by the BPS?
- *Content* Does the method adequately sample the appropriate behaviour within the task or job, or behaviour or skills relevant to this management development context?
- *Construct* Does the tool measure what it sets out to measure, does it correlate with other tests or tools that measure the same thing?
- *Concurrent* When this tool is applied to the task that the management development is preparing people for (or the people currently conducting the task), does it accord with other data we have about the task and the performance of these people.
- *Predictive* Does the tool predict how well someone goes on to perform on the management development programme or in the task for which it is preparing people?

A number of textbooks examine the issue of validity and reliability in greater detail (for example see Cronbach, 1970; Shackleton and Fletcher, 1984; Vernon, 1953). Validity assessment has advanced a great deal over the last few years as new techniques such as meta-analysis have been developed (for further information see

Hunter and Schmidt, 1989; Hunter et al., 1982; Tenopyr, 1989). Meta-analysis is essentially a method for using cumulative research to escape the problems of sampling error and other errors of measurement by collating the findings from several studies, thus enabling sample sizes to become large enough to draw more conclusive findings. Prior to meta-analysis researchers were reduced either to selective review studies so that only studies with certain characteristics were included, which still had the problem of what to do about contradictory conclusions; or to produce comprehensive narrative reviews producing often vague and ambivalent conclusions (see Hunter and Schmidt, 1989). As a result meta-analysis enables research to comment more deeply on the validity of, for example, ability or personality characteristics as a measurement of job performance.

Although most of the research conducted using meta-analysis on validity is based on selection centres, it does show that assessment centres in general are superior to all other methods of predicting performance ratings, with a meta-analytic estimate of their validity generally quoted around 0.4 (for example see Schmitt et al., 1984), compared for example to personality measures with a mean validity of 0.15 (Schmitt et al., 1984), and to interviews with validity around 0.2 (for example see Reilly and Chao, 1982). The possible range could extend from 0 (totally invalid) to 1 (perfect validity), but it would be rare for a measure to achieve over 0.5. We must also bear in mind that these figures have many potential errors of measurement, for example the performance ratings which usually use supervisor's ratings are prone to subjectivity, bias and inaccuracy, and rating scales for performance evaluation and for assessment centre evaluation may not have been the same.

Woodruffe (1993, pp. 45–6) has also reviewed a process called 'utility analysis' to demonstrate the financial benefits of using assessment centres in selection, suggesting that it is possible to claim that, for each participant, the centre can yield a utility gain of £3,360 per person over random selection, and £1,680 over the interview alone in the first year.

However, there is a problem with the stretching of research into new realms of statistical analysis which require considerable understanding of psychology and statistics. It can act to disempower those responsible for management development strategy, as they necessarily become more reliant on the expert occupational psychologist for help in designing and using tools of assessing development needs. Increasingly organizations are becoming more reliant on external consultants and psychometric testing organizations to provide the tools needed. As the proliferation of psychometric instruments expands above the 4,000 currently available in the UK, it is no wonder that the developments can act to confuse rather than clarify what an organization needs to do to diagnose the management development needs of its employees.

Another issue which must ultimately cause ripples on the ocean of research on assessment and diagnosis for management development is that of the clash between subjective and objective assessment. Irrespective of research findings on validity, what really matters is the subjective view of the stakeholders themselves. Ultimately, the prime concern is whether the organization's senior managers believe their assessment tools are effective, and whether the individuals being subjected to them believe that the information produced on learning needs and management development inputs required are relevant and useful to them. Even where a tool has aimed for as great an objectivity as possible, there is always room for subjective judgement to influence the process. For example, if a questionnaire is being used to assess the personality or attitudes of someone as a vehicle for understanding their development needs, subjectivity in the mind of the person filling in the questionnaire will affect the process. Likewise an instrument for job analysis and matching a person's skills to a job will have subjectivity in the way a person scores the questionnaire as they take judgements about the skills used in the role.

While it could be perceived as an intrusion into objectivity, subjective judgements can be used to enhance the assessment process. A number of techniques are evolving to increase the validity of qualitative and subjective data. 'Triangulation' is an approach which typically comprises a mixture of qualitative and quantitative approaches and combines methodologies allowing for multiple viewpoints and the collection of different kinds of data. It has been suggested that this improves the accuracy where these different sources relate to the same phenomenon. 'Within-method' triangulation allows for cross-validation for internal consistency or reliability, whereas 'between-method' triangulation tests the degree of external validity (Denzin, 1978; Jick, 1983; Smith, 1975). An example of within-method triangulation would be checking the correlation of two different interviewers of one individual within an assessment centre (not unlike test-retest reliability), or checking back the viewpoint of the interviewer with that of the respondent. An example of between-method triangulation would be to compare the assessments of different exercises to see whether they provide a consistent picture (as with construct validity). The main difference of these methods compared with more quantitative ones is that this can be done in a more informal way, and can be used where there may be fewer respondents being assessed in a customized centre where it would be unrealistic to do a more detailed statistical validation exercise.

There are other ways in which the more qualitative approaches can be used for checking the validity of the methods for assessing development needs, including the following.

- Where multiple individuals are having their development needs assessed, a common format followed by all will reduce the chances of bias, for example where an appraisal interview is being conducted, a pro forma of the schedule and types of questions to be asked can be provided to all appraisers.
- Pre-testing and piloting assessment techniques can improve their design.
- Thorough training of assessors, for example for appraisal interviewers in learning the necessity of putting aside one's own prejudices and presuppositions and allowing one to feel surprised by the data.
- The use of standardized criteria within the assessment process, which are clearly communicated to all assessors; for example, where a verbal presentation is being used to assess an individual's development needs the assessor has a clear idea of the criteria they are using to evaluate the presentation.
- Full documentation of the development process, with findings communicated to the assessors and the individual, to ensure clarity over development needs and to enable ongoing monitoring and review.

•••• **Summary** ••••

In this chapter we have looked at a range of ways of identifying individual management development needs. The most common is of course the individual performance review process which utilizes an appraisal interview to identify development needs, often alongside other requirements such as the identification of potential and the rating for performance-related pay. The problems associated with this process were discussed in relation to the incompatibility of assessing development and reward together, the key role played by the line manager, and their subjectivity, bias and lack of training.

Large organizations, wary of the problems of reliability and validity in managerial judgement, have increasingly had recourse to more 'scientific' instruments such as psychometric instruments and tests and other tools commonly used in assessment centres. These enable them to clarify competencies or other qualities required of particular categories of managers, and thereby to have more control over their selection and assessment. However, there is a price attached to the accuracy and consistency of assessment in terms of both resources and of a growing dependence on specialist expertise. In addition, there is a danger that the assessment process will end up 'driving' development, or even drive out development. Individual assessment instruments may be ideal for sorting out the sheep from the goats, but their developmental worth can only be justified by the link with individual learning opportunities and individual motivation to learn. We now turn to consider this in Part III.

EXERCISES

(1) In pairs, assume that you were both asked to conduct a performance review interview with the other in order to identify their development needs.
  • Work out what information you would require and what kind of questions you would need to ask (for example with relation to the performance objectives for their current role, their career plans, current personal development plans, and areas of strength and weakness in their current role).
  • If you have access to the information needed, you could go on to role play the interview itself, and identify an action plan as an output of the interview.
  • What tools would be most useful to gain any extra information you need? Why?

(2) Taking your own current job or one known to you, and choosing one psychometric instrument:

- try to find out how use of that instrument could help you to understand your development needs with relation to that job;
- what research and other work has been conducted on it to identify its reliability and validity for use in such a way?

•••• References ••••

Alimo-Metcalfe, B. 1993: Women in management: organizational socialization and assessment practices that prevent career advancement. *International Journal of Selection and Assessment* 1, 2, pp. 68–83.

Alimo-Metcalfe, B. 1995: Leadership and assessment. In Vinnicombe, S. and Colwill, N. L. (eds), *The Essence of Women in Management*, Hemel Hempstead: Prentice-Hall.

Audit Commission 1995: *Calling the Tune: performance management in local government.* London: HMSO.

Baker, B. and Cooper, J. 1995: Fair or foul: a survey of occupational test practices in the UK. *Personnel Review*, 24, pp. 67–82.

Bayne, R. 1990: A new direction for the Myers-Briggs Type Indicator. *Personnel Management*, March, pp. 48–51.

Belbin R. M. 1981: *Management Teams – Why they Succeed or Fail.* Oxford: Heinemann.

Belbin R. M. 1993: *Team Roles at Work.* Oxford: Butterworth Heinemann, p. 21.

Bevan, S. and Thompson, M. 1992a: An overview of policy and practice. Part 1 of *Performance Management in the UK: an analysis of the issues*, London, IPM (now Institute of Personnel and Development.), pp. 1–141.

Bevan, S. and Thompson, M. 1992b: Merit pay, performance appraisal and attitudes to women's work. Report no. 234, Brighton, Institute of Employment Studies.

Boyle, S. et al. 1993: The rise of the assessment centre: a survey of AC useage in the UK *Selection and Development Review* 9, 3, pp. 1–4.

Cattell, R., Elser, H. and Tatsuoka, M. 1988: *The 16PF Handbook.* Illinois, Institute for Personality and Ability Testing.

Cronbach L. 1970: *Essentials of Psychological Testing.* 3rd edn, New York: Harper.

Denzin, N. K. 1978: *The Research Act.* 2nd edn, New York: McGraw-Hill.

Fletcher, C. 1989: A test by any other name. *Personnel Management*, March, pp. 47–51.

Fletcher, C. 1993: Testing times for the world of psychometrics. *Personnel Management*, December, pp. 46–50.

Fletcher, C. and Williams, R. 1992: Organizational experience. Part 2 of *Performance Management in the UK: an analysis of the issues*, London: IPM (now Institute of Personnel and Development.)

Gaugler, B. B., Rosenthal, D., Thornton, G. and Bentson, C. 1987: Meta-analysis of assessment center validity. *Journal of Applied Psychology*, 72, 3, pp. 493–511.

Gill, D. 1977: *Appraising Performance: present trends and the next decade.* London: IPM (now Institute of Personnel and Development).

Gill, D., Ungerson, B. and Thakur, M., 1973: *Performance Appraisal in Perspective.* London: IPM (now Institute of Personnel and Development).

Hunter, J. E. and Schmidt, F. L. 1989: Meta-analysis: facts and theories. In Smith, M. and Robertson, I. (eds), *Advances in Selection and Assessment*, Chichester: John Wiley and Sons.

Hunter, J. E., Schmidt, F. L. and Jackson, G. B. 1982: *Meta-analysis*. Beverly Hills: Sage.

Jick, T. 1983: Mixing qualitative and quantitative methods: triangulation in action. In Van Maanen, J. (ed.), *Qualitative Methodology*, London: Sage.

Johnson, C., Wood, R. and Blinkhorn, S. 1988: Spuriouser and spuriouser: the use of ipsative personality tests. *Journal of Occupational Psychology*, 16, pp. 153–62.

Jung, C. 1966: Psychological types. In Semeonoff, B. (ed.), *Readings in Personality Assessment*, Harmondsworth: Penguin. 15.

Kiersey, D. and Bates, M. 1978: *Please Understand Me*. 3rd edn, Del Mar, CA: Prometheus Nemesis Book Co.

Lee, G. and Beard, D. 1994: *Development Centres: realizing the potential of your employees through assessment and development*. London: McGraw-Hill.

Lewin, K. 1951: *Field Theory in Social Science* London: Harper and Row.

Long, P. 1986: *Performance Appraisal Revisited*. London: IPM (now Institute of Personnel and Development.)

Mabey, B. 1989: The majority of large companies use occupational tests. *Guidance and Assessment Review*, 5, 3, June, pp. 1–4.

McHenry, R. 1994: Myers-Briggs reverts to types. *Personnel Management*, October, p. 97.

Margerison, C. J. and McCann, D. 1989: *How to Improve Team Management*. Bradford: MCB University Press.

Myers, I. B. and McCaulley, M. 1985: *Manual: a guide to the development and use of the Myers-Briggs Type Indicator*. Palo Alto, CA: Consulting Psychologists Press.

Redman, T. and Snape, E. 1992: Upward and onward: can staff appraise their managers? *Personnel Review*, 21, 7, pp. 32–46.

Reilly, R. R. and Chao, G. T. 1982: Validity and fairness of some alternative employee selection procedures. *Personnel Psychology*, 35, pp. 1–62.

Robertson, I. T. and Makin, P. J. 1986: Management selection in Britain: a survey and critique. *Journal of Occupational Psychology*, 56, pp. 45–57.

Schmitt, N., Gooding, R. Z., Noe, R. A. and Kirsch, M. 1984: Meta-analysis of validity studies published between 1964 and 1982 and the investigation of study characteristics. *Personnel Psychology*, 37, pp. 407–22.

Shackleton, V. and Fletcher, C. 1984: *Individual Differences: theories and applications*. London: Methuen.

Smith, H. W. 1975: *Strategies of Social Research: the methodological imagination*. New York: Prentice-Hall.

Tenopyr, M. 1989: Comment on meta-analysis: facts and theories. In Smith, M. and Robertson, I. (eds), *Advances in Selection and Assessment*, Chichester: John Wiley and Sons.

Tornow, W. (ed.) 1993: Special issue on 360 degree feedback. *Human Resource Management*, 32, 2/3, pp. 209–407.

Townley, B. 1990: A discriminating approach to appraisal. *Personnel Management*, December, pp. 34–7.

Vernon, P. E. 1953: *Personality Tests and Assessment*. London: Methuen.

Woodruffe, C. 1993: *Assessment Centres: identifying and developing competence*. 2nd edn, London: IPM (now Institute of Personnel and Development).

Wright, P. M. 1989: The structured interview: additional studies and a meta analysis. *Journal of Occupational Psychology* 62, 3, September, pp. 191–9.

•••• Further Sources of Information ••••

The EAR, the MBTI and the CP1-309, can be obtained from Oxford Psychologists Press Ltd, Lambourne House, 311–321 Banbury Road, Oxford, OX2 7JH. Tel: 01865 510203.

The 16PF including the 16PF5 (the UK variant) and the MBTI are available from ASE (Asessment and Selection for Employment), a division of NFER-NELSON, Darville House, 2 Oxford Road East, Windsor, Berkshire SL4 1DA. Tel: 01753 858961.

The OPQ and the Saville and Holdsworth's Management Interest Inventory are available from Saville and Holdsworth Ltd., 3AC Court, High Street, Thames Ditton, Surrey KT7 OSR. Tel: 0181 398 4170.

The PRISM is available from Development, Strategy and Assessment (DSA), Ltd, 17 Chester Crescent, London E8 2PH. Tel: 0171 241 4704.

The Insight Inventory is available from The Test Agency Ltd, Cray House, Woodlands Road, Henley-on-Thames, Oxford RG9 4AE. Tel: 01491 413413.

The Margerison McCann Team Management Profile is available from TMS Development International Ltd, 128 Holgate Road, York YO2 4DL Tel: 01904 641640

PART III

Management Development
Interventions

CHAPTER 7

The Managerial Learning Process and its Context

•••• Introduction ••••

We have shown how the current stress on strategically focused management development meeting both individual and organizational needs places a heavy emphasis on accurate analysis of these needs. In the last two chapters we have demonstrated how this analysis requires some methodological rigour in identifying managerial roles and competencies around which development can take place and in developing approaches to identify appropriate learning interventions. However, the purpose of management development is only one area which requires our attention. Equally important is the choice of effective development solutions. It is important to avoid the danger of management development solutions following favourite tried and tested remedies. As we shall see in chapters 8 and 9, there is an extensive repertoire of management development methods, and the key skill is knowing what is appropriate for specific individual and organizational circumstances.

There are fads and fashions in management development. For the last ten years work-related informal measures have been fashionable, and formal off-the-job development activities have on the whole been relegated to a secondary position (despite evidence of their continuing extensive use within management education – see chapter 8). A primary reason for this is the belief that effective management rests on the foundation of changes in behaviour and attitude rather than just knowledge and skill (Mumford, 1994), and that these changes are more effectively delivered through work-related development activities. Another reason for the popularity of work-related development is the emphasis on the role of the individual learner in the development process and the scope for them to exercise their preferences and choice over how they learn. Yet it is important to remember that this is the current fashion, and that it is not the first time that there has been tremendous enthusiasm for work-related learning (there was a similar, albeit more low-key, response to proposals for action learning in the mid 1970s, outlined further in chapter 9). Furthermore, we should bear in mind that the complete range of management development methods is itself a product of management history. As Burgoyne and Stuart (1978) point out, management learning methods have evolved through a process of 'natural selection' with new methods emerging in reaction against or in compensation for the weaknesses of older methods. Thus, for example, the business case study seminar method was a reaction against highly theoretical and formal trainer-centred management learning, and action learning was 'invented' to compensate for the remoteness and institutionalization of management development professionals. So, a historical perspective on the current fad for individual experiential learning or self-development is perhaps a healthy thing. It is wise to be circumspect in endorsing any particular approach to management development, and much more prudent to reflect upon what we know about management learning in different contexts before selecting development methods.

•••• Learning Objectives ••••

After reading this chapter you should be able to:

- identify the main positions in the debate over individual managerial learning;
- explore the relationship between individual managerial and organizational learning;
- identify potential barriers to effective management learning;
- develop your own diagnostic tool for ways in which individual managers might be assisted to learn within the constraints of an organizational context.

•••• From Training and Development to Individual •••• Managerial Learning

The last 20 years have witnessed a transition from management training to management learning. The shift of emphasis is away from developing the capacity of the instructor to transfer knowledge effectively to a passive learner, and towards facilitating learning, and helping the learner to learn. This is reflected in the displacement of the dominance of cognitive learning theory (see below) by experiential learning theory. Gone are the attempts to classify the different forms of knowledge, skills and attitudes and to explore how the instructor might influence the mental processes of their trainees to achieve optimal knowledge transfer, skill development and attitudinal change. Instead, the emphasis is upon understanding the internal frame of reference of the individual and giving them the knowledge and skills to find a solution for themselves. However, a number of issues have become entangled: individual learning styles, the essential features of adult learning, learning from experience, learner-centred development and learning in a collective group or wider organizational context. In this section we shall try to differentiate these.

Deference to individual managerial learning style preferences has become the received wisdom of management development. This is largely due to the popularization of David Kolb's (1984) model of experiential learning by Peter Honey and Alan Mumford (1992). Kolb described a four-stage model of learning which is popularly known in its simplified form as outlined in figure 7.1.

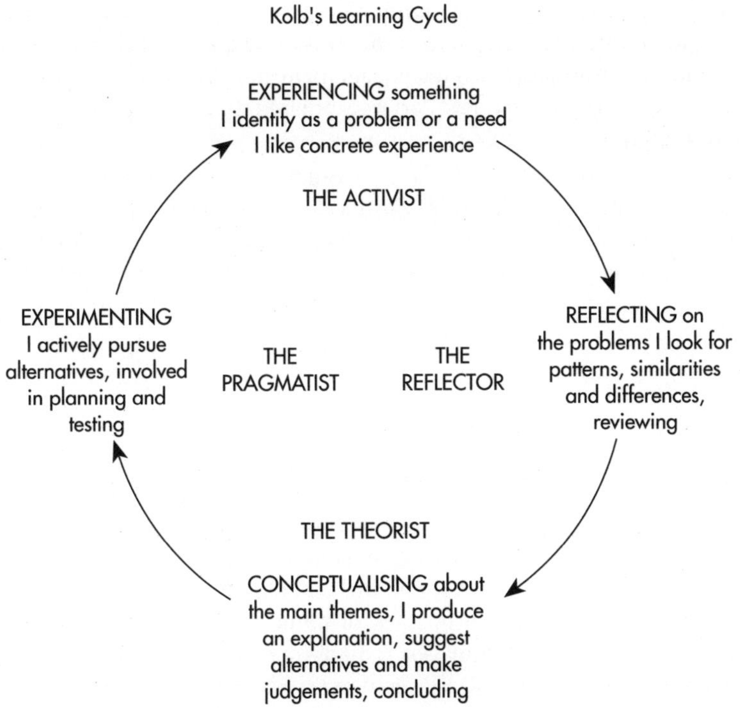

Kolb's Learning Cycle

Figure 7.1 Kolb's learning cycle
Source: Kolb, 1984, Honey and Mumford, 1992

Kolb's model rests on a number of principles.

- The learner is involved in active exploration of the experience.
- The learner must reflect upon their experience in a critical and selective way.
- The learner must be committed to the process of exploring and learning.
- There must be scope for the learner to achieve some independence from the teacher.
- The trainer imposes some structure on the learning process so that the learner is not left to discover by random chance.
- Exposure to experience is necessary for the learner.
- The learner must feel safe and supported so that they are encouraged to value their own experience.
- Experiential learning follows a linked cycle so the trainer must provide appropriate learning activities and teaching methods to support each stage.

Honey and Mumford (1992, 1996) modified Kolb's Learning Style Inventory, transforming it into a user-friendly 80-item learning styles questionnaire. In turn, Kolb's four stages of 'concrete experience', 'reflective observation', 'abstract conceptualization', and 'active experimentation' became four learning styles: the 'activist', 'reflector', 'theorist' and 'pragmatist' respectively. This has become the best-known tool for classifying different learning styles and linking them to the type of learning activities which each 'type' enjoys or dislikes. It provided the basis for Mumford's idea of using learning opportunities to develop personal effectiveness. He claimed that situated midway between formal planned managerial development processes and informal accidental management development activities, 'integrated opportunistic management development' would enable more effective learning if individuals followed the principles of self-development. Thus Honey and Mumford (1992) took the view that every managerial event and personal experience could be of benefit, if the main principles of the learning cycle are followed, namely:

- review;
- conclude;
- plan;
- act again;
- review;
- plan.

However, the move towards interest in individual learning styles is not just a consequence of Kolb's influence. Other developments in personal psychology and learning have also been instrumental, and in particular the work of Malcolm Knowles (1985) on 'andragogy', or the principles of adult learning, and the work of Carl Rogers (1969) advocating 'student-centred learning' as a parallel to his well-known developmental psychology method, 'client-centred therapy'. Another earlier influence was Ralph Coverdale, whose programme of 'Coverdale Training' (Taylor, 1979) emphasized the need to develop a cycle of preparation, action and review to assist people in learning from experience, and practising the skills that are relevant to successful co-operation with others. Indeed, it is interesting that most of the theorists currently influencing the prevailing approach to management learning are American. For over 100 years a number of US writers have been advocating an approach to adult learning that is student centred, pragmatic, lifelong, group based, and self-directed, supported by a facilitative teaching style. As Knowles (1989 p. 37) comments: 'By 1940, most of the elements for a comprehensive theory of adult learning had been discovered, but they had not yet been brought into a unified theory'.

It is Knowles's (1989) synthesis of this in his principles of andragogy that has had a profound influence on approaches to management learning. His coining of the term 'andragogy' in opposition to 'pedagogy' is deliberate. The latter – the 'art and science of teaching children' – draws upon a model which is teacher centred and learner dependent. Knowles rejects theories of teaching that are based upon behaviourist principles (such as classical conditioning and operant conditioning), gestalt psychology and cognitive theory, and motivation and personality theory. He argues that these were based upon studies of animals and children – not adults. Although he acknowledges some exceptions, such as discovery learning (also known as self-directed learning) and Bandura's (1969) system of social learning advocating learning through observation and imitation (a form of modified reinforcement theory allowing for individual regulation of behaviour), Knowles (1989) pays major tribute to the psychologist, Carl Rogers. Rogers (1969) argued that in an ever-changing environment, teachers must become 'facilitators of learning', setting a climate of trust, eliciting individual and group aims, providing access to resources, accepting and sharing emotional as well as intellectual contributions and, above all, accepting their own limitations. Knowles (1989) employed these different sources to create a synthesis of the distinctive principles of adult learning: andragogy (pp. 55–61):

- *the need to know* – adults need to be made aware of why they should learn something;
- *the learner's self-concept* – adults want to be self-directing rather than passive learners;
- *the role of learners' experiences* – adults have a wealth of experience which can be a rich learning resource, can require individual learning strategies, but which at the same time may require unlearning past habits, biases and presuppositions;
- *readiness to learn* – adults are usually most ready to learn those things that they need to know, and so the timing of development is extremely important;
- *orientation to learning* – adults are life centred (or task or problem centred) rather than subject centred, and so learn best when the context affords access to real-life situations;
- *motivation* – while external motivators such as better jobs, promotion, etc. can apply, the most powerful motivators are internal and intrinsic, such as increased job satisfaction, self-esteem, quality of life, etc. (This is an extremely important point which has been recognized by other educational and organizational psychologists (see Deci and Ryan, 1985, 1992; Newell, 1995; Warr, 1987).

Knowles has thus fortuitously managed to pull together the individual qualities that require prior attention before an organization can induce them to maximize the benefits of their learning-style preferences. His influence is openly acknowledged by Alan Mumford, and so it is possible to see how Honey and Mumford's work on learning styles is a timely synthesis of different strands of thought about individual development. But, as we noted earlier, there are other strands of thought in addition to the focus upon individual learning styles and the essential features of adult learning. At one extreme, individual, leaner-centred management development and, at the other, group and organizational learning focus attention upon the organizational context. We will go through each of these in turn, beginning with the individual level, and then moving on to examine group and organizational processes.

···· Maximizing Individual Managerial Learning in ····
Organizational Context: Learning Contracts and
Self-Development

Whereas current thinking about managerial learning has transferred attention from the trainer to the individual managerial adult, it simultaneously requires considerable attention to the context in which the learning takes place. Besides the physical

···· Exhibit 7.1 ····
A model learning contract

Goal	This should cover the general focus of the contract, e.g. the manager's leadership style; the development of a broader strategic awareness.
Learning objectives	These should describe in more detail the knowledge and skills to be acquired.
Action plan	This should identify what the manager will do to achieve this and the roles of other organizational members in facilitating their learning.
Resources	This should outline what is required in terms of time, help, opportunities and other resources.
Learning outcomes	This should specify the knowledge and skill behaviours required, how these should be demonstrated and how evidence will be collected to assess them.

environment, the interpersonal and organizational climate which encourages and rewards development is unanimously regarded as an essential precondition. But by itself, it is not sufficient. There is a need for a framework within which individual manager-centred learning can take place. Individual learning contracts are the main tools to enable individuals (and groups) to tailor make their own personal development plans as a basis for self-development.

Learning contracts are formal agreements negotiated between a learner and their managers or between the learner and a management development specialist. They can also incorporate off-the-job learning experiences and even qualifications-based courses. They usually consist of an agreement on overall goals, learning objectives, and involve drawing up an action plan backed up by a resource statement and agreed measures of achievement (Boak, 1994; Cunningham, 1994a). They assist in securing individual 'ownership' of learning objectives, provide a mechanism for indicating the potential to choose from a wide range of learning resources, and provide a mechanism for the individual learner to monitor and review their own learning. For an example of a model learning contract see exhibit 7.1.

Self-development is a concept that complements current thinking about managerial learning processes and the context within which this takes place. On the one hand the emphasis upon individual learning styles, the distinctive features of adult learning and the importance of reflection upon experience highlight the importance of self-direction in the learning process (Boydell and Pedler, 1981; Megginson and Pedlar, 1992). Conversely, the scale and pace of change within large organizations, and the constraints of resources within small business, make self-development a very important approach. Personal development plans provide a framework around which the individual manager takes control of their own learning and career development.

The personal development plan and development record shown in exhibit 7.2 illustrate the organizational procedures operated by Royal Mail in 1996 to provide a

• • • • Exhibit 7.2 • • • •

Example of a personal development plan and development record: Royal Mail

DEVELOPMENT PLAN

DEVELOPMENT OBJECTIVES (inc. specific learning objectives)	STATE LINK TO BUSINESS PLAN, PEOPLE PLAN OR PERSONAL DEVELOPMENT NEED (inc. the capability standard code from Self Assessment Summary)	PROPOSED DEVELOPMENT ACTION Place tick in the 'DC' box if you would like to discuss this with your Development Consultant (Marketers – include Competence Unit number)				DATE FOR REVIEW
		FORMAL/INFORMAL DEVELOPMENT to be organized by development consultant	INFORMAL, SELF DIRECTED DEVELOPMENT	Time scale 3, 6, or 12	D C √	
Short term development (ie. development in current role)						
Long-term development (ie. in existing role and/or career development)						

Please complete the reverse side of this form and obtain your line manager's authorization before forwarding on to your Development Consultant

• • • • Exhibit 7.2 continued • • • •

DEVELOPMENT RECORD

NAME . . . . LOCATION . . . . TEL NO . . . .

DATE	DEVELOPMENT EXPERIENCE (Describe what you did, why and whether the course was accredited)	TIME SPENT (approx)	LEARNING OBJECTIVES (Were they all met?)	WHAT ELSE DID YOU LEARN	HOW HAVE/WILL YOU USE THIS?	DATE REVIEWED

Please update this record on an ongoing basis and retain it in your Personal Appraisal & Development Plan pack

Source: Royal Mail

framework to support the individual in planning their self-development. Each individual has a capability standards self-assessment pack which they, with their review manager, use to identify their job description capability profile and their personal capability profile. These capability profiles are used as the basis for each individual's personal development plan and are also assessed in appraisal with the review manager and then sent to the individual's development consultant who provides support for achieving the personal development plan. Not all organizations have the extent of support for self-development shown in Exhibit 7.2. This also demonstrates how the process of identifying competencies or capabilities discussed in chapters 4 and 5 can be tied into development.

Although self-development has much in common with learning contracts, unfortunately the context in which it has been developed in many organizations has meant that in practice the promotion of self-development is more a matter of expediency than commitment. Organizational restructuring involving downsizing and delayering, and the retreat from career management and psychological contracts based around organizational commitment to long-term job security (see chapter 3) are usually accompanied by organizational commitment to self-development, personal development planning, career workshops and outplacement counselling. There is much evidence of a gap between rhetoric and practice, and many managers feel disappointed about the support they receive for self-development (Ebadan and Winstanley, 1997; Legge, 1995).

Conversely, learning contracts have made a more successful transition from theory to practice. Although the concept is increasingly used in a work-related context, Cunningham (1994b) has applied the idea of the learning contract to off-the-job development activities, including management education. A learning contract can provide a bridge between an academic institution providing educational support, and the learner and their sponsoring organization. Examples of this can be found in the management programmes offered by university business schools (Middlesex), private management colleges (Roffey Park), and professional teaching institutes (The Kings Fund).

•••• Maximizing Group Learning Among Managers: ••••
Organization Development and Action Learning

The current emphasis upon team working, either cross-functionally or as a member of a project or unit work team, has focused attention upon how managers can learn from and support each other. There are two main sets of techniques to deal with this: organization development and action learning.

Organization development (OD) is an approach that arose out of the conjunction of research into group dynamics, the development of survey research and feedback, and action research. The focus of attention is usually upon formal work team temporary team and inter-group relations (French and Bell, 1990), with an emphasis on the collaborative management of teams compatible with theory Y assumptions of management. The emphasis is on process rather than content, using an action research model of try, evaluate and try again, where change is viewed as an ongoing process. The management of culture is seen as crucial, although attention is paid to social systems ramifications. Thus OD techniques can be very useful in assisting with communication problems and conflict resolution within project teams, and between teams and organizational units. The key assumption is that working on the values, beliefs and norms held by people is the key to lasting change in behaviour. Many of the techniques are useful in stimulating group learning among managers. It is not possible to do full justice to the full range of OD techniques in this book. They are covered more fully elsewhere in specialist texts on organization and human resource development (French and Bell, 1990).

Action learning, popularized by Revans (1982) in the 1960s, is a method which is learner rather than trainer led and yet is able to provide a great deal of structure with minimal direction. It aims to create a collective learning experience through the creation of learning sets which meet to discuss, provide feedback, and approve and evaluate individual development plans and learning contracts. The method is outlined in more detail in chapter 9. However, by far the most frequently cited proposal for integrating individual managerial learning with that of the organization is the concept of the learning organization.

•••• Managerial Learning in Organizational Context: ••••
the Learning Organization

The 'learning organization' is in fact an umbrella term for many different concepts. A simple definition is 'an organization which facilitates the learning of all its members and continuously transforms itself' (Pedler et al., 1991). This simple 'vision' can be elaborated, in that a learning organization:

- has a climate in which individual members are encouraged to learn and develop their full potential;
- extends this learning culture to include customers, suppliers and other significant stakeholders;
- makes human resource development strategy central to business policy;
- is in a continuous process of organizational transformation.

In fact there are many different versions of what a learning organization is (see, for example, Pedler et al., 1991; Garratt, 1987; Senge, 1990), and there is much inconsistency. Easterby-Smith (1995) argues that there are basically two perspectives: the psychological and the systems. The common features of these are outlined in exhibit 7.3.

The psychological perspective focuses very much on getting conditions right for individuals, while the systems approach stresses the importance of functional integration of processes and behaviour. These ultimately lead to an emphasis upon different approaches towards implementing a learning organization. Yet both perspectives are highly prescriptive. Learning how to learn, living with and welcoming change, and creating harmony out of confusion and diversity are all very

• • • • Exhibit 7.3 • • • •
The learning organization: psychological and systems perspectives

The psychological perspective stresses:

- the different hierarchical levels to individual learning;
- the importance of context;
- the assumption that ideas about individual learning can be adjusted to relate to organizational learning;
- concern about the difficulties of implementing organizational learning;
- the view that the main problems are individuals' lack of self-awareness and poor communication ability.

The systems perspective stresses:

- levels of learning that are progressively desirable;
- the problem of 'defensive routines' leading to short-term narrow thinking;
- the primacy of 'informating' (gathering the correct information from outside the organization and ensuring its interpretation, distribution and control through systems which support rather than hinder organizational learning);
- the role of teams in mediating between individual and organizational learning;
- a holistic view of the organizational learning process.

Source: Adapted from Easterby-Smith, 1995

desirable but none the less elusive aims. The very wide perspective embraces nearly all aspects of good management practice, and the emphasis upon 'transformational' as opposed to 'incremental' learning begs the question of how the transition is made to this from the very incremental processes characteristic of individual managerial learning (see above). Furthermore, as with the total quality management (TQM) concept of continuous improvement, the learning organization may be a 'race without end' – it is an aspiration to be approached in small steps, rather than a final destination. Many organizations have made the commitment, but few have confidentally claimed to have become a learning organization. Nonetheless, the learning organization has proven to be very popular with management gurus and consultants who never fail to tantalize their audiences with the prospect that their organization too can join that select club of learning organizations if only they follow the requisite number of easy lessons!

The fact that, on closer inspection, so few organizations can be seen to conform to any learning organization model (Dolan, 1995), raises questions about whether it is indeed either achievable or sustainable. Most accounts of implementation report success stories, usually provided by the organizational champion or change agent responsible for a learning organization initiative. There is a strong likelihood that problems and failure are under-reported, and there is no hard evidence that organizational success or survival was due to becoming a learning organization. Much evidence focuses upon a specific one-off organizational transformation rather than a sustained effort over time, for example the video case of the 'Stairway' project from the retailer Next (TV Choice, 1992), or Peters' (1993) famous case of the spaghetti organization Oticon. In many organizations, line managers are at best sceptical of what they perceive to be yet another training and development fad, and at worst resentful of what appears to be a direct attack on prevailing management style. Human resource managers also find themselves without the resources and tools to initiate, develop and sustain such a large-scale approach. Honey and Mumford (1996) have argued that it is very important that managers at all levels consider the roles and underlying behaviours required of them to build a learning environment.

Elusive prescriptions apart, the current interest in organizational learning reflects a deeper interest in the relationship between managerial learning and organizational culture. This is a symbiotic relationship: on the one hand organizational culture can place limitations upon managerial learning, and on the other managers are the bearers of culture change. It is this latter point that is perhaps the real explanation of the pursuit of the learning organization. After all, management development is a very important instrument of value change. The claim that culture management is an essential ingredient in corporate success is a compelling argument, but none the less one that rests upon shaky foundations (Martin, 1992; Meek, 1988; Woodall, 1996). However, while it is debateable as to whether culture can be consciously manipulated, the cultural context of all organizations exerts a profound influence on the ability of employees to learn. Very often it creates barriers, and these can have significant implications for managerial learning. We now turn to examine these.

•••• Barriers to Self-Development and Organizational •••• Learning

The problem with the experiential learning approach to management development is that it is seldom self-critical. On the contrary it is very critical of off-the-job learning, and especially management education. The underlying assumptions are that the subject to be learnt must be useful and relevant, and that 'action is good and theory is bad'. So when the subject matter is heavily theoretical or knowledge based it is assumed that managers will only learn when learning has an obvious and practical application. Academic or theoretical learning is thereby given a pejorative connotation. Salaman and Butler (1990) have shown that this assumption is given uncritical acceptance, and:

> It argues, implicitly, that to be a manager means one is trained and rewarded to learn only under very restricted conditions: lots of variety, short input sessions, powerful professional and immediate presentation, lots of activities and exercises, obvious relevance to learners' own experiences, maximum emphasis on practical technique or recommendation (certainty), with theory and conceptual elements reduced (uncertainty). (p. 186)

• • • • Exhibit 7.4 • • • •
Barriers to effective managerial learning

- Poor facilitation by line manager or trainer
- Lack of reflection on mistakes
- Inadequate space for 'personal transition'
- Practical difficulties in remedying unbalanced learning styles
- Skilled incompetence and organizational defences
- Organizational performance and reward management structures
- Organizational culture and subcultures:
  - peer pressure and group dynamics
  - climate of distrust
  - uncertainty and insecurity.

They go on to argue that such an approach, while superficially active, actually places the learner in a passive learning position, as it involves little effort on the part of the learner to find out for themselves the relevance, application and practical suitability of general propositions to their own situation. Prevailing theories of managerial learning assert that managers absorb new information only in the above way. This perhaps suggests that managers are stuck at the 'activist' part of Kolb's learning cycle (see above). There are a number of other obstacles to this. These are listed in exhibit 7.4, and the main ones are outlined in more detail below.

Poor facilitation Despite Honey's efforts to demonstrate how remedial self-development activity can be applied by individual managers to work on their own learning styles, those who do so are the exception. Unless individually coached, managers will commit the same sins of either over-indulging themselves in new experiences without reflection and drawing conclusions from the experience, or limiting or avoiding active experimentation as much as possible in preference to tried and tested courses of action. For this is a model of learning that is highly individualistic, yet assumes that managers will have recourse to a trained facilitator or support group to provide counselling and feedback. There is much evidence that organizations neglect this aspect. There is evidence that the current trend towards passing increased responsibility for development on to line managers does not result in better development (Institute of Personnel and Development, 1995).

Learning from successes and mistakes The assumption is that managers learn best through action and, wherever possible, through experience. This has an intuitive appeal to practising managers. While there is evidence that tough challenges and difficulties can have a greater impact on individual managerial learning than successes (Smith and Morphey, 1991), the school-of-hard-knocks approach does not always mean that we learn from our mistakes (Snell, 1992). Making a big mistake, work overload, challenges to our principles, as well as work-life's everyday injustices can be a key channel for personal and moral development, but learning from them does depend upon being able to see them as opportunities for development. In the long term too many hard knocks can have a numbing psychological effect. To maintain experiential learning, it is thus important to engage in less damaging activities which derive from keeping an open curious mind, inviting constructive criticism, and using observations of oneself and others. As Snell (1992) notes, the problem is that most organizations fail to support these forms of learning. This is apparent even in those organizations which like to present themselves as 'learning organizations'. There is evidence that much personal feedback is negative (for example that received through the appraisal process) and that learning from mistakes requires skilled facilitation to provide positive and constructive support. Furthermore, a common 'organizational defence' (Argyris, 1990 – see below) is for negative messages to be obscured by the desire to give positive feedback.

Personal transition cycles   There is a growing awareness of the importance of the psychological processes that individuals experience when having to deal with any major change in their lives. Nicholson (1985) identified 'personal transition cycles' requiring individuals to pass through stages of denial, anger and despair before they can let go of old ways and move on to embrace new ones. As learning is a form of internal change management, this insight has particular significance. The implications are threefold: all individuals need sufficient space to pass through the transition cycle; individuals will pass through each stage at different rates, and so need a flexible and tolerant environment; and, finally, some individuals can never let go, and get blocked at different stages. Thus overcoming resistance to change, and the achievement of effective learning, can only be effective if it gives individual managers the space to pass through the whole personal transition cycle (see figure 3.5 for an example).

Remedying an unbalanced learning style   Another perspective that answers the question why managers have difficulty in remedying the imbalance in their learning style draws attention to the social context in which management learning takes place. The appeal of Kolb's (1984) Learning Cycle and Honey and Mumford's (1992, 1996) application of this masks some confusion over how it is used. There are two potential, but distinct uses.

(1)   To identify an individual's *preferred learning style* in order that managerial learning activities can be adapted to this. So, for example, those pragmatists who prefer active experimentation should be given the opportunity to try out different approaches to a managerial problem rather than be expected to accept a preferred solution without question. (For a fuller explanation of this see Honey, 1994.)

(2)   To help identify an individual's *weakness in the learning cycle* prior to identifyijng remedial development activities. In the case of the pragmatist cited above, their learning preference might present them with a barrier to effective learning in certain situations, and should not be over-indulged. Thus they will

probably need remedial help in 'reflective observation' and 'abstract conceptualization'. Ways in which this might be achieved are again outlined in Honey (1991).

In practice this gives rise to a tension between these two uses. Responding to the diverse preferred learning styles of a large group of managers can be a daunting task for those responsible for management development, and it is all too easy to leave the responsibility to the individual learner or their immediate manager. Alternatively, resource and policy constraints mean that certain individual learning preferences cannot be fully indulged, or are over indulged. This means that remedial work on weaknesses in the learning cycle will not take place. Hardly a management education programme, let alone in-company training event now takes places without a preliminary application of the Learning Styles Questionnaire. However, the extent to which organizational management development activities are able to respond to both individual learning preferences and remedy weaknesses is questionable.

Skilled incompetence and organizational defences   Argyris's work, going back over 20 years, has drawn attention to the limitations of a narrow definition of management learning tied to problem solving (which is implicit in the work of Honey and Mumford and Revans). This leads managers to over-focus on identifying and correcting errors in their external environment rather than questioning and confronting the way in which the problem is defined. Drawing heavily upon group dynamics, Argyris and Schon (1974) and more recently Argyris (1990, 1994) describe how even highly intelligent professionals and managers will explicitly espouse theories – private assumptions – which they think they use every day, but which in fact they do not. Furthermore, managers and professionals are usually unaware of those that they do use to design and manage their actions. In this situation, the difference between 'espoused theory' and theory in use' means that unwittingly they screen out certain information. Consequently they attempt to control and manage their environment, and in turn are forced to indulge in defensive routines' as they display skilled incompetence in avoiding surprise, embarrassment or threats. The outcome is single-loop learning which until there is a crisis or revolution from within or outside the organization leads to declining organizational effectiveness. Single-loop learning is a response to a problem which does not change assumptions, norms and values, all of which may be challenged in double-loop learning.

To avoid skilled incompetence managers have to learn new skills, and principally to question and confront assumptions. This is not just an exhortation for change in individual managerial behaviour, but also raises questions around interpersonal behaviour within management structures and the wider organizational learning systems that created or permitted the problems to occur in the first place. In particular, senior management have to be willing to listen to negative messages and to encourage a high freedom of choice and risk-taking without reigning in control when such behaviour results in a negative outcome. If this is possible, then double-loop learning can occur. Yet as Argyris and Schon (1974) acknowledge, management professionals are amongst those most resistant to double-loop learning because of a strong motive to avoid failure and a high task focus on work. For this reason, grounding individual managerial learning within problem solving can reinforce single-loop learning, and therefore the model of experiential learning may not be completely satisfactory by itself.

Organizational performance and reward management structures   Structures for evaluating and rewarding managerial performance can actually inhibit managerial learning. Salaman and Butler (1990) draw attention to the importance of organizational structure, culture reward and evaluation systems which together act to condition the extent to which individual managers will respond to change and learn. Resistance to learning can come from many sources: existing practices, procedures and assumptions inherent in everyday work. Development interventions to encourage innovation, creativity and risk taking (be they informal or formal; on-the-job or off-the-job) might engender considerable resistance in an organization where success is defined in terms of compliance and deference, and where there is a hierarchical system of authority with centralized decision making. Performance management systems that focus upon strict adherence to pre-set targets or behaviours;, pay systems that reward individual as opposed to team or inter-group performance, can all build up resistance to learning. The key point is that managers are learning all the time, and if they learn that survival depends upon compliance and deference, then this acts as a block to transferring learning to be innovative, or to take risks, into everyday practice.

Organizational cultures and subcultures   Furthermore, the internal differentiation of organizations into departments, specialisms and subgroups can pose a significant barrier. A hierarchy in which power, resources, prestige and rewards are distributed also generates organizational politics. Thus organizational learning that stresses change in behaviour or sharing information and resources is perceived as a threat to sectional interests:

> Thus organizational structures and cultures, and the common internal differentiation (formal and informal) into specialisms and subgroups, may generate conceptions of interest and in-group loyalty, out-group resistance, which seriously gets in the way of managers' willingness to learn. (Salaman and Butler, 1990, p. 190)

It is but a short step to show how conditions of 'groupthink' (Janis, 1972) can come to prevail and to present an impregnable barrier to organizational learning. Yet while Senge (1990) would argue that team learning is the key to the learning organization, we know infinitely more about group dynamics and decision making than team learning (Marsick, 1994).

So, while the organizational context of learning needs to be taken into account, it is important not to fall in to the naïve trap of assuming away organizational power and politics. As Snell (1992) pointed out, failure to foster learning from experience can commonly occur if the prevailing values stress furthering one's own self-interest, concentrating on building a good image by opting for what appears safe and reliable, and avoiding confrontation. In addition, Mumford (1993b) notes that, even in learning organizations, rarely are learning opportunities identified in advance, and the 'developmental' job move is often an ex-post rationalization of expediency. On the other hand, he places a great deal of faith in the ability of the line manager to support work-related development (Mumford, 1993) and experiential learning.

However, current changes in managerial work loads due to downsizing and delayering and heavily task-focused short-term performance management systems place a limit upon the line manager's ability to do this (Institute of Personnel Development, 1995). For example, a recent project on the introduction of empowerment programmes at Rank Xerox (Winstanley and Ojeifo, 1997) has shown that the delayering has resulted in a lack of development support for these teams from more experienced managers within the organization.

•••• Selecting Appropriate Management Development ••••
Interventions

From the preceding discussion it can be seen that it is important to clarify our assumptions about how different groups of managers learn, and also to verify these in practice. To assist in the selection of appropriate interventions we have presented a number of the best-known ones on a simple grid in exhibit 7.5. They are classified according to whether the method is delivered in a work-related or off-the-job environment, and will be examined in more detail in the next two chapters.

While it is possible to identify individual learning needs with a considerable degree of precision, and to gain insight into individual learning styles, much care is needed to ensure that the organization's capacity to support learning is adequate.

•••• Summary ••••

This chapter has provided a general overview of management learning and cautioned against an uncritical acceptance of prevailing fashion. In particular, the self-sustaining learning organization may be the espoused goal of many management teams, but other pressures on the organization may make this difficult to attain. Furthermore, while the merits of experiential and work-related learning are currently perceived to be of superior worth in comparison with formal off-the-job development and management education, effective implementation of such approaches can be problematic. Learning opportunities may well be present in rich abundance in everyday working life, but there is much evidence that making individuals responsible for their own learning does not always result in the best use of these learning opportunities. Indeed, in a world of growing employment insecurity, where self-development and unemployment are likely experiences for most, managers may not just want to learn from the work-related learning opportunity, but may also value the social learning and formal credentials that come with off-the-job development and management education. In practice the dichotomy between work-related development and off-the-job management education and development is not so clear cut. The next two chapters will now review what formal off the job development and education and work-related management development have to offer.

•••• Exhibit 7.5 ••••
Management development interventions

On-the-job experiential methods

- Action learning
- Coaching
- Mentoring
- Sponsorship
- Role modelling
- Job enrichment
- Job rotation
- Secondment
- Special projects
- Task forces
- Deputizing
- Networking
- Visioning

Off-the-job

- Management education
  - Qualifications
  - Short courses
  - Seminars
- In-company management training
  - Workshops
  - Seminars
  - 'Academies'
- External providers
  - specialist packages
  - customized
  - outdoor development

Techniques used in off-the-job management development

- Lectures/presentations
- Case study
- Syndicate/discussion groups
- Distance/open learning materials
- Work-related projects
- Games and simulations
- Role plays
- Individual/group presentations
- External speakers

EXERCISES

(1) If we are able to identify individual management learning styles, to what extent can the organization meet individual learning preferences and provide remedial support for correcting learning difficulties?

For questions 2–5 take your own organization or an organization known to you.

(2) Does the overall organizational culture promote double-loop learning? Can the factors that inhibit this and which lead to single loop learning be identified?

(3) Examine the list of barriers to effective organizational learning and examine the evidence for their existence in your organization.

(4) How do these inhibiting factors relate to the organization's power structure? Who are the stakeholders in the learning process and to what extent do they have conflicting aims?

(5) What do the answers to questions 2, 3 and 4 tell you about the strategic significance of management development for your organization (refer back to chapter 2).

•••• References ••••

Argyris, C. 1990: *Overcoming Organizational Defences: facilitating organizational learning.* Boston: Allyn and Bacon.

Argyris, C. 1994: *On Organizational Learning.* Oxford: Blackwell.

Argyris, C. and Schon, D. 1974: *Theory in Practice: increasing professional effectiveness.* London: Jossey–Bass.

Bandura, A. 1969: *Principles of Behaviour Modification.* New York: Holt, Rinehart and Winston.

Boak, G. 1994: Management learning contracts. In Mumford, A. (ed.), *Gower Handbook of Management Development.* Aldershot: Gower.

Boydell, T. and Pedlar, M. (eds) 1981: *Management Self-development: concepts and practices.* Aldershot: Gower.

Burgoyne, J. and Stuart, R. 1978: Teaching and learning methods in management development. *Personnel Review,* 7, 1, Winter, pp. 53–8.

Cunningham, I. 1994a: *The Wisdom of Strategic Learning: the self-managed learning solution.* Maidenhead: McGraw-Hill.

Cunningham, I. 1994b: Self-managed learning. In Mumford, A. (ed.), *Gower Handbook of Management Development.* Aldershot: Gower.

Deci, E. L. and Ryan, R. M. 1985: *Intrinsic Motivation and Self-Determination in Human Behaviour.* New York: Plenum Press.

Deci, E. L. and Ryan, M. R. 1992: The initiation and regulation of intrinsically motivated learning and achievement. In Boggianos, A. K. and Pittman, T. S. (eds), *Achievement and Motivation: a social development perspective*. Cambridge: Cambridge University Press.

Dolan, S. 1995: A different use of natural resources'. *People Management*, 5 October.

Easterby-Smith, M. 1995: Organizational learning: less than meets the eye? Paper presented to the Annual Conference of the British Academy of Management, Sheffield, September.

Ebadan, G. and Winstanley, D. 1997: Downsizing, delayering and careers – the survivors' perspective. *Human Resource Management Journal*, 7, 1, pp. 79–91.

French, W. L. and Bell, C. H. 1990: *Organization Development: Behavioural Science Interventions for Organization Improvement*. Englewood Cliffs, NJ: Prentice-Hall.

Garratt, R. 1987: *The Learning Organisation*. London: Fontana.

Honey, P. 1991: How people learn. In Prior, J. (ed.), *Gower Handbook of Training and Development*. Aldershot: Gower.

Honey, P. 1994: Styles of Learning. In Mumford, A. (ed.), *Gower Handbook of Management Development*, Aldershot: Gower.

Honey, P. and Mumford, A. 1992: *Manual of Learning Styles*. 3rd edn, Maidenhead: Honey.

Honey, P. and Mumford, A. 1996: *Managing Your Learning Environment*. Maidenhead, Honey.

Institute of Personnel and Development, 1995: *Personnel and the Line: developing the new relationship*. London: Institute of Personnel and Development.

Janis, I. 1972: *Victims of Groupthink*. Boston: Houghton Mifflin.

Knowles, M. 1985: *Androgogy in Action* London: Jossey-Bass.

Knowles, M. 1989: *The Adult Learner: A Neglected Species*. Houston: Gulf Publishing Company.

Kolb, D. 1984: *Experiential Learning*. Englewood Cliffs, NJ: Prentice-Hall.

Legge, K. 1995: *Human Resource Management: rhetorics and realities*. Basingstoke Macmillan.

Marsick, V. J. 1994: Trends in managerial reinvention: creating a learning map. *Management Learning*, 25, 1, pp. 11–34.

Martin, J. 1992: *Cultures in Organizations: three perspectives*. New York: Oxford University Press.

Meek, V. L. 1988: Organizational culture: origins and weaknesses. *Organization Studies*, 9, 4, pp. 453–73.

Megginson, D. and Pedlar, M. 1992: *Self-development: a facilitator's guide*. London: McGraw-Hill.

Mumford, A. 1993b: How managers can become developers. *Personnel Management*, June, pp. 42–5.

Mumford, A. 1994: Effectiveness in management development. In Mumford, A. (ed.), *The Gower Handbook of Management Development*, 4th edn, Aldershot: Gower.

Newell, S. 1995: *The Healthy Organization*. London: Routledge.

Nicholson, N. 1985: A theory of work role transitions. *Administrative Sciences Quarterly*, 29, pp. 172–91.

Pedler, M. 1978: Negotiating skills training part 4: learning to negotiate. *Journal of European Industrial Training*, 2, 1, pp. 20–5.

Pedler, M., Burgoyne, J. and Boydell, T. 1991: *The Learning Company*. London: McGraw-Hill.

Peters, T. 1993: *Management Revolution and Corporate Reinvention*. London, New York and Sydney: BBC for Business, p. 26.

Revans, R. 1982: *The Origins and Growth of Action Learning*. Bromley: Chartwell Bratt.

Rogers, C. 1969: *Freedom to Learn*. Columbus, Ohio: Charles E. Merrill.

Salaman, G. and Butler, J. 1990: Why managers won't learn. *Management Education and Development*, 21, 3, pp. 183–91.

Senge, P. 1990: *The Fifth Discipline: the Art and Practice of the Learning Organization*. New York: Doubleday.

Smith, B. and Morphey, G. 1991: Tough challenges: how big a learning gap? *Journal of Management Development*, 13, 9, pp. 5–13.

Snell, R. 1992: Experiential learning at work: why can't it be painless? *Personnel Review*, 21, 4, pp. 12–26.

Taylor, M. 1979: *Coverdale on Management*. London: Heinemann.

TV Choice 1992: *The Learning Organization: How 'learning' replaced 'training' and changed a department*. London: TV Choice Productions.

Warr, P. 1987: *Work, Unemployment and Mental Health*, Oxford: Oxford University Press, quoted in Newell, S., *The Healthy Organization*, ch. 5, Work, positive health and improved performance, London: Routledge, pp. 90–118.

Winstanley, D. and Ojeifo, E. 1997: 'Negotiated reality: the meaning of empowerment. London: Imperial College Management School Working Paper.

Woodall, J. 1996: Managing culture change: can it ever be ethical? *Personnel Review*, special issue on ethical issues in contemporary human resource management, 25, 6, pp. 26–40.

CHAPTER 8

Using Formal Off-the-Job Management Development

• • • • Introduction • • • •

Our introduction to management learning in the previous chapter noted the way in which specific management development methods and approaches to management learning have gone in and out of fashion. Today it seems incredible that, as late as the early 1980s, there was a strong preference for formal off-the-job management development solutions devised and delivered within company by teams of management development specialists. However, changes within both the corporate and public sectors have questioned the flexibility and sustainability of this approach. Now the pendulum has swung in the other direction. Internal management development departments have all but disappeared, and those that remain are run by a skeleton staff of specialists who draw in external providers and consultants when appropriate. At the same time, there has been a growing emphasis on the role of the line manager in development and individual responsibility for self-development.

Yet, as we noted in chapter 7, an uncritical acceptance of experiential on the job development and work-related management development as more 'real', 'valid' and 'useful' is dangerous. There is still a case to be made for off-the-job management development in various forms. These can involve in-company workshops and seminars, and also a wide variety of management education and outdoor development. The main common feature is that they take managers out of the workplace for most of the learning experience. Indeed they can provide a welcome antidote to managers in an organization where barriers to experiential learning arise and where the constraints of organizational politics and resources create job insecurity and lead to unreliable on-the-job coaching. Rather than outright dismissal of off-the-job management development, or even adoption of the contrary position, we would argue that there is currently a place for off-the-job management development to complement and enhance experiential work-related development activities.

We argue that the polarization between work-related and formal off-the-job management development is artificial, as in practice both types of methods are used in conjunction with one another (for example MBA programmes make use of work-related projects, and off-the-job workshops in organizations are often followed up in the workplace). While we shall examine the two sets of methods in isolation, the advantages and disadvantages of a method can only be assessed in the context of the whole learning experience. For example, by itself a lecture may not be a useful learning experience, but may be a very effective learning device as part of a thoughtfully constructed learning programme. The danger is that in the absence of planned formal development, the current move towards self-development and continuing professional development means that many managers will need to take responsibility for constructing their learning experiences. The effectiveness of this will depend upon achieving the right combination of off-the-job and work-related management development.

This chapter begins by examining the use of management education at the postgraduate and undergraduate levels, and then proceeds to review in-house management development programmes. We then move on to consider the various methods and activities used by both sets of programmes for delivering management development. This should illustrate the way in which the distinction between company-based management development and higher education is increasingly blurred as academic providers and organizations enter a variety of new collaborative partnerships.

•••• Learning Objectives ••••

After reading this chapter, you should be able to:

- identify appropriate forms of management education for different groups of managers, and formulate a strategy for liaising with providers of management education;
- identify when there is a need for the use of in-company workshops, seminars and other forms of off-the-job management development, and develop a programme of off-the-job learning activities that complements work-related managerial learning;
- appreciate where both open/distance learning and outdoor development activities may be appropriately used and designed;
- identify potential sources of off-the-job development activity for small business owner-managers and their managerial staff.

•••• Management Education Provision ••••

THE DEBATE

The specialist professional and academic literature on management development regularly includes articles bemoaning the perceived failure of business schools. They are held to produce managers who are good at developing policy but very weak on dealing with everyday issues of policy implementation (see, for example Margerison, 1991; Mumford, 1994; Mumford, 1996; Warner, 1990). Another source of criticism comes from within higher education – mainly sociologists espousing critical theory

(Willmott, 1994; Reed and Anthony, 1992) who are concerned at the inappropriateness of a 'technicist' curriculum for a world where decisions have to be made in conditions of considerable uncertainty and moral confusion. A third source of criticism comes from researchers such as Burgoyne and Stuart (1978) and Argyris (1994) who are concerned with the perpetuation of single-loop learning (see chapter 7). We shall argue here that some of the criticism of UK management education is both unwarranted and unfair; that there are a wide variety of management education programmes that are delivered in many different ways; and that on balance these are no more inferior than other in-company or externally provided off-the-job development programmes.

Finally, criticism also derives from the observation that, in the UK, management education is provided 'too little, too late and for too few', with lower participation rates than for other countries. For example there are comparatively low rates of participation in higher education in the UK compared with the USA. For the last 40 years the American education system has been geared towards getting over 30 per cent of high-school leavers into higher education. By contrast, the UK had only approached this level by 1992. It must not be forgotten that, as recently as 20 years ago, only half this proportion (15 per cent) entered higher education in the UK, and just under 7 per cent in 1962. This explains why such a low percentage of top managers in the UK hold a degree in comparison with our major competitors: 24 per cent compared with 85 per cent in the USA and Japan (see Handy et al., 1988: p. 2), a factor which has universally been seen as a potential explanation of the poor performance of British business. It also explains some of the reluctance of British companies to hire MBA graduates, and demonstrates the way in which the history of management education in the UK is linked to that of higher education, and our 'anti-industrial' cultural history (Wiener, 1981; Locke, 1981; Hayes, 1993).

THE MBA

Why then is there this critique of management education? Much stems from an over-focus on the MBA. However, it must not be forgotten that the MBA is an American import, and that before 1963 neither management education nor MBAs occupied a place in UK universities, and it was only after 1971 that the polytechnics became the pioneers of large-scale undergraduate business education. The MBA is very much a new product in the UK. In the early 1980s there were only a small number of management schools who awarded MBAs, with around 1,200 candidates graduating each year (Handy et al., 1988, p. 3). Ten years later there were 116 higher education business schools awarding over 8,000 MBAs per annum (Council for National Academic Awards, 1992), and involving around 18,000 students of whom only 3,000 were attending full time (Cannon, 1994). Until the early 1980s MBAs were provided by only a score of older UK universities and mainly on the basis of full-time course attendance.

The critique of management education has been fuelled by the fact that since the mid 1980s MBAs and university business schools in the USA have come under heavy criticism (Porter and McKibbon, 1988; Linder and Smith, 1992). In the United

States there had been a groundswell of criticism of management education which provided the cue for the attack upon management education in the UK. However, the criticisms applying in the USA, that business schools were turning out people overly focused on 'hard' analysis and with overly ambitious expectations of being invited to 'turn around' the company's corporate strategy the minute they got their feet under their desk, were not entirely merited there, nor here in the case of the UK. Here there has always been some emphasis upon understanding human behaviour and human resource management. The use of work-related projects and assignments, especially in respect of those on part-time MBAs, has also encouraged students to address issues of business policy implementation, as opposed to just policy development. There is also considerable diversity in the design of MBA programmes.

One major source of difference is over whether the MBA should provide a general management foundation or whether it should permit specialization in certain functional areas such as business finance, marketing or human resource management. In addition, some MBAs adopt a much more international curriculum and teaching faculty than others (Arkin, 1991). Prestigious business schools have conducted market research and re-engineered themselves in terms of both curriculum and teaching methods. This involves teaching subjects in a cross-functional, thematic way with multi-disciplinary staff teams. The expansion since then has been mainly in the form of 'executive' part-time, distance learning and in-company or consortia programmes (Ashton, 1989; Institute of Personnel Management, 1988), whose participants would be practising managers. The overall aim has been to make the MBA more accessible and more relevant. The label MBA now covers a wide variety of very flexible programmes in terms of focus upon different sectors and industries, modes of delivery, focus upon business issues rather than academic subject specialisms, and forms of assessment that interrelate with workplace assignments and projects.

This flexibility and diversity has not been achieved at the price of quality. While there is no single accrediting body in the UK for MBAs akin to the American Assembly of Collegiate Schools of Business to agree a common standard for the MBA (only 31 of the 116 business schools are members of the UK association of MBAs – The Association of Masters in Business Administration – all MBA programmes have to pass through a process of academic quality assurance. AMBA's criteria for membership include limits on the number of recruits without work experience, and ensuring appropriate and rigorous forms of assessment. This less rigid approach to quality assurance has permitted considerable innovation in curriculum and delivery methods in the UK. The MBA by Self-Managed Learning jointly awarded between Roffey Park Management College and the University of Sussex since 1990, and the Open University's Open Business School MBA (launched in 1989) which permits accreditation of prior learning, are well-respected programmes, but probably would not have existed had such centralized standard setting operated along the lines adopted in the USA.

Thus, despite its detractors, the MBA is increasingly popular. It has become the currency for management career development. If new psychological contracts are orientated towards the guarantee of employability on the external labour market at the expense of job security in the internal labour market (Herriot and Pemberton, 1995), as suggested in chapters 1 and 3, then managers need to construct good curricula vitae. Also formal qualifications become more reliable credentials in the eyes of the external world than learning acquired through on-the-job experience or through other formal company management development programmes. MBAs are prized credentials among practising managers because they are quality assured through the mechanisms for external validation and accreditation. They provide a breadth of knowledge and organizational awareness that stretches beyond immediate organizational experience; and they are a vehicle for individual reflection and value change. However, MBAs are not the only products of management education. We now turn to examine some of these.

UNDERGRADUATE BUSINESS DEGREES

While undergraduate business education is not normally considered to be part of an organization's repertoire of management development methods, it does impinge on them. For a start, there has been considerable innovation in undergraduate higher education, and this affects the quality of graduate management recruits. Many, but not all, BA and BSc business studies degrees incorporate at least one lengthy work-experience placement as well as (increasingly) foreign language skill development and work experience outside the UK. Also, there has been a growth in joint honours degrees that combine business management education with other subjects such as information technology, chemistry, engineering, languages, etc. European Union policy initiatives such as the ERASMUS programme have greatly facilitated the networking between UK and other European universities, so that many under-graduates can complete part of their study outside the UK. Thus, it pays for the management development specialist to take an interest in graduate selection practice within their own and other organizations, and to keep abreast of trends in higher education. This can be done in a variety of ways – from involvement in the graduate milk round, to consulting course directories, prospectuses and handbooks, and attending university open days.

HIGHER SPECIALIST POST-GRADUATE QUALIFICATIONS

Over the last five years new forms of masters courses have evolved. These are professional rather than academic masters courses targeted at the experienced, already-qualified mid-career manager, and often accrediting prior experience and learning. From strategic financial management, to managing human resources and marketing, to name but a few, these are designed to be a useful means of professional and career development for middle-level managers, while at the same time offering an academic learning experience at masters level. Currently these courses feature prominently in the schemes of continuing professional development operated by professional bodies (see chapter 10).

POST-EXPERIENCE AND POST-GRADUATE CERTIFICATES AND DIPLOMAS

The MBA accounts for only a fraction of the provision of management education for mature students. The majority are engaged in some form of certificate or diploma, either as an introduction to general management such as the Certificate and Diploma in Management Studies, or as specialist professional management qualifications such as for the Institute of Personnel and Development, the Association of Accountancy Technicians, or the Institute of Bankers. Most students entering such courses have never had any prior higher education, or are returning to study after a lengthy break. Thus they require much attention to study skill support and different ways of learning.

Contrary to the opinion of the critics of management education, in these programmes a great deal of attention is devoted to ensuring integration of work and classroom learning. Group work, work-related assignments, personal learning diaries and log books, and the use of organizational mentors are now common practice, and 'chalk and talk' the exception. Indeed, the quality of individual student learning experience is an area where quality assurance from the professional and statutory bodies such as the IPD or Higher Education Funding Council applies. In particular, post-experience management education at certificate and diploma level has been influenced by the 'competence movement'. Many courses are tied to either NVQs (at levels 4 and 5) or to the MCI framework (see chapter 4). As universities need to market and promote their post-experience management education, there are usually ample opportunities for organizations to meet course directors or attend open days/ evenings.

EXECUTIVE EDUCATION

All the preceding programmes are qualification based, and these form the bulk of management education. However, despite the criticisms of management education for being 'narrow and one dimensional based . . . on their faculty structures . . . which reflect the major business functions – finance, marketing, information technology, human resource management' (Warner, 1990), many corporate clients have remained undeterred and have commissioned various forms of executive education from business schools. Whilst once the preserve of only the elite UK business schools, and independent management colleges, most UK higher education establishments now provide some form of in-company executive education. This can vary from introductory management courses for first-line managers (often accredited by the award of a diploma or certificate) through to more specialized courses for middle managers who need to deepen their knowledge of financial and strategic management, and finally to special seminars for senior executives, or for women managers. While the scale of this is novel and independent consultancies have captured the lion's share of this market (Cannon, 1994), the recognition of the possibility of fruitful collaboration between business and management education goes back a long way (Margerison, 1991).

···· Flexibility in Meeting Business and Individual Needs ····

THE FRAMEWORK FOR PARTNERSHIP BETWEEN MANAGEMENT EDUCATION PROVIDERS AND BUSINESS

As we have shown above, British business schools are very active in offering a range of management development activities. Rather than get dragged down into the sterile and endless debate about whether British business schools do meet business needs, we will conclude this section with a consideration of how a working partnership between management education and business organizations might be built. This is best done by an open exchange of aims. Based on the authors' experience of collaboration between business and management education, the aims and objectives of the two sides often differ quite considerably, as outlined in exhibit 8.1.

At first it might seem that there are some irreconcilable points of difference, but only if they are openly acknowledged can a suitable compromise be reached. It is also possible for quite innovative solutions to arise from government-sponsored collaboration between universities and companies such as the Teaching Company Scheme (Peattie, 1993), and MBAs by self-managed learning (Cunningham, 1994) or action learning (see chapter 9).

FLEXIBLE LEARNING

As we have already noted, the drive to be responsive to the needs of organizations and also participants has encouraged the development of more flexible models of delivery. The oldest of these is distance learning, pioneered by the National Extension College and the Rapid Results College. While the initial thrust of these organizations was in technical education, by the late 1980s distance learning became a more popular means of delivering management education. While often the terms distance learning and open learning are used interchangeably, there is in principle a difference between the two. Open learning is much more flexible about the timing of study in terms of start dates and duration. It is also very student centred in terms of catering for student learning preferences and the media used to deliver learning (from videos and cassette tapes to multi-media technology). Most of what passes as open learning in management education is more accurately labelled distance learning as there are quite specific start and completion dates for the constituent parts of the programme. Distance learning materials are supplemented by tutor-facilitated study sessions, telephone hot-lines, study groups or learning sets (see chapter 9), and individual mentors.

The boundaries between distance/open learning approaches to management education and more conventional courses is becoming increasingly fluid. Most providers use study packs of materials and encourage the use of study groups or action learning sets and individual mentors. There is even evidence to suggest that far

···· Exhibit 8.1 ····
Working with providers of management education

What providers want:

- sufficient lead time for development, and time to get to know the organizational context and immediate work environment of participants;
- an ongoing commitment and guarantee on minimum numbers attending;
- fee payment that covers development costs;
- a committed project liaison officer in the organization;
- consultation over arrangements for nomination of participants, and some control over criteria for participant entry (including minimum qualifications);
- clarification of requirements for follow-up assignments and feedback;
- a key role in assessing individual participant performance (this may have to be exclusive, if the course leads to an accredited award);
- nomination of organizational mentors for participants;
- time off for participants to attend lectures and workshops, to carry out project work and assignments, or a proportionate reduction in working hours;
- support for participants in respect of fees and access to computing facilities;
- assistance with identifying work-related projects or finding a project placement for the student.

What organizations want:

- a fast response with respect to development;
- avoidance of an open-ended commitment;
- a committed academic course director and academic administrators dedicated to the programme;
- discretion over nomination of course participants;
- minimization of development costs, in case the course is unable to run as planned;
- flexibility over numbers attending without incurring financial penalties;
- fees charged per capita;
- follow-up assignments and projects that are achievable within the constraints of work, and availability of in-company counselling and support;
- involvement in assessing participant performance.

from wanting to avoid attending class, students value participative classroom learning, especially when their work situation leaves them isolated. So, while provision of management education has moved away from full-time courses or day release, and there are even signs that evening study is much less appealing, participative tutor-led forms of delivery are still popular because of the opportunities they afford for social learning and networking.

THE ACCREDITATION OF PRIOR LEARNING

The expansion of management education provision has occurred despite the large number of applicants without appropriate prior qualifications. This was a problem confronted particularly by the National Council for Vocational Qualifications and the Management Charter Initiative, and it was these organizations that sponsored the development of systems for the Accreditation of Prior Learning (APL) and the Accreditation of Prior Experiential Learning (APEL). These rest upon arrangements between an assessor and an applicant whereby the latter is assisted in assembling a portfolio of evidence of prior achievements that can be interpreted as meeting the requirement of specific management competencies. In the case of APEL, this evidence can be drawn from everyday experience as well as formal learning situations. Thus voluntary activities such as running a play group could be seen as involving the exercise of basic management skills. All that needs to be done is to assemble paper evidence and testimony verifying this. Many new universities use this process for the admission of candidates without formal qualifications, but the long-winded nature of the process and the demands in terms of staff time are an obstacle to its extensive use.

•••• In-House Management Development Programmes ••••

The swing away from formal off-the-job management development has also affected what organizations themselves provide in-house. It has long been recognized that leading organizations have shifted way from formalized to focused management development (see chapter 2) because of the need to respond quickly to change and the need to cut overheads. Thus organizations are less likely to have a well-established suite of courses through which individual managers can progress as their job roles change. Internal developments such as the creation of autonomous business units or the introduction of an internal market, as in the National Health Service, have resulted in the dismantling of corporate management development pro-grammes. What exists is much more likely to be targeted at key managers and to be flexible in terms of both content and mode of delivery. It is now very common for such programmes to be linked in with culture change initiatives and workplace development activities. Some organizations, such as global pharmaceutical giant SmithKline Beecham, have provided a framework to synthesize their on- and off-the-job management development, and enhance its status by creating corporate universities and academies (see exhibit 8.2).

•••• Management Development Methods ••••

Whether conducted in a university classroom or a company training room, whether led by an academic or by a management trainer, off-the-job management develop-ment requires careful choice of methods. In the previous chapter we noted that

---

• • • • Exhibit 8.2 • • • •
Vignette of SmithKline Beecham Academy

SmithKline Beecham was formed in 1989 as the result of the merger of a very traditional research-led UK pharmaceutical company and a more market-driven American counterpart. It was the first of a series of mergers and acquisitions throughout the pharmaceutical industry prompted by the need to command the market share required to sustain product development in a world of escalating R&D costs and increasing government regulation and price controls.

SmithKline Beecham International (SKBI) manufactures, markets and sells prescription and over-the-counter health-care products in over 130 countries worldwide (with the exception of Europe and North America, which are covered by other divisions). Over recent years SKBI has restructured its sales network and set up an extensive sales training network run from its headquarters in West London. A key change is the adoption of a distance learning approach for product training in place of traditional classroom-style training for sales representatives. This distance learning is supported by a network of around 100 tutors situated in various countries, and the organization and communications are managed by a headquarters-based team of trainers and project managers.

In order to bring academic rigour to this sales training initiative, and to assist in setting and maintaining standards of achievement, a quasi-academic institution called the SB Academy was set up and empowered to confer various grades of membership upon employees who complete courses offered on the Academy syllabus.

---

management development methods tend to go in and out of fashion through an evolutionary process (Burgoyne and Stuart, 1978). There are in fact an enormous number of management learning methods which were classified over ten years ago by Huczynski (1983). While not updated to include some of the newer (primarily work-related) methods that have been developed over the last ten years, this provides an excellent summary of the techniques and their learning use. A more recent review of the main methods of management development is included in a special issue of the Management Development Review (1989). We cannot, of course, do justice to all of these here, but provide an introduction to the main methods moving from those that are most trainer centred and familiar to those that are less trainer centred and least familiar. The key point to remember is that none of the methods is intrinsically good or worthless – they need to be selected and combined according to the type of learning required.

LECTURE METHOD AND PRESENTATIONS

These are often dismissed as an example of the worst practice of transferring information and learning to be found in business schools. However, they can take on a variety of forms from the promotion of a set of values as in a corporate video, or indeed an inspirational video from a management guru such as Tom Peters, or the keynote address at a conference, to providing an introductory overview of a learning event and even as a device to challenge established assumptions and provoke debate (see Huczynski, 1983). In practice such presentations are linked with workshops and seminars and are usually followed by 'break-out' sessions allowing fuller discussion. Lectures can also be used to transfer information about a new activity or skill effectively, if time is allowed for questions and discussion afterwards (Griffin and Cashin, 1989). Much maligned, the lecture and presentation always play some role in off-the-job management development activity.

CASE STUDIES VIGNETTES AND CRITICAL INCIDENTS

These are all linked, because they all emphasize practical, applied and participative learning. Case studies are lengthy, comprehensively written and provide detailed information about some past managerial experience. In contrast, vignettes and critical incidents are short, precisely written, and contains fewer complex issues. They can be as short as a paragraph, and even be based upon a press cutting. They are an excellent way of soliciting attitudes and beliefs regarding abstract issues and ideas. This makes them excellent teaching devices for business ethics. However, they can have drawbacks in that they encourage students to jump to conclusions too quickly. This, however, can be remedied by feeding in additional information during the discussion. Exhibit 8.3 summarizes the advantages and disadvantages of using vignettes.

• • • • Exhibit 8.3 • • • •
The advantages and disadvantages of using vignettes

Advantages

- They are an effective means of raising interest and generating a productive discussion.
- Where there is a shortage of specific information on organizations and business contexts, they are an easy way to rectify the situation.
- They can add flexibility to classes, workshops and seminars, enabling the facilitator to pursue a point not raised in the discussion or outside the main themes covered.
- They provide a specific example in practice of a process or construct discussed in the literature.
- They can promote discovery learning, especially when dealing with theoretical issues

Disadvantages

- They can encourage short cuts in learning, compared with case studies.
- The quality of discussion may depend a great deal upon participants' existing knowledge of that issue or similar issues.
- They encourage gut responses, compared with case study analysis which demands prior preparation and reflection.

The case study method emerged via Harvard Law School, and later Harvard Business School, and has become a standard teaching device in management education. It can also be used for in-company management training with the case material generated by real-live company issues. Usually, though, it is more normal for critical incidents to be used in-company. There is a heated debate about the worth of case studies as a teaching device. The advantages and disadvantages of case studies have been summarized by Osigweh Yg (1989). The appeal of case studies and potential problems with these are set out in exhibit 8.4.

Case study use is currently very popular in management education. In the UK there is a central clearing house operated by Cranfield University School of Management, and there are also journals that specialize in publishing case studies for teaching purposes. Published collections of case studies for specialized management functions such as human resource management are also increasingly common (Winstanley and Woodall, 1992; Legge et al., 1991; Tyson and Kakabadse, 1987; Corbett, 1994;) They invite the student to analyse data or reported behaviour and to provide a reasoned set of recommendations for action based on this (see introduction to Winstanley and Woodall, 1992). Case studies also have their use for in-company management development seminars and workshops. These have the advantage that they can usually be written with inside information, and can be much richer and more valid than those written solely on the basis of just company reports and press cuttings.

MANAGEMENT GAMES

This covers a wide range of activities (Institute of Personnel Management, 1989) including simulations and exercises. The main categories are outlined below.

Business games These which focus upon business–economic decision making, usually inviting participants to make a decision on what policies should be adopted. They tend to involve computers and be iterative as each set of decisions has consequences which create a new situation and hence the need for new decisions. They work both at the level of cognitive awareness and team working. They:

- show those whose experience is in just one department how the whole enterprise fits together;
- increase understanding of business finance and how the functional activities contribute to a financial objective;
- stretch people by giving them a demanding, extended and work-related task;
- cause a management team to work closely together on a common task.

University business schools are often the main source of business games, which they often use for in-company work with junior and middle management (and, more recently, as at Kingston University, with Russian managers), and for induction into a management education programme (such as at Imperial College Management School).

•••• Exhibit 8.4 ••••
The appeal of the case study approach and possible problems

Reasons for the appeal of the case study approach

The case study approach:

- Focuses on 'doing' in a classroom setting as a way to improve development.
- Enhances learner development of verbal and written communication.
- Fosters mastery through the invitation to solve a mystery.
- Possesses an illustrative quality.
- Exposes learners to a wide range of true-to-life management problems.
- Enables learning without confronting actual sensitive issues because of their artificial character.
- Promotes constructive change in the management of the organization.
- Inspires interest in otherwise theoretical and abstract training material.
- Provides concrete reference points that foster learning by association, to help bridge the gap between theory and practice.
- Helps unlearn 'skilled incompetence'.

Potential problems with case study approach

The case study approach:

- diminishes the teaching role of the trainer;
- focuses on past and static considerations;
- inhibits double-loop learning;
- reduces the learner's ability to draw effective generalizations;
- diminishes individual responsibility for learning and encourages lazy thinking based on past experience;
- may reinforce norms of non-criticism and thus inhibit the growth of knowledge;
- may foster 'groupthink';
- may compromise quality for quantity of interactive learning;
- may produce unrealistic responses which reflect more the student's rationalization of what a desirable response should be than the solution or course of action they would actually be likely to pursue in practice.

Source: developed from Osigweh Yg, 1989

Board games   Not all games involve a computer simulation. Board games using dice can have a similar effect, and are particularly useful in training in such matters as employment law and business ethics. They use a game approach for helping memorize or revise facts, or for exploring a subject and developing discussion. This has proven to be particularly useful in assisting recall of complex legal information relating to employee relations. For example, an ethical dilemma board game has been developed by Strategic People, an HRD consultancy.

Structured experiences These are exercises designed to focus attention upon transactions between individuals, and the ways in which these can shape group efficiency. They arise out of the group dynamics movement, especially T groups or sensitivity training which involve unstructured agendaless group sessions of 10 to 12 members, where the facilitator assists the group to review the pattern of actions, reactions, interactions and associated feelings of members (Bradford et al., 1964). The aim of these and structured experiences is to increase the ability of members to appreciate how others react to their own behaviour; to increase the ability to gauge the state of relationships between others; and to increase the ability to carry out skilfully the behaviour required by the situation. The content is relatively unimportant compared with the process, and the tasks are often simple, requiring little documentation, but are easily grasped and will generate discussion and differences of opinion. The trainer observes and feeds back their observations, inviting participants to reflect and respond. Sample group tasks would be 'building a paper aeroplane that could stay airborne for five seconds' or 'building a paper tower' (see exhibit 8.5). There are also team analysis games such as 'Lost at sea' or 'Lost on the Moon', which help identify team roles and understand team dynamics and decision making. While tremendous fun, care is needed to ensure that such games are appropriately used, as participants may fear exposure and ridicule, or get caught up in the fun of the game and lose sight of the purpose of the learning experience.

Role play Role play is a device to bridge the gap between cognitive (i.e. thinking); affective (i.e. feelings and values) and behavioural skills. While participants may know how to solve a problem practically, they may not have internalized the feelings that resolving it in real life might generate. Participants have to take on some of the feelings and attitudes associated with a role, and act it out in relation to one another. Role plays can be both structured and spontaneous. They can be very specific, such as in sales training, or highly complex as in simulations of high-level decision making at board level. However, very often role play is used as an essential part of interpersonal skills training, such as handling staff grievances, discipline, appraisal or selection interviews and is even used in management development and assessment centres. With role plays it is important to ensure appropriate use of closed circuit television (CCTV) or camcorder and playback to help participants learn from the experience.

The use of management games is not without pitfalls. Whereas lectures and case studies use pre-existing experience and knowledge of outcomes, games do not, and their success is very much dependent upon participant action and interest and the facilitation skills of the tutor. Games are also less predictable than conventional methods in terms of ensuring learning outcomes. Thus the overall effectiveness of games is dependent upon the willingness of participants to role play and their commitment. However, there are a number of advantages in that they free

•••• Exhibit 8.5 ••••
Paper tower exercise

Brief for teams

Using only the materials provided your task is to construct a paper tower. Your team's performance will be judged on the:

- *height* of your tower;
- *quality* of your design.

The exercise has two parts:

(1) *Planning* You have . . . minutes to plan the construction of your tower. You may try out elements of your design but please remember that *no additional resources are available*.
   You are not allowed to reconstruct any elements of your tower.
(2) *Construction* You have . . . minutes to construct your tower. It must remain standing for two minutes at the end of the construction period.

Facilitator's brief

(1) *Set-up* For this exercise to work it is necessary to have enough people to create at least three teams of four to seven people.
(2) *Materials needed* Several newspapers and sticky tape.
(3) *Objectives* This is a competitive team exercise where the objective for the team is to win, having the highest and best-quality tower.
   The learning objectives include enhancement of team performance by:

   - observation and reflection of team roles;
   - team interaction;
   - positive and negative behaviour;
   - team co-ordination;
   - ideas development;
   - problem solving;
   - time management.

(4) *Support input* Usually the exercise will be accompanied by lectures and exercises to identify team roles, for example the Belbin (1981 and 1993) team role exercises and discussion of positive and negative team behaviour and processes.
(5) *Observer* The role of observer is allocated to one team member in each team, where they will fill in the observer sheet and, at the end of the exercise, feed back to the team their observations.
(6) *Debriefing* This should consist of the observer feedback and a facilitator-led discussion on effective and ineffective team behaviour and how processes identified in the lecture were in evidence in the exercise. A conclusion should be drawn from participants of what they have learnt and how they would do things differently another time.

Paper towers/team roles review

(1) Which roles are represented in your group?
(2) How effectively did you use the resource represented by the people in your group?
(3) Review the role preferences of each individual in your group.
(4) As a group what are your areas of strength and weakness? What type of tasks would you easily perform well and what type of tasks would you have to work harder to achieve?
(5) If asked to undertake the same or a similar project tomorrow what would you do differently in order to be more effective?

participants from passive or 'surface' learning (Chaharbaghi and Cox, 1995); and there is evidence that the learning achieved is at a deep level and can have long-term effects – especially in changing interpersonal behaviour (see exhibit 8.6).

Choosing and using appropriate games is not easy, but usually requires the following:

- clear objectives – is the aim to develop theoretical knowledge and understanding of ideas, or is it to develop interpersonal behaviour or change individual attitudes?;
- a thorough understanding of individual motivation and group dynamics, so as to ensure the optimal conditions for game play;
- advance preparation and rehearsal, so that the game can be properly introduced and potential problems can be anticipated;
- appropriate room layout;
- taking account of organizational culture so that participants are not expected to behave in a way that is totally inconsistent with the norms that apply back at work.

OUTDOOR DEVELOPMENT

There has been a massive growth of interest in outdoor training over the last ten years in the UK. Outdoor training, and organizations such as Outward Bound and the Leadership Trust, have a long history of combining personal development with physical fitness. However, the advent of UK government training programmes in the 1980s, which recommended outdoor development as a vehicle for personal development, led to a growth in the number and type of providers, of varying quality. The distinctive nature of the learning experience is that it is usually built around the learning cycle (see chapter 7) with an emphasis upon 'doing' followed by opportunities for reflection, concluding, and planning ahead, and that it also works at the affective or emotional level – occasioned by the stressful experience of physical discomfort or even danger. Although the tasks are very different from managerial work, they are none the less real and can lay bare underlying management processes. While most programmes use staff qualified in outdoor pursuits, the best also use experienced training consultants and will build in a complementary programme of indoor activities and self-assessment instruments covering such aspects as communication, leadership style, team roles, conflict management and other interpersonal skill development. Before embarking on any outdoor development activity it is very important to justify the reason for its use (Bank, 1994; Teire, 1994).

There are basically two types of outdoor programme: management teamwork and personal development. The former provides the opportunity for a whole work team from an organization to go away as a group. However, this requires very careful handling as on the one hand it is advisable for all participants to be of the same status (the presence of more senior staff can be disruptive to group dynamics) but on the other hand an unintended outcome of the enhanced group solidarity can reinforce an 'us-and-them' situation on return to work. Ensuring an effective transfer of learning back to the workplace also requires time to be allowed for follow-up, especially in respect of the reviewing, concluding and planning stages of the learning cycle. Unless

•••• Exhibit 8.6 ••••
Deep, surface and strategic learning

Surface learning

Directs attention towards learning *content*:

- focuses on detailed information;
- focuses on information in sequence;
- focus on discrete elements without integration;
- concentrates upon memorizing detail;
- aims to reproduce information;
- fails to distinguish principles from examples;
- treats task as an external imposition;
- focuses exclusively on completing task requirements;
- unreflective about purpose or strategies.

Deep learning

Directs attention towards *underlying meaning and comprehension*:

- focuses on the overall meaning of information;
- tries to understand;
- vigorous interaction with the content;
- attempts to identify the underlying principles and concepts;
- examines the logic of the argument;
- identifies the essence of an argument and the supporting facts;
- relates new ideas to previous knowledge;
- relates concepts to everyday experience;
- relates evidence to conclusions.

Strategic learning

(Note: occurs more on examined courses.) Strategic Learning:

- has aims based around achieving highest possible grades;
- organizes time and effort to greatest effect;
- ensures conditions and materials for learning are appropriate;
- attempts to predict test or exam questions;
- finds out details of marking schemes.

Source: Drawn from Entwistle, 1987.

there is the organizational and structural support back at work, and the workforce is stable, with a low turnover, outdoor development for management teams may not be cost effective. One study (Lowe, 1991) has evaluated such courses for supervisory management and in terms of levels of evaluation methodology (see chapter 2). It found that they were viewed as very effective in terms of immediate reactions, and their impact upon participant learning and job behaviour, but of much less determinate value in terms of wider organization benefit.

The sheer cost of such management team programmes explains why organizations often sponsor individuals on personal development programmes where they will mix with participants from other companies. This can be an effective means of removing the impediments to development that are reinforced by the normal work environment and presence of peers (such as low self-esteem, lack of self-confidence, fear of failure, fear of shame and fear of social disapproval). However, unless there are arrangements to support the transfer of the individual manager's experience back to the workplace, the benefits for both individual and organization can be lost.

•••• Off-the-Job Development for Small-Business Managers ••••

Much of the literature on off-the-job development activities assumes that organizations are sufficiently large to be able to sponsor sufficient numbers of managers as participants. This is clearly not possible for small businesses, where very often there may be a very small management team of a handful of people, or even just an owner-manager. As we have already seen (see chapter 4) it is not possible to make any generalizations about the management development needs of small businesses. Some (for example, small software development houses, small accountancy practices and even NHS general practice fundholders) may be staffed by highly trained technical and professional staff, while others (kitchen design companies, restaurants, etc.) may have been set up and run by people with few formal qualifications who are self-taught and have little predisposition towards management training. Thus it is very difficult to generalize about small-business requirements for formal management development. However, research on the development of management teams in owner-managed firms shows that expertise needed at the start-up stage usually includes production/operations management, research and development, marketing and general management. Usually the need for financial skills is met through external recruitment and personnel skills by means of internal promotion (very often of secretarial staff).

Usually time to attend programmes and to study is the problem, and so flexible delivery of learning is a major consideration. It may be possible for managers from these organizations to attend open programmes in management education, or short courses provided by management consultancies and organizations such as the Industrial Society. This is a particularly acute problem for owner–managers (see also chapter 13) whose business development may have outstripped their management knowledge and skills. A useful source of support can be found in membership of networks and associations such as the Institute of Directors and the Institute of

Management who provide suitable seminars and breakfast meetings, where experience can be shared.

•••• Summary ••••

This chapter has examined the most common types of off-the-job management development. Overall, off-the-job management development is alive and kicking despite the current fashion for experiential learning at work. Indeed, there are equally good justifications for its use, and management education in particular has been unfairly treated by some management consultants and radical academics. It should not be forgotten that many managers learn in spite of rather than because of their employers, and that the balance between meeting individual and organizational needs will never be a totally happy one. This is more so today than it has ever been. Organizational restructuring makes the balance of commitment between organizations and their managers very uneven, and probably explains the current enthusiasm for management education that can provide managers with recognized, transferable higher-education management qualifications. Increasingly the onus will be upon the individual manager to put together packages of off-the-job and work-related learning methods in a meaningful way. If they are lucky they may receive some assistance from the organization in terms of assessment centres, career development workshops and the construction of personal development plans. At the same time the boundary between the learning experience within management education and in-company or other externally provided off-the-job learning is much more fluid. Yet choice of solutions needs very careful consideration, and the following questions should be posed:

- What are the main learning objectives of the different organizational stakeholders in respect of management development?
- What is the prevailing climate of opinion with respect to off-the-job management development, and which forms are acceptable?
- Is an off-the-job learning solution more desirable or more resource intensive than experiential work-related development?
- What range of provision could be considered, and who would be potential providers (both internal and external) and participants?

EXERCISE

Work through the above list of questions in the Summary section of this chapter. Identify one off-the-job management development method that you have experienced. Review and analyse the strengths and weaknesses of this approach, drawing on your own experience. Identify how this method could have been adapted to meet your needs more fully.

•••• References ••••

Argyris, C. 1994: *On Organizational Learning*. Oxford: Blackwell.

Arkin, A. 1991: How international are Britain's business schools? *Personnel Management*, November, pp. 28–31.

Ashton, D. 1989: The case for tailor-made MBAs. *Personnel Management*, July, pp. 32–5.

Bank, J. 1994: *Outdoor Development for Managers*. 2nd edn, Aldershot: Gower.

Belbin, R. M. 1981: *Management Teams, why they succeed or fail*. Oxford: Butterworth Heinemann.

Belbin, R. M. 1993: *Team Roles at Work*. Oxford: Butterworth Heinemann.

Bradford, L. P., Gibb, J. R., and Benne, K. D. (eds) 1964: *T Group Theory and Laboratory Method*. New York: John Wiley.

Burgoyne, J. and Stuart, R. 1978: Teaching and learning methods in management development. *Personnel Review*, 7, 1, Winter, pp. 53–8.

Cannon, T. 1994: *Management Development for the Millennium*. Corby: Institute of Management.

Chaharbaghi, K. and Cox, R. 1995: Problem based learning: potential and implementation issues. *British Journal of Management*, 6, 4, pp. 249–56.

Corbett, J. M. 1994: *Critical Cases in Organisational Behaviour*. Basingstoke: Macmillan.

Council for National Academic Awards 1992: *The MBA*. London: CNAA.

Cunningham, I. 1994: Self-managed learning. In Mumford, A. (ed.), *Gower Handbook of Management Development*, 4th edn, Aldershot: Gower.

Entwistle, N. 1987: A model of the teaching–learning process. In Richardson, J. T. E., Eysenck, M. W. and Warren-Piper, D. (eds) *Student Learning*, ch. 2, Milton Keynes: SRHE and Open University.

Griffin, R. W. and Cashin, J. L. 1989: The lecture and discussion method of management education: pros and cons. *Management Development Review*, 8, 2, pp. 25–32.

Handy, C., Gordon, C., Gow, I. and Randlesome, C. 1988: *Making Managers*. London: Pitman.

Hayes, J. 1993: The role of the business school in management development. *Personnel Review*, 22, 1, pp. 4–17.

Herriot, P. and Pemberton, C. 1995: *New Deals: the revolution in management careers*. New York: John Wiley.

Huczynski, A. 1983: *Encyclopedia of Management Development Methods*. Aldershot: Gower.

Institute of Personnel Management 1988: *MBAs*. Personnel Management Factsheet No. 12, London: Institute of Personnel Management (now Institute of Personnel and Development).

Institute of Personnel Management 1989: *Management Games*. IPM Factsheet No. 15, London: Institute of Personnel Management (now Institute of Personnel and Development).

Legge, K. Clegg, C.W. and Kemp, N. 1991: *Case Studies in Information Technology, People and Organisations*. Manchester: NCC Blackwell.

Linder, J. C. and Smith, H. J. 1992: The complex case of management education. *Harvard Business Review*, September–October, pp. 16–33.

Locke, R. 1981: *Management and Higher Education since 1940*. Cambridge: Cambridge University Press.

Lowe, J. 1991: Teambuilding via outdoor training: experiences from a UK automotive plant. *Human Resource Management Journal*, 2, 1, pp. 42–59.

Management Development Review 1989: special issue on management development methods, 8, 2.

Margerison, C. 1991: *Making Management Development Work: Achieving Success in the Nineties*. Maidenhead: McGraw-Hill.

Mumford, A. 1994: *Management Development: Strategies for Action*. 2nd edn, London: IPD.

Mumford, A. 1996: Could do bettter. *People Management*, 24 October, p. 27.

Osigweh Yg, C. A. B. 1989: Casing the case approach in management development. *Management Development Review*, 8, 2, pp. 66–76.

Peattie, K. 1993: The teaching company scheme: effecting organizational change through academic/practitioner collaboration. *Journal of Management Development*, 12, 4, pp. 59–72.

Porter, L. W. and McKibbon, L. E. 1988: *Management Education and Development: Drift or Thrust into the 21st Century?* New York: McGraw-Hill.

Reed, M. and Anthony, P. 1992: Professionalising management and managing professionalisation: British management in the 1980s. *Journal of Management Studies*, 29, 5, September, pp. 591–693.

Teire, J. 1994: Using the outdoors. In Mumford, A. (ed.), *Gower Handbook of Management Development*, 4th edn, Aldershot: Gower.

Tyson, S. and Kakabadse, A. 1987: *Case Studies in Human Resource Management*. London: Heinemann.

Warner, M. 1990: Where business schools fail to meet business needs. *Personnel Management*, July, 52–6.

Wiener, M. 1981: *English Culture and the Decline of the Industrial Spirit (1880–1980)*. Cambridge: Cambridge University Press.

Willmott, H. 1994: Management education: provocation to a debate. *Management Learning*, 5, 1, pp. 105–36.

Winstanley, D. and Woodall, J. (eds) 1992: *Case Studies in Personnel*. London: IPM (now Institute of Personnel and Development).

····CHAPTER 9····

Work-Based Management Development Methods: Informal and Incidental Learning

···· Introduction ····

Faced with a choice of management development methods, it is easy to concentrate on the formal management development programmes and courses that are provided away from everyday work and often conducted through educational and training establishments. In our introduction to chapter 7 we acknowledged how this approach dominated management development for many years, despite much criticism of its being irrelevant and 'too little, too late for too few' (Handy et al., 1987). In this chapter we move on to consider the informal and incidental development activities which automatically take place on a daily basis, without necessarily receiving recognition or being linked to the formal development policies and processes for managers within organizations. While our view is that recent fashion has swung away from formal off-the-job development towards work-based management development, we also feel that it has done so in an uncritical manner. Work-based management development requires some planning and plenty of conscious reflection and support. This chapter will address these issues directly.

The true scale of work-based management development methods is both huge and hidden. For this reason it is extremely difficult to quantify and to assess the contribution made by such methods to the overall effectiveness of managers. In the USA, over ten years ago, it was estimated that of the $210 billion spent on training in industry, $180 billion was spent on informal or on-the-job training (Carnevale, 1984). Although comparable reliable estimates for the UK are unavailable (total employer spend on training and development has been variously estimated as anything between £20 billion in 1987 and £10–£11 billion in 1993), it is fair to assume a similar pattern applies, particularly with respect to management development.

In this chapter we will review what is meant by work-based management development and why it is seen as such a powerful tool in developing managerial effectiveness at the individual, group and organizational level. The range of work-based development methods will then be outlined, followed by an evaluation of their appropriateness in different contexts. The chapter will conclude with a consideration of the support mechanisms required to achieve both effective work-based managerial learning and to integrate it within wider organizational management development strategy.

•••• Learning Objectives ••••

After reading this chapter, you should be able to:

- define what is encompassed by work-based management development and explain its significance in relation to theories of managerial learning;
- identify appropriate informal work-based learning opportunities for the needs of both different individual managers, work groups and the wider organization;
- devise appropriate support mechanisms to optimize managerial learning from both informal and incidental work-based learning experiences.

•••• The Meaning and Utility of Work-Based ••••
Management Development

There is a great deal of confusion surrounding terminology: 'work-based learning', 'work-related learning', 'natural learning', 'experiential learning', 'informal learning' and 'incidental learning' are just some examples of the most frequently used terms. Until very recently there has also been relatively little systematic research focusing upon the learning events and experiences that are significant in a manager's career (Davies and Easterby-Smith, 1984; McCall et al., 1988; McCauley et al., 1994), so we cannot with certainty say that work-based management development methods will always be effective, or will even be perceived to be so by those experiencing them. This is because they do not involve just conscious learning, but also unconscious and subconscious learning.

Yet work-based learning activities are increasingly an important component in corporate management development strategy. Much of the research into managerial roles has revealed that leading-edge companies developed their managers by devoting substantial effort to:

> adding responsibilities to jobs, creating special jobs . . . transferring people between functions and divisions, mentoring and coaching employees, giving these people feedback on development progress, and giving them instruction into how to manage their own development. (Kotter, 1988: pp. 81–2)

Yet there is much anecdotal evidence that by themselves such activities do not always make a difference. Much appears to depend on the circumstances in which they are used, the timing, and above all who perceives the need for them. We shall return to this theme later in the chapter.

In the UK the interest in work-based development can be traced back ten years to a concern about the competence of the general workforce in the context of growing youth unemployment. The government sponsored research into the identification of 'core skills' in the early 1980s in the hope that trainees could be assisted to develop them and thereby acquire transferable skills. At the time this research showed that these skills were best developed through everyday practical work experience. This research drew upon the earlier experience in the USA in competency-based learning for secondary-school pupils and for managers. While in the UK the definition of occupational competency as the basis for vocational and managerial qualifications was different from the US model (see chapters 4 and 5), it shared a similar emphasis on developing and assessing competency in relation to behaviours and tasks exhibited at work. Work-based learning and assessment thus became a major component in the delivery of National Vocational Qualifications and the Management Charter Initiative standards for managers. Many organizations adopting a competency-based approach to human resource development would thus be looking towards the use of work-based development.

There is also a much more fundamental reason for the current interest in work-based development for managers. This lies in the accelerating rate and scope of organizational change since the late 1980s. In the corporate sector, the scale of merger, acquisition and divestment activity has made organizational restructuring a more frequent and common phenomenon. The downsizing and delayering associated with this has resulted in a considerable reduction of white-collar managerial jobs discussed in chapter 2. This has three implications. First, managers who are entering restructured (and usually much larger) job roles have a need for rapid and relevant development support that is not easily met solely by off-the-job management development and education. Second, the numbers of managers involved makes such off-the-job provision impracticable within the time scales and training and development budgets operating. Finally, the identification and effective use of work-based learning are central to strategies of organizational learning, which frequently accompany such restructuring.

However, as previously noted, work-based learning is open to several definitions. At the most basic it can be seen as something that occurs naturally as people go about their jobs. They can learn from their mistakes, by trial and error, from their interactions with other employees and customers, etc., as well as from their successes. They can learn from all of these, but they do not always do so. As we saw in chapter 7, there is much evidence that while managers can learn from experience, they are not always able to do so. For a start, organizational defensive routines may encourage only single-loop learning (Argyris, 1990). Thus, even if the manager does make a mistake, she or he may be conditioned to search for an alternative solution among a restricted number of options. Similarly, learning from a success can lead to the complacent assumption that the same behaviour will result in the same outcomes in all circumstances, and encourages over-confidence in individual ability (McCall et al., 1988). Also, Knowles (1989) reminds us that, as adults, managers will only be motivated to learn when they perceive a felt need, and that this involves perceiving the direct utility of what is being learned and having the opportunity to try it out in practice. In addition, the context of the experience is important. There is much evidence that adults are more likely to learn from non-routine experiences than from the routine (Marsick and Watkins, 1990, pp. 21–3) and that, finally, the opportunity for reflection is essential. As few managers are naturally predisposed to reflectiveness as opposed to action, it is not surprising that left to themselves they will forego the opportunity to reflect in favour of immediately taking some form of action. For these reasons, then, experiential learning in the workplace is not always 'naturally' effective.

There is also a further distinction to be made between informal and incidental learning (Marsick and Watkins, 1990). Incidental learning is usually the by-product of some other activity such as carrying out a task or interactions with other people. As such it is never planned or intentional. In contrast, informal learning, although it is often accidental, can be planned or intentional even though it is predominantly experiential, non-institutional and controlled by the learner rather than the trainer. Incidental learning may be seen as a subset of informal learning which is tacit, taken for granted, and is implicit in everyday management assumptions and actions. Both informal and incidental learning (but particularly the latter) are denoted by the task through which they are achieved and by the capacity of the individual (in terms of both other work demands and their attitudes and perceptions). This obviously raises questions around how best to take advantage of opportunities for informal and incidental learning. We shall return to this at the end of this chapter, but at this point it is necessary to review some examples of work-based learning.

•••• A Review of Work-Based Development Methods ••••

What follows is a categorization of informal work-based learning methods. However, it is important to recognize that, in both principle and practice, they are not always well distinguished from each other in the literature. We have attempted to acknowledge this. At the same time we have provided a classification that groups the methods according to three categories: one-to-one relationships, real-work tasks and learning in groups. Table 9.1 provides an overview of the different methods mentioned in this chapter, and outlines the different ways in which learning takes place, and the different roles played by the participants in the learning process.

•••• Learning from One-to-One Relationships: Coaching, •••• Mentoring, Sponsorship and Role Models

COACHING

Perhaps the most important source of development is the immediate line manager. They can counsel, provide insight, give frank feedback and open doors, or they may only do some or none of these. Coaching skills are the essential means by which this can be done, but while they are a natural component of a line manager's style for some, many have consciously to acquire these skills. This usually requires off-the-job training involving observation of others, role play and reflection. Good coaching involves showing an interest in people and always being on the look-out for learning

Table 9.1 An overview of work-based development methods

Method	Learning process
Learning from another person	
Coaching	Feedback, reflection, challenge
Mentoring and sponsorship	Support, advice, feedback, opportunity, challenge
Role models	Observation, reflection, imitation
Learning from tasks	
Special projects	Problem solving, taking responsibility, taking risks and making decisions, managing without mastering
Job rotation	Exposure to other cultures and points of view
Shadowing	Observation of tasks, new techniques, skills
Secondment	Exposure to other cultures and points of view
Acting up delegation	Trial of new tasks and skills, challenge
Learning with others	
Task forces/working parties	Strategic understanding, building awareness and confidence
Action learning	Problem solving, interaction, influencing
Networking	Interaction and building awareness

opportunities at work. Above all, it requires that managers show confidence in their staff and are 'person centred' rather than 'task focused'. An impatience to get on with a job or an intolerance of mistakes are big obstacles to effective coaching. Superficially, coaching skills appear to be quite simple (Singer, 1979; Rae, 1987), but their application requires considerable sensitivity towards the individual being coached, and in some situations a more directive style is required. Coaching is often regarded as something that is carried out primarily with non-managerial employees, but it is also the foundation for most other forms of work-based learning for managers. The main coaching skills are listed in exhibit 9.1.

MENTORING AND SPONSORSHIP

Mentoring occurs where an experienced manager offers guidance, stimulus, encouragement, feedback and support to a younger or less experienced employee. Mentors are usually found outside the line management relationship, and mentoring can be either a formal or an informal activity. Sometimes it is done in an informal *ad hoc* way at the instigation of the individual manager. In this situation, it often leads to sponsorship where a manager takes an active role in creating and communicating career opportunities to an individual and acts as their advocate, giving them 'visibility' within the wider organization and outside. However, mentoring can also be incorporated into formal management development programmes. Some organizations build formal mentoring schemes into graduate training or executive development programmes, but widespread formal organizational mentoring is not common, and most schemes fall into decay. Informal mentoring tends to be most successful, and there is much literature supporting its value (for example see Clutterbuck, 1985; Cunningham and Eberle, 1993; Hunt and Michael, 1988), and exploring its various

---

• • • • Exhibit 9.1 • • • •
The skills of coaching

Observation

This involves the coach standing back dispassionately to review the situation and their role before taking action.

Active listening

This involves not just hearing what the employee says, but making an effort to understand what lies behind it. Being able to empathize and yet to distinguish between fact and fantasy are essential. Appropriate body language and noises are usually required to maintain rapport.

Discussion

The skill here is to ensure that it is the employee who diagnoses the basic problem and formulates a solution, not the coach. The coach summarizes and reflects back the ideas of the employee while simultaneously concealing their own ideas as to the nature of solutions. Occasionally the coach may need to challenge and confront (see below), particularly if it appears that the employee is unable to respond or has chosen an option that is highly risky.

Challenging and questioning

The skilful use of questioning techniques (knowing when to used open, closed, probing and leading questions) forces the employee to reflect upon and justify their ideas.

Delegation

This involves transferring the initiative and responsibility for action to the employee. The basic techniques are agreeing achievable objectives and expected results, giving authority for action, avoiding interference when events do not turn out as expected, and providing opportunities for review and feedback.

Timing

The coach has to set aside time from other duties to ensure that they can carry out their duties properly, and also has to ensure that the employee has sufficient time in order to be able to take advantage of learning opportunities as they arise.

---

dimensions in more depth (Bates, 1993; Noe, 1988; Megginson, 1988). Mentoring can also be a good work-related development opportunity for the mentor themselves. It can help a newly appointed junior manager acquire confidence if they are asked to mentor other employees, and it can also keep a senior manager in touch with what is happening elsewhere in the organization.

ROLE MODELLING

Line managers or mentors can be useful role models, but there are many other sources of role models within organizations, both positive and negative. Often unwittingly, role models are observed and studied for their qualities, attitudes and behaviour, and will accordingly be perceived as effective or ineffective by the observer. These observers may then consciously or unconsciously try to imitate their good qualities or shun their poor ones. It seems that most managers learn from watching those around them and use their observations to form positive or negative role models even though they may not be working with these as explicit constructs. It is interesting to note that a recent study of senior managers in the NHS (Dawson et al., 1995) found that, without prompting, over 70 per cent of the sample mentioned positive role models as being influential in their development and 13 per cent negative role models. This stands in direct contrast to only 10 per cent who cited training and development programmes. Clearly the qualities of positive and negative role models are highly context dependent in terms of both the organization's history and current stage of development and the individual observer's disposition (there is much evidence that we seek out role models who have similar traits to ourselves). But it is important to remember that negative role models can be very instructive: they teach patience and the need to be aware of managerial impact on others (McCall et al., 1988).

···· Learning from Tasks: Special Projects, Job Rotation, ···· Shadowing, Secondments and Acting Up

Task-based management development methods all draw upon the principle of job enrichment and need theories of motivation. Earlier needs theories such as that of Herzberg et al. (1959) and Maslow (1943, 1987) have been evolved into more complex systems used to promote better job design, such as Hackman and Oldham (1980) and Warr's (1987) popular vitamin model. The motivators of greater responsibility, recognition and personal growth can all be activated through job enrichment in order to assist individual learning.

SPECIAL PROJECTS

These can include a wide variety of activities. Some may be a direct component of the manager's job, such as starting up a unit from scratch, turning around an underperforming unit or managing an operation of a much larger scope. Such developmental assignments all emphasize the ability to stand alone, make decisions and shoulder responsibility. They involve learning new skills 'on the run', learning to act when there is a high risk of failure, learning to work with difficult people under trying circumstances, and learning to cope with an extremely exhausting workload. These are the 'stretch' assignments given to develop potential and assist succession planning from middle to senior management positions. Within restructured organizations and small businesses, such special projects are the norm in everyday managerial life, even though their primary purpose may not have been development so much as expediency.

However, not all work-related projects are as ambitious. More modest tasks include investigating the cause of a problem or developing a new approach to the work of a unit. Sometimes the manager will be temporarily assigned to this on a full-time basis, but very often the project can be carried on alongside normal work duties. Sometimes the project may take the individual out of their normal work environment and involve fact finding and liaison with other units. In this case the manager may be assigned to a task force or working party (see below). Projects that are sufficiently testing (as opposed to just an excuse for dumping work) can help a manager learn that although they cannot master every issue, they are none the less able to manage the assignment and work with others over whom they have very little control. Combining this with support from a coach or mentor can be a very powerful form of development.

JOB ROTATION

This involves moving an individual or cohort of managers into different roles and tasks within different work groups and environments, with the aim of broadening their knowledge and skill base. It can either be done on a regular and structured basis or in an *ad hoc* fashion, in response to circumstances. It is most commonly used in graduate trainee and executive development schemes in the UK, as a form of induction into the organization. Job rotation is more widely used in Japan as a key element in management development, in order to provide wider exposure to the organization and its various activities. On an *ad hoc* basis, it is a valuable way of meeting the needs of plateaued managers – especially in delayered organizations, and of counteracting insular attitudes common among those who have been doing the same type of work for a long time.

SHADOWING

Shadowing is more limited and passive than job rotation or secondment but more active and conscious than role modelling. Unlike role modelling the observation is more concerned with task than with qualities. In the manual area this is more known as 'Sitting next to Nellie'. The emphasis is upon observing new skills and tasks being carried out in an unfamiliar job role. An example is where a manager visits another site or company and spends time observing the work of a peer over a period of days or even weeks. This is sometimes used internationally as a form of development for doctors visiting overseas practices or for managers interested in learning new forms of quality management from peers in other countries.

SECONDMENT

This is a form of work-based development that takes the individual out of the normal work unit and places them within a different working environment for a defined period of time. Usually this involves a placement within a different organization, but it can include placements within different parts of a large organization. Sometimes the secondment takes the form of a job-swap between two individuals who then both have an opportunity to try out a different role but can use each other for consultation and advice. In the changing world of flexible customer-focused organizations, secondments can serve a positive purpose (Chater and Stokes, 1992). Individual managers can be seconded to suppliers, customers and manufacturers to acquire know-how that will facilitate interorganizational learning. They can also even be used to provide a service to the community. Organizations such as Business in the Community (see Exhibit 9.2) act as the broker of such secondments in their Employee Community Involvement Programme. However, the success of any secondment depends on careful management of the exit process from the parent organization and entry into the host organization, as the expectations of all parties need to be clear at the outset for the secondment to be successful. Similarly, the re-entry of the secondees into their parent organization needs to be handled sensitively. All too often secondees return to the same job, and to deaf ears. The situation can easily degenerate into a syndrome of dissatisfaction, demotivation and ultimately departure from the organization. While this might be appropriate in some situations, it can also be a costly waste of resources. Thus secondments require very careful support at all stages.

ACTING UP

This occurs when, for reasons of maternity leave, illness, recruitment difficulties and, increasingly, the delayed replacement of a departed employee, an individual temporarily assumes the responsibilities of a more senior position. The developmental value is the opportunity to learn new skills and to explore the suitability of such a career move from both the perspective of the individual manager and the organization. Such developmental opportunities depend for their success on effective delegation by offering challenge, responsibility and autonomy. Unfortunately, there are too many occasions when delegation becomes dumping and when the manager does not get the full credit for what they have achieved. One example is in the NHS where a director temporarily takes on the role of a chief executive, or where a non-executive director takes over the role of chair, pending recruitment of a new replacement. Potential difficulties arise on return to previous roles as the new incumbent takes over, particularly when a manager then has to work below them. They may have different ways of working, and it is not always easy to relinquish power once it has been tasted.

•••• Learning from Others: Task Forces, Action Learning •••• and Networking

These are all methods that rely upon social interaction with more than one person, and where the social learning involves changes in values and perspectives as much as the achievement of tasks.

···· Exhibit 9.2 ····
Employee Community Involvement as a management development tool

Employee Community Involvement (ECI) is the involvement of company employees and managers in their local communities, supported by their employers. It can involve employees at any level, can take a variety of forms, and is a practical and effective way of developing individual and team skills. By taking staff out of their work environment to work on projects of real value to the community, it provides intensive development of initiative, communications, influencing, decision making and self management skills.

ECI opportunities include:

- Development Assignments, typically of 100 hours, focused on problems in community or educational organisations, and linked directly to the development needs of the individual.
- Team Development Assignments, tailored to assist team building, usually undertaking a mix of practical and strategic work in a host organisation, where participants have the additional motivation of 'putting something back'. This approach is at its most effective when accompanied by pre-project workshops on roles and the nature of team working.
- Mentoring – one to one association with people from all sectors of the community, supporting education, helping to enhance the management of schools and charities and developing coaching, interpersonal and listening skills.
- Business on Board – placement of employees and managers on the boards of trustees of charities or of school governors, to develop general management and influencing skills.

This practical and growing way of developing managers provides benefits:

- For employers:
  - intensive development of skills in real life situations
  - enhances the ability to initiate and cope with change
  - develops teamwork and inter-developmental co-operation
  - raises morale
  - improves competitiveness
  - helps to create healthier communities in which to do business
- For managers:
  - the satisfaction of making a genuine contribution
  - development of new and existing skills
  - broadens horizons by taking manager out of company culture
  - exposes managers to risk and decision-making
  - introduces them to new ways of managing with slender resources

Business In The Community is the leading broker of community involvement for development, and provides a national support service including:

- advice and consultancy
- workshops and seminars
- brokerage and matching of appropriate opportunities
- full management service for placements, including matching, induction, monitoring and evaluation.

Employee Community Involvement for development supports the MCI's Model of Personal Competency. More that 150 Marks and Spencer staff take part in BiTC's Development Assignment programme each year. Other companies using Employee Community Involvement for development include KPMG, Sony, Sun Alliance, SBC Warburg, Shell UK and British Aerospace.

Source: Business in The Community. 0171 224 1600. 44 Baker St, London W1M 1DH. Employee Community Involvement as a Management Development tool.

TASK FORCES AND WORKING PARTIES

These are often set up to deal with a pressing organizational problem, the solution to which requires input from a number of managers, often from diverse parts of the organization. They are an increasingly familiar phenomenon in organizations facing change, and provide an opportunity for participants to gain a wider perspective. They are also a great means for ambitious young managers to acquire organizational visibility, and hence career advancement. Ultimately this depends upon the significance of the working party's tasks and outputs. However, care is needed to ensure the nomination of participants is both considered and fair. It is easy for those who are strong in impression management to get assigned, but not for equally acceptable, but not so noticeable, candidates.

ACTION LEARNING

Action learning was an approach first coined by Revans (1982) in the 1960s to describe groups of managers with a facilitator learning through exchanging experiences on real-life problems. Revans believed the most effective managerial learning took place within the context of real-life problems, which were of a non-routine nature and which presented a challenge to the manager concerned. He thus draws heavily upon Rogers' (1969) humanistic philosophy that true development is achieved only by helping individuals to help themselves. Furthermore, the manager would be more inclined to go beyond analysing and making recommendations and actually implement a course of action if they 'owned' the problem and if they received encouragement from others in similar positions. For this reason, action learning sets are formed, whereby a groups of managers with different problems agree to regular meetings in which they present their problems, listen to one another and offer advice.

There are a variety of ways in which action learning can be implemented (Pedler, 1991; McGill and Beaty, 1992). Learning sets usually consist of five to six people who negotiate the use of their meeting time to test and question each other about a challenging work-related problem to which they have been assigned. They are usually assisted by a facilitator who will point them in the direction of an appropriate source of expertise and will assist with group learning when requested. The key point is that managers are motivated to take responsibility for their own learning and to be focused upon action rather than just analysis. While supportive, the learning set culture is not 'soft'. There is emphasis on learning by doing and working together to reframe problems. There is only a marginal tolerance of failure.

Since its inception action learning has always had a committed following, but since the late 1980s interest has grown. It complements many Japanese management practices, such as continuous improvement and organizational restructuring, and the broadening of managerial job roles has made it increasingly popular as a means of supporting organizational initiatives to encourage self-development. Action learning has a relationship to management development that is similar to the relationship between quality circles and quality management. Both start with a focus on work problems and utilize a team approach to identifying, analysing and solving problems, and ultimately the implementation and evaluation of the preferred solutions. However, action learning sets differ markedly from quality circles in that they bring together managers from different work areas or even different employers. They are comrades in adversity rather than members of the same work unit or having similar expertise.

NETWORKING

Finally, there is a growing recognition that it is not what we know but whom we know that affects how we get on at work. This indicates the importance of old boys' clubs, such as the Freemasons, and occasionally old girls' clubs, such as Forum, the network for high-earning women. On the negative side this can degenerate into nepotism where membership guarantees a passport to career success within an organization. We have acknowledged their growing significance to career development in changing organizations (see chapter 3), and shall see that informal male networks can be a major obstacle to career advancement for women (see chapter 11).

However, besides the more obvious function of career advancement, networking is a useful way of getting things done, and getting a fresh perspective on problems (Smith, 1989; Thatcher, 1996). Quality management, internal markets, downsizing and delayering all place more emphasis upon the management of relationships outside the vertical chain of command. Good influencing skills are important, but need to be complemented by the ability to network. Sometimes, external networks can be very helpful to learning at work. Many senior HR professionals are using a variety of networks for this purpose (Thatcher, 1996). It is common for such networks to be a spin-off from formal off-the-job management development programmes and educational courses. It is very common for study-group members on MBA and other management education courses to continue to meet regularly as a basis for learning from one another. This is particularly important where such managers often work in relative isolation from others who share the same concerns, such as is the position of many human resource managers who are working within business units or for small firms.

•••• Making Effective Use of Work-Based Management •••• Development

We have outlined some of the most frequently used forms of work-based management development, but there are many others. Yet despite continuing exhortations from management development literature that informal and incidental learning processes are worthwhile and are cost effective (Mumford, 1993a; Mumford 1993b; Pedler et al., 1990), they are implemented only in a very patchy fashion in most organizations. We now turn to consider why this is so, and what is required for successful work-based management development.

One reason may be that where it is practised the learning is based upon informal and incidental processes. These do not appear in formal organizational management development policy statements or plans, and in consequence may also be under-reported in research. Managers are involved in informal and incidental development, but they do not always know they are doing it (Mumford, 1993c), and so do not necessarily report that they do so. Although this may be true, there is a big difference between a process being informal and its being *ad hoc* or incidental as we noted earlier. Informal processes can become institutionalized and part of the organizational culture, and senior managers are important in communicating this. Unfortunately, this is all too rare, or else the good intentions are frustrated by pressure at the middle-management level.

So another reason could be inadequate practical support from line managers. Earlier in this chapter we noted the fundamental role of the line manager in supporting informal and incidental learning. This is extremely important and extends beyond a formal organizational policy of intermittently appraising performance and identifying development needs, into everyday managerial activity, as outlined in exhibit 9.3.

The problem is that helpful bosses are rare, liable to move on, and the current changes in organizations make them all the more elusive. Performance management systems which are highly task focused, and the intensification of managerial work, push out the available time for development, as borne out by recent research findings (Hutchinson and Wood, 1995). This is ironical, given that such organizations are often those where the human resource strategy is to place the responsibility for most development firmly on to the line manager, with the human resource manager acting as an internal consultant.

Another reason that informal and incidental management development is under-valued and ignored, may be to do with formal training itself. Managers who themselves are not trained to use the workplace for their own and their colleagues' learning are unlikely to perceive its worth. A formal training culture breeds a demand for formal training and creates blindness to informal and incidental management development.

Therefore, if an organization believes that work-based management development is important, it needs to:

- communicate why it is important;
- instigate training in how to do it;
- ensure that it is integrated with other formal development and human resource activities such as appraisal and rewards;
- clarify the roles and responsibilities, especially those of the human resource specialist, the line manager and the individual manager to be developed;
- ensure that these roles are reinforced in the wider organizational culture.

Yet caution is needed when following such a route towards formalizing and acknowledging the value of work-based development. Some organizations make a conscious choice to stay informal, creative, unrestrained by procedure and un-shackled by the need to formulate detailed policies tightly related to overall organizational strategy. These organizations may thus choose to reinforce the

•••• **Exhibit 9.3** ••••
Role of a manager in developing subordinates

Within formal system of development

- Appraisal of performance
- Appraisal of potential
- Analysis of development needs and goals
- Recognizing opportunities
- Facilitating those opportunities
- Giving learning a priority
- Selecting opportunities in tune with learning styles

Within the direct managerial context

- Using management activities as learning
- Establishing learning goals
- Accepting risks in subordinate performance
- Monitoring learning achievement
- Providing feedback on performance
- Acting as a model for managerial behaviour
- Acting as a model of learning behaviour
- Using learning styles and learning cycle
- Offering help
- Direct coaching
- Looking for deputizing/delegating opportunities

Source: Mumford, 1993b

importance of work-based management development in a different way, through their culture, role modelling and particularly by the example played by senior managers. This will be the case in many small firms, where intuitive and informal processes would become lifeless and constricting if driven to be formalized in any way. This is why there cannot be a blanket charter for good practice.

More specifically, three factors have to be present to overcome any contextual constraints on work-based management development: creativity, proactivity and critical reflectivity (Marsick and Watkins, 1990).

CREATIVITY

As McCall et al. (1988, p. 58) argued, 'the essence of development is that diversity and adversity beat repetition every time'. This has two aspects. First, the manager has to be exposed to new experiences, but at the same time usually needs help in recognizing these as learning opportunities. Performance management makes managers focus upon tasks rather than their learning content. They thus need assistance in becoming aware that these are not mutually exclusive, and also in thinking creatively (Schon, 1983). The ability to think beyond the point of view that they normally hold requires not only a great deal of effort on the part of the manager but also an encouraging organizational and immediate work environment.

PROACTIVITY AND SELF-DEVELOPMENT

Proactivity is the readiness to take initiative, and in this instance means the ability to take responsibility for one's learning. The current management philosophy of empowerment is associated with the emphasis upon self-development (Pedler et al., 1990). Currently the creation of personal development plans and learning contracts is at the heart of much formal management development within organizations. Individual managers need to be clear what is required of them in this respect, and also where to go for help. A typical personal development plan format is included in exhibit 7.2 in chapter 7.

While immediate line managers may be responsible, there is often a need for additional professional human resources support and counselling. The kind of discussion raised in career counselling could focus on the career direction and area of development the person is interested in and why; whether they restrict themselves to a particular job or consider several areas of interest, such as projects using particular skills. The discussion could cover ways their current role can be broadened and also their skills and capabilities for this role, and those they need to develop, including development action which could be taken.

There is also the danger that over-formalizing what is essentially informal and incidental will undermine the necessary spontaneity and responsiveness that is essential to the effectiveness of this form of management development. On the other hand, it is important to recall that the readiness of the individual manager will determine what is appropriate, as Gabarro (1985) noted when he looked at the experience of managers entering a new job. Each of the different stages – 'taking hold', immersion, reshaping, consolidation and refinement – will contain different learning needs and opportunities and requirements for support.

CRITICAL REFLECTIVITY

Despite the above comments on being proactive, it remains true that retrospective learning by means of reviewing will be more likely in the case of work-based learning than planning for the future. Yet it is also ironical that studies of managerial work have all shown how naturally unreflective an activity it is. Thus managers usually require support to reflect in a variety of ways: individually, with a counsellor or with a group. A recent study in the USA showed that in comparison with those who were asked to reflect alone, those who had an individual helper or were part of a group were much better able to recall and analyse their learning from a highly developmental experience (Wood-Daudelin, 1996).

•••• The Limits of Work-Based Management Development ••••

Finally, it is important to avoid an uncritical advocacy of work-based management development. There are certain circumstances where it is not suitable. For example, unless individual managers are seconded outside an organization, work-based development will not be any use in developing knowledge skills and insights not currently available within the existing organization. Nor is work-based learning likely to provide a means of acquiring the knowledge, skills and insights suitable for promotion, unless it involves acting up or participation in strategic-level task forces or working parties. It is also more likely to be effective in the short run on negative learning (i.e. learning how not to do something), and may be partial, accidental and difficult to transfer. Work-based learning is also generally less effective and efficient where new skills and knowledge need to be speedily learnt.

The other major drawback is that informal, incidental and often subconscious processes by their nature are sometimes more accessible to some managers than others. This becomes a particular problem when management development activity is linked to promotion and succession opportunities within an organization. In the same way as the use of word-of-mouth and grapevine methods in recruitment have been judged as discriminatory in the light of UK equal opportunity legislation, so might informal and incidental management development activities. Despite their success, there is a belief that such systems can sometimes have a disadvantageous impact upon women and ethnic minorities.

•••• Summary ••••

Most organizations are potentially a rich source of work-related development opportunities. The problem in using them effectively thus appears to rest upon having access to appropriate sources of support, and also on ensuring equitable access. Both of these are serious obstacles and ultimately mean that work-related development can be a precarious foundation on which to construct an entire management development strategy. However, despite the swings of fashion between off-the-job and work-related management development, it is important to recognize that the two can be complementary. What is most important is selecting development interventions suitable for a range of individual managers within a specific organizational context. Sometimes this requires particular thought, as we shall see in Part IV when we look at general requirements of management development for professionals, women, international managers and board-level management.

EXERCISES

(1) What work-related development activities do you currently engage in?
(2) Which ones does your employer encourage?
(3) To what extent are the range of work-related development activities available appropriate for both the organization and yourself?

•••• References ••••

Argyris, C. 1990: *Overcoming Organizational Defenses: Facilitating Organizational Learning.* Boston, MA: Allyn and Bacon.

Carnevale, A. 1984: *Jobs for the Nation: challenge for a society based on work.* Alexandra, VA: American Society for Training and Development.

Bates, T. 1993: How external mentoring operates. *Management Development Review,* 6, 4, pp. 6–9.

Chater, S. and Stokes, H. 1992: *Sharing Skills: making the most of secondments.* Cambridge: Careers Research and Advisory Centre.

Clutterbuck, D. 1985: *Everyone Needs a Mentor: how to foster talent within the organisation.* London: IPM (now Institute of Personnel and Development).

Cunningham, J. B. and Eberle, T. 1993: Characteristics of the mentoring experience: a qualitative study. *Personnel Review* 22, 4, pp. 54–66.

Davies, J. and Easterby-Smith, M. 1984: Learning and developing from managerial work experiences. *Journal of Management Studies,* 21, 2, pp. 169–83.

Dawson, S., Winstanley, D., Mole, V. and Sherval, J. 1995: *Managing in the NHS: a study of senior executives.* London: HMSO.

Gabarro, J. 1985: *The Dynamics of Taking Charge.* Boston: Harvard Business School Press.

Hackman, J. R. and Oldham, G. R. 1980: *Work Redesign.* London: Addison-Wesley.

Handy, C., Gow, I., Gordon, C., Randlesome, C. and Moloney, M. 1987: *The Making of Managers.* London: National Economic Development Office.

Herzberg, F., Mausner, B. and Synderman, B. 1959: *The Motivation to Work.* 2nd edn, London: Chapman and Hall.

Hunt, D. M. and Michael, C. 1988: Mentorship: a career training and development tool. *Academy of Management Review,* 8, 3, pp. 475–85.

Hutchinson, S. and Wood, S. 1995: *Personnel and the Line: developing the new relationship.* London: Institute of Personnel and Development.

Knowles, M. 1989: *The Adult Learner: A Neglected Species.* Houston: Gulf.

Kotter, J. 1988: *The Leadership Factor.* New York: Free Press.

McCall, M. W. Jr, Lombardo, M. and Morrison, A. 1988: *The Lessons of Experience: how successful executives develop on the job.* Massachusetts: Lexington.

McCauley, C. D., Ruderman, M. N., Ohlott, P. J. and Morrow, J. E. 1994: Assessing the developmental components of managerial jobs. *Journal of Applied Psychology* 79, pp. 544–60.

Marsick, V. J. and Watkins, K. 1990: *Informal and Incidental Learning in the Workplace*. London: Routledge.

Maslow, A. H. 1943: A theory of human motivation. *Psychological Review*, 50, pp. 370–96.

Maslow, A. H. 1987: *Motivation and Personality*. 3rd edn New York, NY: Harper and Row.

Megginson, D. 1988: Instructor, coach, mentor: three ways of helping managers. *Management Education and Development*, 19, 1, pp. 33–46.

McGill, I. and Beaty, L. 1992: *Action Learning: A Practitioners Guide*. London: Kogan Page.

Mumford, A. 1993a: *Management Development: Strategies for Action*. 2nd edn, London: Institute of Personnel and Development.

Mumford, A. 1993b: *How Managers can Develop Managers*. Aldershot: Gower.

Mumford, A. 1993c: How managers can become developers. *Personnel Management*, June, pp. 42–5.

Noe, R. 1988: Women and mentoring: a review and research agenda. *Academy of Management Review*, 13, 1, January, pp. 65–78.

Pedler, M. 1991: *Action Learning in Practice*. 2nd edn, Aldershot: Gower.

Pedler, M., Burgoyne, J., Boydell, T. and Welshman, G. 1990: *Self-Development in Organisations*. Maidenhead: McGraw-Hill.

Rae, L. 1987: *Coaching for Results*. London: Industrial Society.

Revans, R. 1982: *The Origins and Growth of Action Learning*. Bromley: Chartwell Bratt.

Rogers, C. R. 1969: *Freedom to Learn*. Columbus, OH: Charles E. Merrill.

Schon, D. A. 1983: *The Reflective Practitioner*. New York: Basic Books.

Singer, E. 1979: *Effective Management Coaching*. London: PM (now Institute of Personnel and Development.

Smith, B. 1989: Networking for real. *Journal of European Industrial Training*, 13, 4, pp. 11–17.

Thatcher, M. 1996: Networks create a professional buzz. *People Management*, 2, 17, 29 August, pp. 22–5.

Warr, P. 1987: *Work, Unemployment and Mental Health*. Oxford: Oxford University Press: Quoted in Newell, S. 1995: *The Healthy Organization*, ch. 5, Work, Positive Health and Improved Performance, London: Routledge, pp. 90–118.

Wood-Daudelin, M. 1996: Learning from experience through reflection. *Organizational Dynamics*, 24, 3, Winter, pp.36–49.

PART IV

Meeting Different Management Development Needs

CHAPTER 10

Management Development for Professionals

•••• **Introduction** ••••

Some of the fastest growing sectors of the economy are dominated by knowledge-based organizations (Handy, 1989) and 'know-how' organizations (Sveiby and Lloyd, 1987), in which a large proportion of the workforce is made up of professional employees. Likewise, in terms of occupations and employment, an increasing proportion of the UK workforce is engaged in 'professional' occupations, and employment in higher level occupations is projected to grow most rapidly between 1996 and 2001 (see table 10.1 Lindley and Wilson, 1997).

About 80 per cent of the professional workforce is employed in large organizations, and for some (such as health or software services) this constitutes the majority of their employees, while in other organizations they can still be a very small percentage of the overall workforce (as in multiple retailing). A further 10 per cent of all professionals are self-employed. For these and many other reasons, it is important to highlight the particular management development needs of professionals.

Table 10.1 Occupational employment projections, percentage change 1996–2001

SOC sub-major groups	%
1. Managers and administrators	+7.3
2. Professional occupations	+12.1
3. Associate professional and technical occupations	+8.5
4. Clerical and secretarial occupations	+1.0
5. Craft and related occupations	–1.6
6. Personal and protective service occupations	+16.7
7. Sales occupations	+4.1
8. Plant and machine operatives	+1.0
9. Other occupations	–2.6
All occupations	4.9

Source: Lindley, R.M. and R.A. Wilson (eds) (1997). *Labour Market Assessment: Review of the Economy and Employment 1996/97*. Institute for Employment Research, University of Warwick: Coventry.

This chapter will begin with an outline of what is meant by 'profession' and 'professionals', and then go on to elaborate why management is becoming an increasingly important topic in education and development for professionals. Some of the dilemmas and problems faced by professionals in management, and the reasons why their relationship with management is traditionally a difficult one are then explored. The growing interest in continuing professional development (CPD) is then examined, and finally, some specific recommendations are made for tailoring management development to the needs of professionals.

•••• Learning Objectives ••••

As a result of reading this chapter, you should be able to:

- explain how, in some ways, the management development requirements of professionals are different from those of other managers;
- appreciate that not all professionals have the same management development requirements;
- identify and provide suggestions of ways to overcome particular dilemmas faced by professionals entering management.

•••• What are Professionals? ••••

Defining professional work is very difficult. Definitions will vary depending upon whether there is a focus upon *traits*, or the historical *process* whereby an occupation becomes a profession, or the *power* needed to acquire professional recognition. One way is to take a trait approach and list what they generally have in common. Common characteristics cited for professions are (Dawson, 1992; Johnson, 1972; Kerr and Von Glinow, 1977; Millerson, 1964):

- expertise based on a distinct body of knowledge, and specific, lengthy and systematic training and education;
- altruistic service, expressed in 'service orientation';
- autonomy: value placed on autonomy and independence in work and decision-making;
- restrictive entry: through the use of occupational closure, that is, limiting entry to the profession to those gaining certain qualifications or serving an apprenticeship;
- collective organization: peer group and collegial maintenance of standards, control and evaluation;
- ethics: adherence to a professional code of ethics and standards of behaviour;
- commitment to and identification with the profession.

However, such a trait approach ignores the fact that this is very much an ideal type, and most professions only exhibit some of the characteristics mentioned. The trait approach also underplays their differences in history, development, culture, and type of work. It could be argued that there are degrees of professionalization rather than a simple dichotomy between professions and non-professions (Ritzer, 1986).

A 'process' or 'power' perspective will lead to a different categorization, for example between (Reiss, 1955):

- old established professions such as physicians, lawyers, university professors;
- new professions such as natural and social scientists;
- semi-professions, lacking power to achieve widespread recognition, such as teachers, nurses, social workers, librarians;
- would-be professions, those aspiring to professional status such as personnel managers and funeral directors;
- marginal professions, working alongside professionals, for example laboratory and scientific technicians, paramedics.

In addition, the definition of the term professional in the UK has been dogged by being dragged into a debate over status. For example, in engineering, the development of the profession has, in one way, been influenced by attempts to raise the status of the engineer, and in another has been marked by its failure to do so, with the resultant concentration being on its problems of 'low status'. A parallel development can be observed with the personnel management profession. However, it is important to note that the understanding of the word 'professional' in the English speaking world, is very different to that in the rest of Europe. For example, in Germany, there is no distinct word for the word 'profession', it is usually referred to as *Beruf*, which also means occupation or employment. In most of Europe, the professions are closely linked with state service, and are subject to much stronger regulation, although there have been some moves in this direction in the UK over the last 15 years.

Guy (1985) provides us with a useful alternative summation of the role of professionals in organizations. She suggests that traditional theory assumes three core points:

(1) Professionals, by virtue of their expertise, demand the right to influence not only the decision-making of the organizations that employ them but also the structure of the organization itself (Mintzberg, 1979).
(2) Membership of a profession brings with it a set of values unique to itself, and this membership connotes an exclusivity, as well as a homogeneity among its members (March and Simon, 1958; Simon, 1945).
(3) Members of a profession adopt their professional goals and rank those as more important than the organization's goals (Satow, 1975; Etzioni, 1959).

She comments that these are a function of the attributive process rather than based on reality, and that 'it is more accurate to attribute professionals' behaviour in organizations to the exigencies of the work site and the task in hand than to their respective professional identification' (Guy, 1985, p. 9).

There are huge differences between professions in terms of both their organizational context and the extent of incorporation into managerial hierarchies. They also vary according to how the relationship with management has been developed. For example, some types of engineers (mechanical and chemical, for example) have largely been incorporated into lower and middle management hierarchies within large corporations. Lawyers have more traditionally worked in partnerships with some administrative support. Accountants have achieved considerable status within the ranks of senior management. Human resource specialists have largely bemoaned their problems of lack of status, and perception as administrative support, or welfare go-between, and decried their failure to reach board level in many organizations. The function of human resource management itself has largely been a response to raise the personnel profile at the strategic level.

The role of professionals in management varies, both between professions and organizations. For example a clinical director in mental health is likely to have a very different role depending upon whether the treatment regime within the organization is highly institutionalized or in the form of a partially self-governing community. Other examples of the role of professionals in management are found in the 'professional service firm' (Maister, 1982) or the 'know-how organization' (Sveiby and Lloyd, 1987).

A common career path for professionals is to begin as a junior, undertaking professional tasks, to move into management, for example becoming a project manager, and thence into senior management concerned with client relations (Schriesheim et al., 1977).

This organizational configuration arises from the likelihood of a base of project work, as is often the case in professional partnerships, such as law firms, or even management consultancies. Greenwood et al. (1990) suggest that professional partnerships, such as in accountancy, need to be managed in a very different way from other organizations. This is due in part to their distinctive type of ownership and governance, where ownership, management and operations are fused; and to the fact that most professionals aspire to partnership, and most partners practice at the local office level. In such organizations, 75–80 per cent of the work is done by professionals, and thus requires collegiality, peer evaluation and autonomy. Partnerships are a form of association which protect professionals' independence, promote and maintain professional standards, link market performance with firm reputation, and increase liability for professional negligence by others.

From our discussions of the varying features of professions, their different historical development, power and organization context, and style of work, it becomes evident that these differences need to be taken into account in designing management development. Before we do this, we need to get more information on the nature of professional education and careers, in order to appreciate where management development fits in.

•••• Professionals, their Careers and Education ••••

Over the last 20 years, entry into most professions has become more closely tied to the acquisition of a higher education qualification in a directly related field. Often this qualification is validated by a professional body. At the same time, there has been a move to incorporate more management education within the undergraduate curriculum for various professional groups. In engineering for example, the publication of the Finniston Report (1980) coincided with a wider push for greater emphasis in undergraduate engineering education on management subjects.

To take another example, medicine, there have been changes in the NHS which have alerted people to the importance of management for doctors at both undergraduate and postgraduate level. Of particular impact have been the changes arising from the Griffiths Report (1983) and the concept of 'general management' and later 'resource management' followed by the creation of the internal market in 1991. Short postgraduate courses for doctors in management are now flourishing all over the country, for example the Advanced Certificate in Health Management at Imperial College. Even at the undergraduate level changes are taking place. Doctors have always been a most tightly regulated group in terms of professional qualification, with the General Medical Council (GMC) specifying the general content of the undergraduate curriculum. Although the GMC does not make any direct comments on the incorporation of a managerial component into the curriculum, individual medical schools are now using their flexibility within the GMC requirements to include management topics. For example the new undergraduate curriculum in medicine at Imperial College now includes compulsory modules in management and an optional management stream.

Therefore, it is now common for professionals to have had some exposure to management skills and education prior to embarking on their career. Once they do so, the traditional choice has been between taking one of two alternatives within a 'dual career' ladder. They may either stay as an expert in their own specialist field, the 'professional' or 'techie' route, or they may branch into management. Where this career ladder genuinely exists, then it is possible for a professional to achieve the same level of status, prestige and remuneration as that of the manager, as has sometimes been the case in some small high-technology and computer-based firms. Another way of making the 'dual career ladder' distinction is to distinguish between the role of the professional leader and that of the manager. Where professionals aspire to becoming the professional leader, this can lead to conflict within an organization. This is particularly the case where leaders take on a representational role in management, seeing their role as one of representing their profession and colleagues at the management table. This leads to the potential problem of 'tribalism', which is discussed below. Sveiby and Lloyd (1987) provide an alternative example of the hybrid role and career route followed by professionals in 'know-how' organizations (see figure 10.1). In both approaches to professional careers there are implications for the type of development opportunities that may be required at different career stages.

The main issue we wish to highlight here is that, increasingly, most professionals are expected to have some managerial expertise, even if it is for merely managing their team or department. However, another dimension concerns what is happening to much professional work in large organizations. Delayering of management hierarchies and the growth of cross-functional working mean that professionals can no longer rely on predictable upwards career moves, they may also be more isolated

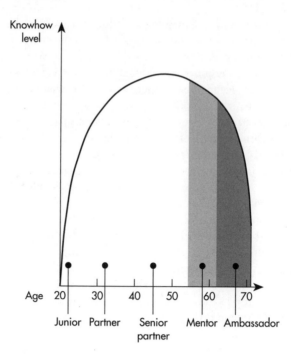

Figure 10.1 The lifecycle of a professional
Source: Sveiby and Lloyd, 1987

from other members of their profession, and may need to be able to work closely with other professionals and general management.

•••• The Roles of Professionals in Management, and •••• Associated Problems

ATTITUDE TOWARDS MANAGEMENT

One problem facing those providing management development for professionals is said to be an *attitudinal* one. Hitherto, many professionals have seen management as a task to endure, or if possible, to ignore or shunt to an administrator. It is neither exciting nor challenging nor important, but is the boring administrative duties which take them away from the real job of treating patients, or designing engines, or saving a child from abuse. To this extent it may be necessary, but it is also low status, unattractive and tedious. Management is thus administration, and should be treated as such.

In some areas of professional work there has been a change of attitude, with some professionals realizing the strategic potential, importance and contribution of management to meeting their key objectives. An example of these contrasting attitudes towards management can be illustrated by two quite different models of clinical directors encountered in research in the NHS (Dawson et al., 1995). In one model the doctor undertook the role of clinical director, either by default because there was no one else of their status to do it, or because it was their turn. They viewed the role as providing representation for their professional group, making sure that their group had a voice in management. Their primary responsibility was to their professional colleagues and to fight their own corner. Although clinical directors of this sort still exist, there is also a type of doctor who views their entry into management as a career move, wherein their primary responsibility is to the organization as a whole, and not to one sectional interest. In order to exercise the art of management, they positively pursue the development of interpersonal, financial, strategic and planning skills. Their career may result in movement into roles such as chief executive or chair of an NHS trust.

The challenges and problems facing these two very different types of doctor in management are very dissimilar. Management development for the former may be more around attitudinal and motivational issues, team building and working across professional boundaries, but is likely to fall by the wayside as professional work spills over to take up all the available time. If anything, this type of doctor is more likely to desire help with delegation, time and stress management, and support in resolving ethical dilemmas where professional and managerial codes conflict. Conversely, the latter type of manager may be more receptive to the development of financial, strategic and change management skills, and more proactive in pursuing help which fits with their own career intentions in management. These contrasting attitudes towards management are not confined just to medical practice. They can be seen in many other areas of professional work, such as social work and university lecturing.

A variety of different relationships can develop between professionals and managers (see table 10.2). In private practice – such as is the case for solicitors, lawyers and dentists – the management role may be interpreted as being largely

Table 10.2 Different professional–managerial relationships

Professional role	Professionals' relationship with manager	Predominant types of control over professional work	Professionals' role in planning and decision-making about the nature of their work
'Proleterian' professional	Subservient	Hierarchical Administrative Technological	Remote
Member of 'professional-managerial class'	Assimilation	Output Personal self Unobtrusive	Participative, with varying power
Private practice	Professional/client	Personal self Unobtrusive	Self-determined, with varying consultation

Source: Dawson, 1992 p. 30

administrative, performed by support staff, with the professional's role in management being to provide professional leadership. A 'proletarian' professional may see a move into management as a step up in the hierarchy, whereas those who have been more assimilated into management without loss of professional status and power, for example engineering directors in engineering companies, or clinical directors in the health service, may pose a challenge. They may view their role as 'representational' or as an ambassador for their specialty, seeing themselves as negotiating with management rather than being part of management. The development required here is of two forms: one relates to the challenge of getting the manager to take the broader view, a helicopter view of what is best for the organization, and thus a unitarist view which may put the organization before their specialty; and the other giving them skills in negotiation and conflict management to help them bring their colleagues and department with them, and tackle dissenters. The problem with this approach is it essentially takes a unitarist view of the organization, assuming that the different view of the professional is a flaw which needs to be mended, rather than a legitimate different view within a plurality of interests.

GIVING UP THE PROFESSIONAL ROLE

A second problem facing professionals entering management is the difficulty they may have with giving up their professional role, and allowing their technical skills to diminish. Many professionals are strongly motivated by public service values, for example doctors, nurses and social workers, and perceive the importance of holding highly developed technical skills and expertise to achieve these ends. Others – such as senior partners in accountancy or legal practices – may feel that it is commercially important to keep up the finer technical details of professional practice, as seniority of status is perceived in terms of professional reputation and expertise. However, the intrusion of management into their time inevitably means the loss of technical development time, with the associated anxiety that they may become obsolescent in their professional skills, and thus find re-entry difficult. Finding the right balance between professional and managerial responsibilities is a constant challenge for most professionals as they progress through their careers.

It is commonly assumed that on entering management, professionals need to develop their inter-personal skills, because they are incapable of dealing with people. In particular engineers, as professional technocrats, are castigated for their lack of human relations skills. However, it is necessary to return to the point that professions differ greatly in this respect, and indeed some professions – for example teaching, nursing and social work – are said to abound in human skills. However it is also important to go beyond professional stereotypes: not all engineers are inarticulate, nor do all doctors have a dreadful bedside manner. Nonetheless, for most professionals, inter-personal skills are an essential component of their work, and this applies just as much to those in managerial positions. Therefore initial professional education and continuing professional development need to incorporate this dimension, bearing in mind that the inter-personal skills needed for professionals in management may be of a particular kind. Team-building, negotiation, persuasion, working across professional boundaries, handling discipline, motivation and leadership through people and values, are all particularly important.

MAINTAINING PROFESSIONAL AUTONOMY

A third problem for professionals becoming incorporated into management is professional autonomy. It has become a truism to say that professionals value their autonomy, and that this autonomy becomes threatened when they are incorporated into managerial hierarchies. We would suggest that this point has been over-played. Certainly many professionals have more discretion time than many non-professional staff, but this is no more than has often been the case for many senior general managers. The reality of work for many professionals is that they are working such long hours and juggling so many tasks, that discretion time is only achieved at times when others are retiring to bed. For example (Dawson et al., 1995) found that 35 per cent of NHS managers work over 55 hours per week, and many of these were doctors in management.

Over the past few years, there have been political moves to bring public service professionals more to account, for example through clinical audit for doctors, performance review for teachers, and performance measures at corporate and organizational levels, such as league tables in health and education. However it would not be true to say that prior to this all professionals enjoyed considerable autonomy. Doctors were themselves trained in a very hierarchical way, certainly junior doctors at the lower levels were highly beholden to their seniors, and likewise accountants and solicitors. Even teachers were to some extent under the authority of the headteacher. What is meant therefore, by professional autonomy, is accountability to professional peers and superiors, but not to others.

It is this form of professional autonomy that has been subject to control, especially in the public sector through greater control over the content of professional work and how it is carried out, for example, the national curriculum in education and protocols in medicine. Other measures include boundary performance controls utilizing positive and negative performance rewards (for example the research selectivity exercise and teaching assessment exercise used in higher education to rate departments and institutions). This has meant that some professionals entering management in the public sector are requesting management development support for conducting appraisals, for dealing with disciplinary situations, and for setting and assessing performance criteria and information.

One reason why there have been attempts by governments to limit the power of professionals in public services is out of concern for their commitment. Questions are raised as to whether there is a conflict between organizational and professional loyalty. This has particularly become an issue where professionals such as doctors and nurses have spoken out within the media against the standards of care in their service, and where some organizations have responded with 'gagging clauses' in employment contracts. Although this is largely an issue for the management of professionals, it is also a problem for professionals in management. How can they reconcile the dilemma, what should they do when their organizational and professional ethics clash? Increasingly, those management development courses focused on sectors dominated by professions run modules on ethics and also on managing professionals. Although there are no easy answers to the question of what happens when professional and organizational codes of conduct clash, management development courses can be a useful venue for discussing and thinking through these issues.

ACCOUNTABILITY, QUALITY AND CUSTOMER SERVICE

Another reason for attempts to limit the power and autonomy of professionals is to do with their relation to client groups. There is a view that professionals have acted as controllers of client groups rather than their servant. Although this arises out of their autonomy, it is also strongly linked to the criticism of restrictive practice: from solicitor control over household conveyancing, to medical practitioner control over diagnosis and referral of patients for specialist treatment, and the signing off of company accounts by a chartered accountant–clients might well regard this as a restriction on their free choice. Conversely, professional groups claim that these restrictions have arisen to ensure quality control. See table 10.3 for an outline of the two perspectives of their power and characteristics. However we would argue that it is not a question of limiting the power of professionals to enable an increase in client-focused services, as pushed by total quality management practices. Changing services to be more client oriented, does not necessarily mean a rout of professionals. Instead it may mean using the art of persuasion, team-building and the use of development and education to enable professionals to adjust to a client focus. It involves working with and through professional colleagues, rather than against them, but it does mean a challenge to a narrow professional view. Although there will inevitably be tensions, it is the ability to manage these creatively rather than with a sledgehammer which will help the professional in management.

It would also be wrong to assume that the only reason why professions have not been subjected to the management controls that apply to other occupations, is because professionals have been successful in guarding their independence in the struggle for power. There are two other powerful reasons. One relates to the view that high trust working relationships yield better performance and motivation, which is undermined when managerial controls are introduced. The second relates to management's difficulty in understanding sufficiently the work of a professional to the extent that it becomes difficult to institute controls. The complexity of the work, and difficulty in controlling it, was illustrated in the legal evidence of the role of the

Table 10.3 Two perspectives on the role of professionals

	The professional view	The client view
Restrictive entry	Increases quality	Decreases client choice Increases price
Peer control	Ensures enlightened feedback	Disempowers clients from providing feedback
Professional autonomy	Enables freedom of expression Produces quality work	Prevents performance being monitored, rewarded or punished

official auditors for Robert Maxwell's group of companies. The difficulty of unravelling the roles and responsibilities demonstrates the difficulties encountered in controlling professionals.

•••• Management Development: Integrating it with •••• Continuing Professional Development

The above problems associated with the role of professionals in management need to be taken into account in the design and choice of management development solutions. Key objectives will be to:

- promote attitudinal change, and encourage a global view of the organization;
- help reconcile differing professional and organizational perspectives;
- develop inter-personal and communication skills;
- deal with conflict; and
- develop professional leadership.

The relative weighting of the content will vary according to organization and professional discipline. There are a number of texts which identify key skill areas for the management development of professionals. For example, Batley (1989) provides an exhaustive list (see exhibit 10.1).

•••• Exhibit 10.1 ••••
Key management skills for professionals

- time management
- personal organization
- effective delegation
- staff motivation and self-motivation
- objective setting and standards
- planning, scheduling and controlling work
- achieving good staff relations
- negotiating and managing conflict
- improving productivity
- decision making and problem solving
- managerial resilience and acceptance of change
- understanding communications

- performance reviews
- counselling staff
- interpersonal skills
- training and coaching
- selection interviews
- career planning and development
- writing for results
- effective meetings
- presenting yourself, a service or a product
- understanding management styles
- managing stress
- keeping up with technical change
- marketing your service and yourself

Source: Batley, 1989

However, a point to note about such lists is that they are very similar to those skills in management utilized on management development courses in general, apart from keeping up with technical change. The big issue for professionals is having such skills taught in a way which is seen to be relevant to them and their service, tailored to their particular organizational environment. Above all, it helps to consider their management development needs within the framework of continuing professional development requirements.

There is currently a growing awareness of the importance of Continuing Professional Development (CPD), not only from the professional bodies which, in some circumstances set the requirement but also from other stakeholders, such as the organizations within which professionals work, providers of courses, and individual professionals themselves. Most professional bodies now have a statement on what they believe the purpose and suitable content of CPD to be. There are two basic approaches: the sanctions model and the benefits model (Clyne, 1995) although there are combinations of the two. The first sets out the obligations of members of a professional body in respect of CPD and monitors compliance. The second is more concerned to offer rewards for the successful achievement of CPD and to encourage members to engage in continuous learning. The Institute of Chartered Accountants (ICA) of England and Wales corresponds to the former model, and the Institute of Personnel and Development (IPD) and the Institution of Electrical Engineers (IEE) to the latter (see exhibit 10.2 for an outline of the IEE's scheme). However, each profession has its own particular requirements, and so it is difficult to generalize about CPD.

Inasmuch as it is possible to generalize, there has been a recognition of the need for flexibility in terms of who provides the development, the context of what is included, the manner in which it is delivered and the timing of the development. Requirements are now usually framed in terms of notional annual hours (usually ranging from 30 to 50) or the 'points' system. The IEE's scheme in exhibit 10.2 suggests 60 units over a three-year period which approximates to 35 to 40 hours per annum. Almost universally, CPD is recognized as involving more than the updating of technical knowledge. The development of managerial skills, commercial aware-ness, and personal effectiveness are all equally desirable components. Also, besides the wide range of acceptable subjects, most professional bodies accept that there are a wide variety of ways of achieving CPD: part-time and short courses; distance learning, in-company programmes, professional meetings, research; presentations to learned societies and publication in learned journals, structured reading, coaching, involvement in mentoring, coaching and teaching, secondments, and voluntary work. Exhibit 10.2 shows how the IEE supports such activities. Some professional bodies are considering linking their CPD requirements to the achievement of NVQ and MCI standards of competence. However, there is a danger that this might constrain individual choice of CPD towards those with only a clearly identifiable and measurable outcome. This could lead to cautiousness and conservatism.

There is a growing awareness that CPD needs to be delivered in such a way that it optimizes professional learning styles. Donald Schon's work on the need to create the opportunity for 'reflection in action' (Schon, 1983) as well as the work of Peter Honey, Alan Mumford, Carl Rogers and Malcolm Knowles (see chapter 7) have highlighted the need for attention to this matter. The delivery of CPD needs to

···· Exhibit 10.2 ····
The Institution of Electrical Engineers
trial continuing professional development scheme

The IEE believes it has a responsibility to provide professional support and guidance to its members. To this end a Continuing Professional Development (CPD) scheme was launched on 1 January 1995. It is fully voluntary. The scheme is being run on a three year trial basis and is likely to change significantly as it seeks to satisfy the needs of individual members and their employees.

Its aim is to assist IEE members in planning and recording the professional development that they undertake throughout their working life. This development encompasses the whole range of learning activities and does not concentrate solely on formal training courses; members find that a large percentage of learning comes through on-the-job experiential training and private study and it is important that this is recorded.

At present the scheme recommends that members undertake a minimum of 60 professional development units (pdus) over a rolling three-year period, at least 25 per cent should be technical and 25 per cent non-technical. Upon successful completion of this recommendation a certificate will be issued and if a member attains 120 pdus or more with the relevant technical/non-technical split a certificate with merit will be issued.

The pdu is the measurement system used for cpd activities and it is a three-tiered system – 1 pdu per hour of formally examined activities; $\frac{3}{4}$ pdu per hour of interactive; and $\frac{1}{2}$ pdu per hour of attendance only.

One of the main initiatives at present is the formal agreement with the Institution of Mechanical Engineers (IMechE) to introduce a common cpd scheme for the two institutions. Integrated in this initiative is the move away from the concept of measuring inputs (i.e. hours and pdus) to measuring outputs. The IEE believes members are progressively coming to appreciate the benefits of cpd, viewing it as: insurance against obsolescence; and a development aid to maximize effectiveness as an engineer.

The IEE operates several support services to assist members in their cpd. These include:

- *Courses information service* – a database of providers of learning opportunities and the activities that they offer.
- *Registered employers* – to date some 270 companies. These are companies who employ IEE members and act as a link between the IEE and the individual members.
- *Career advisory service* – provides free advice and assistance on various aspects of career development and re-direction to members.
- *Professional development record (PDR)* – An A4 folder which assists engineers at all ages, levels and disciplines to plan their career and maintain a record of their aims, objectives and achievements.
- *Professional development series* – booklets to assist members in the cpd, including: working with schools and colleges; developing and implementing a programme of learning; and mentoring.
- *Learning activities* – are available through the Institution including diplomas, short courses, distance learning courses, certificates, technical activities, conferences, vacation schools and symposia, technical briefings colloquia/seminars, fast fora, discussion meetings, lectures and foreign language conversation circles.

Source: Drawn from information provided by the Institution of Electrical Engineers

accommodate different individual learning styles, and above all provide relevance, the opportunity for direct application, self-direction and motivation. As people progress through their professional career, they are more likely to want to use informal learning and learning by means of shadowing or working with other professionals.

Another development is that most professional bodies now place the responsibility for managing CPD on the individual professional. They are required to assess and audit their own CPD needs, maintain a record of these and the learning outcomes, and assemble a portfolio of evidence. In principle, this should permit responsiveness to the individual's circumstances. However, several professional bodies still report problems with the perceived relevance of CPD and individual motivation (Clyne, 1995). Indeed, there is evidence that professionals in large organizations look to personnel and training departments to take the lead on CPD (Croft, 1996). On another note, there is a tension between permitting individual choice and encouraging CPD that is appropriate to the career stage of the individual.

Clyne (1995) contrasts what is desirable in terms of the training needs model with what is likely in CPD for chartered accountants and illustrates how in the CPD they are likely to receive less commercial skills, managerial skills and interpersonal skills and more technical knowledge and skills. This illustrates the point that if the individual has responsibility for their own CPD, then it is critically important that it is linked to their own career plan, rather than just the needs of the organization or the professional body.

Recent research (Clyne, 1995) has shown that individual effort in CPD depends very much on a combination of three factors: motivation, awareness and support. It also depends upon access. This is particularly a problem for women professionals who undertake a career break. Arrangements for maintaining CPD requirements may not be designed to fit in with a career break for raising a family, or with subsequent part-time employment, as is markedly the case for medical practitioners. In addition, such women professionals are doubly disadvantaged by the cost of carrying out CPD, which in all probability they have to bear themselves. However, access to CPD is a problem for almost all professionals. As we noted above, the long hours worked by most professionals mean that there are time constraints. CPD has to be achieved within short intensive bursts or integrated with ongoing work responsibilities. Another problem concerns resources: the growing interest in CPD has occurred at a time when many organizations are having to justify expenditure on training and development, and also spread it more widely across other groups.

It is thus advisable for any organization contemplating management development for its professional employees to attempt to integrate this within CPD requirements. If the organization is able to demonstrate awareness and support for specific CPD requirements, then it will stand a better chance of developing its professionals into effective managers. One way an organization can do this is through collecting information on what CPD schemes exist, which staff they cover, and communicating the requirements of the schemes to those affected, as in the case with one NHS Trust which produced the data shown in table 10.4. Management development can be presented as a legitimate element in CPD at induction, and endorsed by senior professional staff. Integration can be achieved around the process of development reviews resulting in the construction of personal development plans (see chapter 9).

Table 10.4 Data collected by one NHS Trust on CPD schemes covered by staff groups

Professional body	% of Staff	Scheme	Start	V/M **	Suggested study	Benefits
Institute of Biomedical Sciences	5–10	CPD	1992	V	4.0 credits/year Approx. 24 h/y	Improved employment prospects
Royal College of Pathologists*	5–10	CME	1995	V	250 credits/5 y. Approx. 50 h/y	Improved employment prospects
Royal College of Nursing	34	PREP	1994	M	5 days/3 years Approx. 13 h/y	UKCC registration
Institute of Personnel and Development	<1	CPD	1996	M	35 hours/y	Review level of membership

* Equivalent schemes run by other Royal Colleges e.g. R.C. surgeons, R.C. physicians.
** V=Voluntary, M=Mandatory.

Obviously this may necessitate some adaptation of performance review processes, and the provision of adequate support in terms of informed advice from the professional body, opportunities for coaching and mentoring from experienced professionals.

The organization will also need to support on-the-job development through membership of multi-disciplinary project teams with specific terms of reference and report back deadlines. Examples could include teams to raise funds for a new classroom in a school, or to examine integrated care pathways in a hospital, or get market information for testing a new engineering product. Working within teams outside an individual's professional area brings with it benefits and disadvantages. It can open a professional's eyes to new ways of perceiving a situation, or it can get bogged down in dissent and strife. However, well managed, these can provide useful developmental opportunities.

Projects can also be a useful device to develop leadership skills for professionals. Sveiby and Lloyd (1987) are strong proponents of the project route, where potential leaders are given small, interesting projects to champion, where their mistakes will cause little damage. They suggest that development provided through the leadership of projects should occur intermittently and briefly as the primary task is 'to establish his or her professional credentials' so that he or she is accepted by others as a leader when the time comes.

International secondments or even just cross organizational secondments can be a particularly good way of countering the argument that 'it would never work in my area'. If a professional can see that at another organization, or in another country, their speciality is managed differently, it does open the possibility of change. Alternatively secondments can be a way of helping a professional who has entered management to acquire an alternative perspective. For example a clinical director, in a provider unit such as a hospital trust, may benefit from a short spell in their purchaser or commissioning agency, or an engineering director could spend some time in the marketing department to see how priorities are defined and viewed differently.

•••• **Summary** ••••

We have highlighted the difficulties in talking about professionals as one group, identifying that their culture, practices and relationship with management varies according to individual personalities and attributes, their profession, and the organization and sector within which they are situated. We have also provided an overview of current thinking about continuing professional development, indicating the wide variety of approaches to prescribing requirements, and delivering it. As most professional bodies now recognize the need for management development activities as part of an integrated CPD programme, we recommend that organizations attempt to integrate their own management development policies and practices with those of the appropriate professional bodies.

EXERCISES

Drawing on your knowledge of one professional-based organization, answer the following questions:

(1) How far do the professionals in this organization fit the ideal type proposed above?

(2) Is Guy (1985) right in suggesting that professionals and their behaviour and attributes have more to do with their work site, organization and task in hand, than the attributes listed above?

(3) How are the professionals in this organization different from others, and how would you describe their culture and practices and relationship with management?

(4) Do these professionals have a career ladder which incorporates management? Try and draw the career route open to these professionals.

(5) What model of management or leadership do these professionals utilize?

(6) What development activities do you think are appropriate for helping equip these professionals for managerial work?

(7) How could these development activities be accommodated within the CPD requirements of the appropriate professional bodies?

•••• References ••••

Batley, T. 1989: *Management Skills for Professionals*. Oxford: Philip Allan.

Clyne, S. (ed.) 1995: *Continuing Professional Development: Perspectives on CPD in Practice*. London: Kogan Page.

Croft, C. 1996: Pushing against a culture of reliance. *People Management* 2 May, pp. 36–7.

Dawson, S. 1992: *Analysing Organisations*. Hampshire: Macmillan.

Dawson, S., Winstanley, D., Mole, V., Sherval, J. 1995: *Managing in the NHS: a study of senior executives*. London: HMSO.

Etzioni, A. 1959: Authority structure and organizational effectiveness. *Administrative Science Quarterly* v, pp. 43–67.

Finniston Report 1980: *Engineering Our Future*. Report of the committee of inquiry into the engineering profession chaired by Sir Montague Finniston. London: HMSO Cmnd 7794.

Greenwood, R., Hinings, C. R. and Brown, J. 1990: 'P2-form' strategic management: corporate practices in professional partnerships. *Academy of Management Journal* 33, 4 pp. 725–55.

Griffiths, Sir Roy 1983: *NHS Management Inquiry Report to the Secretary of State*. DHSS London: *HMSO*.

Guy M. E. 1985: *Professionals in Organizations: Debunking a Myth*. New York: Praeger.

Handy, C. 1989: *The Age of Unreason*. London: Business Books.

Johnson, T. 1972: *Professions and Power*. London: Macmillan.

Kerr, S., von Glinow, M. A and Schreisheim, J. 1977: Issues in the study of professionals in organizations: the case of scientists and engineers. *Organizational Behavior and Human Performance* 18, pp. 329–45.

Lindley, R. M. and Wilson, R. A. (eds) 1997: Labour Market Assessment: *Review of the Economy and Employment 1996/7*. Coventry: Institute for Employment Research, University of Warwick.

Maister, D. H. 1982: Balancing the professional service firm. *Sloan Management Review* Fall, pp. 15–28.

March, J. G. and Simon, H. 1958: *Organizations*. New York: Wiley.

Millerson, G. 1964: Dilemmas of professionalism. *New Society* 4, June, p. 15.

Mintzberg, H. 1979: *The Structuring of Organizations*. Englewood Cliffs, NJ: Prentice Hall.

Reiss, A. 1955: Occupational mobility of professional workers. *American Sociological Review*, 20, pp. 693–700.

Ritzer, G. 1986: *Working, Conflict and Change* 3rd edn, Englewood Cliffs, NJ: Prentice Hall.

Satow, R. L. 1975: Value-rational authority and professional organizations: Weber's missing type. *Administrative Science Quarterly* 20, pp. 526–31.

Schon, D. 1983: *The Reflective Practitioner: how professionals think in action*. London: Temple Smith.

Schriesheim, J., von Glinow, M. A., and Kerr, S. 'Professionals in Bureaucracies: a structural alternative' in Nystrom, P. and Starbuck, W. 1977: *Prescriptive Models of Organizations*, North Holland TIMS Studies in Management Sciences, Amsterdam, North Holland 5, pp. 55–69.

Simon, H. 1945: *Administrative Behaviour*. New York: Macmillan.

Skills and Enterprise Network 1993: *Skills for Success: A Challenge to Training and Education*. Sheffield: Skills and Enterprise Network.

Sveiby, K. and Lloyd, T. 1987: *Managing 'Know-how'*. London: Bloomsbury Press.

CHAPTER 11

Management Development for Women

···· Introduction ····

Management development for women concerns issues that reach above and beyond personal and organizational development. It is bound up with debates about the nature of the workforce and approaches towards equal opportunity, with attitudes, aspirations and behaviours; and even with the nature of society and the role of work itself. It also involves considerations about career development for both men and women (see chapter 3). Not only are women's attitudes of great concern, but so are those of male managers and organizational values at large. Perhaps it is this which explains the heated debate that often surrounds management development for women. In particular, there has been much talk of glass ceilings – seemingly impenetrable career barriers for most women, who stand by, witnessing often less-qualified and experienced men pass through (Davidson and Cooper, 1992; King, 1993). These days the indignation of well-qualified women managers up against a glass ceiling is confronted by a mixture of paternalism, the politics of patriarchy and a backlash against political correctness.

Yet over the last 15 years there has been a strong interest in improving women's access into management. A variety of approaches, designed to increase their participation in the managerial workforce have been adopted by organizations and championed by national government (Hansard, 1990; McGuire, 1992; Collins, 1992). These have included women-only training courses, scrutiny and modification of human resource policy and practice, special equality units, and the lobbying of board members to make the business case for more effective use of women as a managerial resource. Despite much effort, women's entry into middle management positions has been slow, and almost negligible at the senior level (Hansard, 1990). So our concern in this chapter is to explore the reasons for this lack of success, and current thinking on the range of measures available to assist women in pursuing their managerial careers.

•••• Learning Objectives ••••

After reading this chapter you should be able to:

- Identify the main trends in women's participation in the managerial labour force, and examine the pattern of women's managerial career development, both in terms of their entry into management positions, and their progression into more senior positions.
- Understand that the appropriateness of measures to improve women's participation in the managerial workforce depends very much on diagnosing the problems inherent in each specific situation.
- Identify a range of management development measures targeted at both the individual and organizational level, in order to increase women's participation at all levels in the managerial workforce.
- Explore different strategies to develop women's managerial careers in different individual circumstances and organizational contexts.

•••• Women in the Managerial Workforce ••••

Women now constitute 48 per cent of the employed workforce in the UK, reflecting a steady growth over the last ten years. Indeed, their economic activity rate is steadily approaching that of men (see table 11.1, Sly, 1993), for whom new entrants and those over 50 are particularly vulnerable to unemployment. However, this growth in women's participation in the labour force has been primarily in part-time employment. Even though the rate of growth of part-time employment for men is startling, in absolute terms, it is highest for women (see table 11.2).

In contrast to their general labour force participation rates, women are under-represented in the managerial workforce. In 1988 about 28 per cent of all managerial jobs, but only 11 per cent of all general management jobs, were held by women (Hansard Society, 1990). This illustrates a notable feature of women's entry into management jobs and their subsequent career progression: they enter and progress mainly by means of the functional chimney, and so they are more highly represented in support functions, rather than line positions. Another difference is that women are more likely to be managers in traditionally female occupations such as catering, retail, personnel and training, and office administration. More recently women managers

Table 11.1 Changing economic activity rates of women and men

	1979 %	1984 %	1990 %	1993 %
Women	63	66	71	71
Men	91	88	88	86

Source: Sly, 1993, p. 484.

Table 11.2 Rate of change in economic activity by type of employment

	1979 % (000s)	1984 % (000s)	1990 % (000s)	1993 % (000s)
Full time employees				
Women	–	–7	19	–5
	(5,603)	(5,221)	(6,200)	(5,896)
Men	–	–9	5	–9
	(14,321)	(12,987)	(13,701)	(12,433)
Part time employees				
Women	–	15	13	5
	(3,246)	(3,935)	(4,475)	(4,676)
Men	–	253	40	26
	(117)	(413)	(580)	(733)

Source: Sly, 1993, p. 484.

have become more numerous in public sector services such as health, local government, education, and certain business-related professions such as marketing, advertising and public relations, the law and accountancy. This sectoral concentration illustrates the segmentation of the female managerial labour market, with women concentrated in managerial work in lower status, lower paying, service sector occupations.

Turning to examine how women enter managerial positions, we know that outside the professions, excluding personnel, most have worked their way up from administrative or operational level positions, into the increasingly important supervisory positions that now constitute first line management. While they may have entered with good vocational qualifications, further progression is very dependent upon access to management training and qualifications, and above all, upon recognition of their potential. Both of these aspects have proved to be problematic. In addition, for the last 30 years, both public and private sector organizations have been opening up managerial positions to graduate entry, but there is still evidence that women's share of these jobs does not match their 44 per cent share of the graduate workforce. There is considerable evidence that women managers are more likely to 'leak' out of graduate management training schemes than their male counterparts, and are much less likely to move on to work in the core business areas and line management.

While it is reassuring that women do stand a better chance of entering lower level management positions, they still encounter considerable difficulty in progressing into middle and senior positions. Estimates vary, but the proportion of women in middle management is anywhere between 4 and 8 per cent, and in senior management, it is between 1 and 2 per cent. The causes of this are difficult to pinpoint and have been referred to as a 'glass ceiling' (Davidson and Cooper, 1992; King, 1993). Again, the segmentation of women's managerial work means that they tend to hit a glass ceiling at a lower level than their male counterparts in general management. This can be seen in functional areas such as marketing, accountancy, engineering, the law, and even personnel.

It is particularly interesting to observe that professional underachievement can arise in many different ways. While in engineering, accountancy and finance, women have entered a profession that has always been male dominated, this is not the case for personnel management. Contrary to the assumption that the personnel management terrain is waiting to be conquered by women, Legge (1987) and Gooch and Ledwith (1996, p. 102) demonstrate the way in which men colonized senior positions and marginalized women in what was hitherto a feminized profession. Thus women's managerial career achievement is mediated by the exercise of a combination of professional and organizational power.

The impenetrable nature of the glass ceiling is held to be the reason why many women managers, especially in mid-career, turn to self-employment. This is illustrated by the growth rate of women entering self-employment in the 1980s which far exceeded that for men, and grew by 70 per cent over the period 1981–7. Many of these self-employed women managers will be in traditional employment such as catering or hairdressing, and may even not appear in the statistics because they run bed and breakfast accommodation or help their partners. However, there is a growing group of mid-career, and even senior female managers and professionals who are opting for self-employment and setting up their own businesses (White, et al. 1992; Marshall, 1995).

Perhaps the most significant explanation of why women experience difficulties in career progress and are increasingly inclined to pursue self-employment is the need to interrupt a career because of family commitments. Career breaks for maternity leave, and the subsequent difficulties of childcare arrangements around the working day, often mean that women are forced to mark time on the career ladder or even step down grades at what is often a crucial age for career advancement – from their late twenties to late thirties. In Britain in the late 1980s about 45 per cent of women returned to work within nine months of giving birth, although those who took longer, returned to work in inferior positions to those they left when embarking on maternity leave (Kandola and Fullerton, 1994). Independent of children, there is evidence that in dual career partnerships the woman is less likely to contemplate a career move involving relocation (although there is growing evidence that this also applies to many men). Women managers who seek to achieve balance between personal and work life can encounter the reaction that they are lacking commitment to the organization, a commitment that involves being available for work at all hours in all locations. But is such intensification of work necessary? Recent work from the USA (Bailyn, 1994) has challenged this by using an action research framework to show that, in most organizations, working time can be reorganized in such a way that is beneficial to all employees, enabling them all to enjoy a home life, and still get the job done.

In order for women to be successful in management, they need to jump through hoops (Hirsh and Jackson, 1989). They need to enter management at an early age through training schemes or with appropriate qualifications; they need to have experience in functions which are seen as central to the core business of the organization and move into generalist managerial roles; they need to be continuously employed; they need to be able to work long hours; they need to conform to the organization's age-related concept of careers; they need to be geographically mobile;

and they need to manage the promotion process by conforming to promotion criteria. Thus it should not be surprising that women find career progress more difficult than do most of their male counterparts.

•••• Diagnosing the Problem before Choosing the Solution ••••

THE NEED FOR DIAGNOSIS

Most of what has hitherto been written about measures to develop women's managerial careers has been highly prescriptive. Women managers have received rather short shrift from the authors of the main texts on management development who either ignore the issue or cast around rather superficially for a series of interventions that they have heard can work (Margerison, 1992; Mumford, 1993; Mayo, 1991; McBeath, 1990, for example). Colgan and Ledwith (1996, p. 33) suggest that literature and practice on management education and training programmes are largely gender-blind. Equally, the more specialist literature on management development for women, usually written by experienced women practitioners and academics, tends to generate huge shopping lists of possible interventions in a rather indiscriminate manner (Beck and Steel, 1989), or to push the virtues of favoured techniques such as networking and mentoring (Segerman-Peck, 1991).

Furthermore, women are not the only group who are disadvantaged. More recently, there has been a frantic rush away from equal opportunity policy towards diversity management (Kandola and Fullerton, 1994; Herriot and Pemberton, 1995; Wilson, 1996). Current initiatives from the USA are directing attention towards the recognition and development of a multi-cultural workforce. This switches the primary focus from equal opportunity initiatives focused on gender, to the management of diversity in which gender is but one dimension along with ethnicity, age, disability and sexual preference. A growing interest in the management of diversity in the very different UK cultural context runs the risk of de-emphasizing and devaluing the claim of special attention for women's management development (Woodall, 1996). It also makes it harder to pass on specific needs in specific contexts rather than more generalized issues. In any case there is a lack of evidence as to whether this approach is working effectively (Colgan and Ledwith, 1996).

None of these approaches are satisfactory from either an individual or organizational perspective. To bury the issue of gender within a broader context of equal opportunity, moves one step away from dealing with the problems of women's management development. To move further away into the realms of identifying how workforce diversity can sustain competitive advantage means we lose sight of the problem altogether. As we stated at the outset of this book, choice of appropriate interventions should be preceded by thorough analysis of organizational context, and diagnosis of what is strategically required.

Surprisingly, the need for analysis of strategic requirements within the organizational context was acknowledged at the early stages of investigation into women's management development needs. The Manpower Services Commission (1981) and one of the first main texts on management development for women (Cooper and Davidson, 1983) identified three reasons for the lack of career development for women, each requiring different types of interventions to bring about change. These three reasons were:

- women's attitudes and behaviours;
- formal personnel procedures and career paths;
- the organizational culture.

To our thinking, these three reasons remain highly durable, with the exception that the last category should be expanded to include men's attitudes and behaviours. It is helpful to look at each of the three in turn, as each will suggest the need to consider different types of intervention. The full range of possible interventions is listed in table 11.3.

WOMEN'S ATTITUDES AND BEHAVIOUR

Women's attitudes and behaviours as reasons for women's underachievement in management are most usually cited by those who feel that either no action needs to be taken, or conversely, that women need to be made aware and encouraged to take action for themselves. Early equal opportunity initiatives often focused upon developing women's attitudes and behaviour. Cooper and Davidson (1983) listed four main aspects which can potentially contribute to women's underachievement in management:

- *Lack of confidence* – This is typically seen in women's low career orientation; apparent lack of leadership and initiative; inability to build on success, and unwillingness to seek out and accept promotion relative to men.
- *Competitiveness* – It has been argued that women assume that if they work hard and do a good job, then they will automatically be noticed and singled out for promotion. They are less likely to be self-publicists and indulge in organizational politics.
- *Family roles* – The general tendency for working women to assume the majority of domestic responsibilities, and to place their career as secondary to that of their partner, reinforces their lack of confidence, and places an additional stress upon them in comparison with men.
- *Stereotyping* – The notion of successful managers consists essentially of male characteristics: apart from 'superwoman', women lack role models which acknowledge the co-existence of their career and domestic roles.

However, there are two different underlying explanations that have become confused here. Firstly, there is the issue of whether women's career motivations are different from those of men, and possibly their desire for a better alternative way of living and working. Secondly, there is the issue of whether women have perceptual and aspirational limitations in relation to the options open to them, due to conditioning or poor advice.

Studies have shown (Spencer and Welchman, 1991; Gutek and Larwood, 1987) that because of poor career advice or early conditioning, women have different

Table 11.3 Interventions for developing women managers

	Target		
Intervention	Women's attitudes and behaviours	Career paths and personnel procedures	Organizational climate
Career-life planning	*		
Assertive communication	*		
Influencing skills	*		
Identifying and using power	*		
Managing risk	*		
Stress management	*		
Mentoring and role modelling	*		
Networking:			
new entrants	*		
returners	*		
career developers	*		
career changes			
Self-development groups	*		
Equal opportunity monitoring and audits of:			
selection and assessment criteria		*	
selection and assessment practice		*	
access to work-related development		*	
Family-friendly employment:			
career break schmes	*		
workplace nurseries	*		
child care vouchers	*		
parental leave	*		
enhanced maternity leave	*		
out of school care	*		
flexible working	*		
job sharing	*		
senior level part time work	*		
Positive action:			
women only management development courses	*		
accelerated development for women managers:			
new entrants		*	
returners		*	
mid career		*	
career planning advice		*	
Gender awareness for men			*
Women and men working together			*
Winning board level commitment			*
Promoting and publicizing success			*

Table 11.3 Continued

| | Target | | |
Intervention	Women's attitudes and behaviours	Career paths and personnel procedures	Organizational climate
Building support			*
by identifying:			
'champions' and 'ambassadors'			*
by supporting:			
'kudos seekers' and 'subversives'			*
and neutralizing:			*
'opponents' and 'blockers'			

perceptions of the career options open to them, compared with men. They want to achieve balance between work and other commitments, and intrinsic job satisfaction is more important than getting ahead. Above all, they lack conscious career aims and plans. Such explanations tend to point to a syndrome of underachievement, and yet there is also evidence to suggest that, the opposite might actually be the case, that women actually overachieve in terms of output relative to their direct male comparators. For example, the apparent lack of confidence and low career orientation is not always confirmed. Studies have found that differences can be due both to generational and life cycle effects (Scase and Goffee, 1989, p. 106, p. 111; White et al., 1992). Also, these and other studies (Alban-Metcalfe and Nicholson, 1989; Nicholson and West, 1988) have questioned whether women suffer from a lack of competitiveness.

It is often difficult to separate out the generational and life cycle effects. For example, younger women are more likely to have a conscious career plan, but this may also be due to the fact that they have grown up in a different era, or to their socio-economic class background. Career life cycles are also important (see chapter 3). Men and women make their careers in different ways. While men tend to make gradual regular career moves throughout their career, women tend to make rapid career moves over a shorter period, involving more frequent 'out-spiralling' (sideways moves out of the organization in order to advance elsewhere, and then, possibly return to the original organization at a higher level) than men, in order to achieve promotion. They are often more qualified, ambitious, and (surprisingly) mobile than men (Alban-Metcalfe and Nicholson, 1989; Nicholson and West, 1988; Alban-Metcalfe and West, 1991). They rate their careers as more important than do their male equivalents, but express more frustration over their career outcomes. 'They [women] achieve equivalent status to the men . . . . by being better qualified, more ambitious, and more mobile; not only changing jobs more often, but moving up in status faster than men. They are also younger' (Alban-Metcalfe and Nicholson, 1989, p. 41).

Turning to family role, there are again generational differences. Older women managers are less likely to have married and had children, but for younger women managers it is parenthood rather than marriage that creates the most conflict between home and work. Even here, as we noted previously, dual careers are now much more common, and it could be said that middle aged, middle level male managers are increasingly likely to be 'reluctant managers' in comparison to their younger male counterparts and women at all levels. A false stereotype of men being more able to separate home and work life, to work long hours, and to give unlimited priority to work issues, persists, despite abundant evidence to the contrary.

More generally with respect to stereotyping, research acknowledges the stereotyping of management as a male role (Marshall, 1985; Rothwell, 1985; Schein, 1973; Brenner et al., 1989). It is based upon the foundations of a continuous, unbroken organizational career where work is the primary source of identity. Male managerial styles are seen as directive and task-centred, while female managerial styles are seen as collaborative and people-centred. But again, there is inconclusive evidence to suggest that women automatically collude with these stereotypes. Much has been written about a distinctively female management and leadership style. In particular, Rosener (1990) has argued that women are more disposed to a transformational leadership style (based on the use of personal power) rather than a transactional style (based on the use of structural power) as is common with most men. She argues that women are succeeding because of, rather than in spite of, the use of these characteristics, which have hitherto been generally considered as inappropriate in leaders. However, the ability to adopt a particular leadership style depends upon organization context: a people-centred transformational leadership style is not easy to sustain when organizations are encouraging (despite calls to the contrary) an assertive and task-centred approach to work.

Thus we need to proceed with caution if we want to ascribe women's 'underachievement' in management to lack of confidence, low career orientation, lack of competitiveness and family role. All these may apply at some time to some women managers, but this is by no means universal. It is thus important to carry out some prior analysis, and only then will it be possible to decide which of the suitable interventions might apply. For example, assertiveness training will not help the woman manager who seeks to change the stereotype of successful managerial behaviour rather than herself, and providing appropriate role models may not help a manager cope with role stress. Yet precisely because these issues concern self-image and lack of confidence, and ultimately deeply held values, and secret hopes and fears, they can only be addressed in a 'safe space'. Hence this provides the justification for women-only training or at least individual career counselling and support. This requirement can cause controversy within the organization, among women as well as men – with the former often denying the need for separate treatment, and the latter often resentfully observing that they too might benefit from some similar pro-gramme. In our opinion, these views deserve respect and should not be dismissed out of hand. Indeed, a successful strategy for women's management development requires that the achievements of women pioneers are not devalued, and that personal development needs of all employees are addressed.

Colgan and Ledwith (1996) identify a number of skills which women need to apply in order to get on in organizations, and to be effective change agents. They suggest that women need to develop more political skills, to enable them to read the organization, its agendas and power bases; and to have better understanding of what baggage they are carrying in terms of their own predispositions, identities and influences. They distinguish between wise, clever, inept and innocent behaviour in women's political styles, where those who are wise in their reading of situations, and use networks and alliances combined with personal integrity, are the majority amongst highflying women (White, Cox and Cooper, 1992).

FORMAL PERSONNEL PROCEDURES AND CAREER PATH

The observation in the previous section would suggest that many of the obstacles to women's lack of career development must lie in structural factors. Very often formal personnel policies can act as an indirect barrier to women entering and pursuing careers in management. This has been the main theme underlying liberal equal opportunity measures designed to remove both formal and informal barriers. There are a number of aspects.

First of all recruitment, selection and assessment processes are the major barrier. Organizations can rely on a limited source of candidates and narrow person specifications. Selection processes, such as interviews, can easily be vehicles for unconscious bias and recent research has revealed that even psychometric testing is not above reproach (Mottram, 1987). In particular, Alimo-Metcalfe's work (1995) has revealed a gender bias in the skills, behaviours, and qualities that organizations seek from managers, in the methods used to assess candidates, and finally in the perceptual judgments of assessors. Appraisal schemes and assessment and development centres have also been shown to discriminate against women in terms of their criteria, techniques, and the perceptions of the assessors (Alimo-Metcalfe, 1994; Townley, 1990). The preference for systems based upon personality traits and behaviour as opposed to performance can disadvantage women. Trait systems are more vulnerable to 'halo' and 'horn' effects, and certain behaviours can be perceived as positive for one sex, but negative for the other. For example, assertiveness and initiative perceived in male behaviour can often be viewed as officiousness and interference in a female. Also, the role of the assessors themselves is important. This is particularly so in appraisal processes, where male line managers are likely to rate males and females differently, and can therefore be a major obstacle to women's managerial career development (for example, see Bevan and Thompson, 1992). Thus the supposed neutrality of promotion procedures can be revealed as a form of social closure by specifying prerequisites that women might not necessarily possess, such as specific formal qualifications, length of service, specific types of functional work experience, commitment to work long hours in different locations, and being well-known to the selectors on an informal basis.

Access to organizationally sponsored training and education is often unequal between men and women. A vicious circle operates whereby nomination for course participation depends upon perceptions of potential, or upon having achieved a managerial grade. Despite recent survey evidence that female employees in general are more likely than men to be enroling for formal off the job training and education (Gibbins, 1994), this is certainly not the case at the managerial level. In particular, sponsorship for management education is unequal, enrolment statistics for MBAs compared with diploma level qualifications illustrate the gender differences. Perhaps the only area where training and development opportunities are likely to be the same is for male and female graduate management trainees. Yet women receive less favourable job postings upon completion, often in an unprestigious specialist function, and subsequently leak out of the fast track as they are no longer seen as having high potential (Hirsh and Jackson, 1989), again a vicious circle. Fast track schemes are also exclusionary for those women who are late entrants to management.

In most small and medium sized organizations however, and increasingly in the corporate sector, development opportunities are increasingly work-related (see chapter 9), and the line manager is the main point of access. Development measures such as job rotation, internal secondments – but above all allocation to special development projects, or membership of high profile task forces and working parties – are the main means of developing skills and achieving visibility. Although line managers are very important gatekeepers to this type of activity, research evidence frequently confirms reports that women managers seldom receive positive support from their immediate line manager, and often have to acquire mentors and sponsors at a senior level from elsewhere in the organization (White et al., 1992; Woodall et al., 1995) who become a key means of access to opportunities to prove oneself, by taking on a challenge, and ultimately acquiring the visibility for career progress. This becomes particularly evident in relation to the under-representation of women as international managers, where prejudice and unreasonable hurdles are the main problems (Harris, 1995).

Quite clearly, if formal personnel procedures are perceived to be the source of obstacles to women in management, then actions are required that address the structure of employment policies and practices. This will necessarily involve getting the commitment of at least the human resources director and some other senior management. Initially, the emphasis is upon data collection and analysis by means of equal opportunity monitoring and audits in order to provide the 'ammunition of reason' with which to bombard the glass ceilings that are perpetuated by traditional career paths and personnel procedures. Secondly, there are measures designed to ensure that organizations recognize that the domestic responsibility of child care affects all employees' work patterns, but particularly those of women managers. Finally, there are interventions designed to bring about positive action to redress the effects of the glass ceiling, such as accelerated development programmes for women and the setting of targets.

However, this traditional equal opportunities approach is currently subjected to much criticism for being overly formal, bureaucratic, and out of step with current developments in organizational structure and the location of wider HRM policy-making (Aitkenhead and Liff, 1991; Woodall et al., 1996; Woodall, 1997). The growing use of informal processes in developing and managing employees (especially in small firms) cannot be addressed easily by this approach. In addition, the overall spirit of equal opportunity policies is to increase opportunity, rather than just maintain it. It is thereby more suited to a time of organizational growth, rather than retrenchment. Thus positive action measures have been very controversial and caution is needed to ensure that their effect does not cause a backlash against women's managerial career development programmes.

THE ORGANIZATIONAL CULTURE

The prevailing value system in an organization, and attitudes towards women in general, can be major determinants of whether or not women have easy access into management. It is clear that ultimately all organizational cultures have a gendered basis (Sheppard, 1989). Men and women experience organizations differently, and if gender is perceived as an organizational issue, then this is usually in terms of the problem of integrating 'femaleness' into the organization, rather than of masculinity itself adjusting. Furthermore, while men's sex role behaviour goes unnoticed at work, there is evidence that they use sex more than women, as evidenced in the sex stereotypes to which they resort in their treatment of women: 'pet', 'housekeeper', 'devoted worker', 'iron maiden', and 'siren'. Kanter's (1977) illuminating work showed how the male response to token female managers varied according to the proportion of women in work groups, and she challenged the view that the presence of a few female tokens can pave the way for others in an organization. This is well-illustrated in the example of the first female UK prime minister, Margaret Thatcher.

Top management attitudes are also major determinants of the prevailing sets of values and beliefs within an organization, and top management commitment can be the key to culture change. However, culture is more than values and beliefs. It is also a means for the mediation of power. The organizational climate and culture cannot be viewed in isolation from organizational power structures, which in turn determine access to the opportunity of using informal organizational networks. Coe (1992, p. 22) has identified the 'men's club' as one of the main barriers encountered by women in their managerial careers. Informal organizational networks are essential to the effective performance of managerial roles. Marshall (1985, p. 93) has listed the following functions provided by informal organizational mechanisms: transmitting information; socialization of new recruits; coping with uncertainty; assessing the intangible elements of managerial effectiveness and potential; achieving organizational visibility; problem solving through exchanges involving influence, reciprocity, and conflict; providing prompt and frank feedback about an individual's performance, acceptability and prospects. Indeed, on reflection, it is difficult to conceive of the possibility of effective management without the use of informal networks. This is a sobering thought, especially for those who perceive that formal policies and competences are the main vehicle for equal opportunity management development. The problem is that while such networks are currently held up as being functional to organizational effectiveness, they can also be dysfunctional leading to poor decisions, and above all, be inequitable in respect of those who are outsiders. All too often it is women managers who predominate amongst those on the outside.

Thus, if the problems encountered by women entering management or seeking to develop their managerial careers are found to be located within the organizational culture, then this will need to be addressed. The problem is that the interventions required are the slowest to bring results. Amongst these, raising men's gender awareness is very important, but needs to be handled sensitively to avoid generating either a hostile response, or a smug complacency. While direct training in equal opportunities aspects of management, recruitment, selection, appraisal and so on can be useful to ensure that all are aware of the need to comply with formal requirements, it rarely achieves more than that. Behavioural compliance can mask attitudinal hostility, cynicism, and at best indifference. At this level the most effective interventions are in the form of a public relations campaign, which adopts either a hard sell or soft sell approach as appropriate. The benefits and successes need to be promoted, and the informal organizational power structure has to be tapped to identify and enlist the support of champions and ambassadors (Willis and Daisley, 1992). Willis and Daisley suggest that even those 'kudos seekers' whose motivation is self serving, and the 'subversive' supporters who dare not come out openly in support of measures, should also be welcomed.

From another perspective, women can be encouraged to join and form a variety of networks. There is much mystique and also opprobrium and disapproval surrounding the operation of women's networks. However, they provide a natural antidote to the men's club to which so many male managers unwittingly belong. Women's networks provide a range of benefits from the more instrumental information on job opportunities and business contacts to access to role models, mentors, training, expertise, support and confidence-building (Segerman-Peck, 1991). There are now a variety of formal women's networks ranging from general business networks (some of these are listed in exhibit 11.1) to specific networks for financial services, information technology, medicine, dentistry, architecture, and even networks within large organizations. Most of these address the main work-related needs that women

---

• • • • Exhibit 11.1 • • • •
Some networks for women managers

City Women's Network
European Women's Management Development Network
Forum (for senior women earning above £100,000)
UK Federation of Business and Professional Women
Women in Banking
Women in Information Technology
Women in Management
Women into Public Life
Women's Engineering Society

N.B. Additional information on over 150 women's organisations is produced by the *Women's National Commission*, Cabinet Office, Government Offices, Horse Guards Road, London SW1P 3AL. Tel: 0171 270 5903

face at different stages of their careers: entering management, career development, returning to work after a career break, changing career, and self-employment. The careers register for women managers in the NHS is an example of a very useful network (see chapter 3). If the organizational climate is not oriented to going beyond mere legal compliance on equal opportunity, the very least that those responsible for management development can do is to publicize the availability of networking activities to women managers.

•••• Achieving a Strategic Approach ••••

We have already suggested that a strategic approach is needed, by virtue of our emphasis upon correct diagnosis of the source of women's under-representation in management prior to any action being taken. Obviously no one source prevails in any organization, and in reality a combination of measures are needed to meet each organization's circumstances. This involves more than getting a board level commitment to equal opportunities, setting up an equal opportunity monitoring unit, and collecting statistics. Action-research methodologies are particularly useful as a way of both exploring the dimensions and causes of problems, and as ways in which to build up commitment to change. Thus an iterative cycle of inquiry, analysis, discussion and experimentation is more likely to leave behind new structures and new ways of thinking than an externally imposed solution.

However, our focus on the problem of women managers' under-representation is only a partial acknowledgment of the strategic aspect. It necessarily focuses attention on practices within an organization. However, as we have seen, women are far more likely than men to change organization and career. In particular, they are more likely to incorporate a period of self-employment or work in a small business into their career. For these reasons, management development for women involves going beyond organization-specific measures to those centred on women themselves. The key processes that assist this are networking and its attendant activities of mentoring and self-development.

Finally, there is a prevailing view that a strategic approach to management development for women rests upon 'making the business case'. Demonstrating the potential value-added and current under-utilization of an organization's woman-power is the idea behind current initiatives such as Opportunity 2000, the government campaign launched in 1991 which by 1994 had 278 member employers, representing about 25 per cent of the UK workforce (Opportunity 2000, 1994). But do equal opportunities make good business sense? Dickens (1994) has shown that this is not necessarily so. For example, the business case for encouraging women into management is served if it assists with recruitment difficulties and the image projected to customers, as exemplified in the human resource practices of many high street retail outlets. On the other hand, is the business case for women managers really served if the organization is pursuing a strategy of low-cost employment (as is often the case in retail), and how easy is it to sustain the business case of encouraging women managers in the face of redundancy and redeployment? To make the development of women managers contingent upon enhancing organizational effectiveness is not to make as strong a case as could be made on ethical principles of fairness and social responsibility. Thus, using the business case is a supplementary approach to be used where it is sustainable, but cannot replace the case made on other grounds. We have to see which arguments are most likely to work in the circumstances, otherwise we are in danger of putting from the tee, and using a driver on the green, an approach not likely to gain access into the men's golf club.

A strategic approach to women's management development is therefore highly contingent upon organization politics, business strategy, and ultimately the women concerned. It is therefore impossible to be prescriptive about what action should be taken. The following suggestions should therefore be viewed as an aide memoir:

- What is the pattern of women's representation in management and in supervisory positions?
- What is the 'business case' for women's management development?
- Which women **want** or **need** (these are not necessarily the same) management development?
- What are the structural and cultural constraints of the organization?
- How can organizational politics be used to maximize support (including that of women themselves) and minimize opposition?

•••• Summary ••••

This chapter provides a justification of why the development of women managers deserves special attention. It has attempted to avoid presenting the issue either as a moral crusade or as a minor diversion from main stream management development. It has also stressed the need to recognize that there are many different potential reasons explaining the under-representation of women in management, and drawn attention to the importance of diagnosing the problem before resorting to solutions. The causes of under-representation vary from woman to woman and organization to organization. In particular, we have emphasized the importance of a thorough diagnosis of the need for development before any action is taken. If solutions are to have any benefit, this involves not only focusing attention on the target group of women, but on the wider issues of human resource management policy and practice, and the organizational culture and politics. There is rarely a quick fix, and many interventions require action research to identify what is required and ongoing support to ensure that solutions are implemented and followed up. Above all, we have suggested the importance of encouraging women managers to network, as their more varied and mobile career path makes this more vital.

EXERCISES

(1) What stereotypes of male and female managers have you encountered? Interview a female manager about her attitudes, experiences, and work, and compare this with the stereotype. Now do the same with a male manager. What do your interviews tell you about the accuracy of your stereotype?

(2) Compare you own managerial career path with that of one of your peers of the opposite sex. In what way does this comparison illustrate the differences in the way in which women and men enter and make progress in management?

(3) Is there a business case to be made for improving management development for women in your organization? What action (if any) is required? Outline your justification for this.

•••• References ••••

Aitkenhead, M. and Liff, S. 1991: The effectiveness of equal opportunity policies. In J. Firth-Cozens and M. A. West (eds) *Women at Work: psychological and organizational perspectives*. Milton Keynes: Open University Press.

Alban-Metcalfe, B. and West, M. 1991: Women managers. In J. Firth-Cozens and M. West *Women at Work: psychological and organizational perspectives*. Buckingham: Open University Press.

Alban-Metcalfe, B. and Nicholson, N. 1989: *The Career Development of British Managers*. London: British Institute of Management.

Alimo-Metcalfe, B. 1994: Waiting for fish to grow feet! Removing organizational barriers to women's entry into leadership positions. In M. Tanton (ed.) *Women in Management: a developing presence*. London: Routledge.

Alimo-Metcalfe, B. 1995: Leadership and assessment. In S. Vinnicombe and N. L. Colwill *The Essence of Women in Management*. Hemel Hempstead: Prentice Hall.

Bailyn, L. 1994: *Breaking the Mould: women, men, and time in the new corporate world*. New York: Free Press.

Beck, J. and Steel, M. 1989: *Beyond the Great Divide: introducing equality into the company*. London: Pitman.

Bevan, S. and Thompson, M. 1992: Merit pay, performance appraisal and attitudes to womens' work. Report Number 234, Institute for Employment Studies: Brighton.

Brenner, O. C., Tomkiewicz, J. and Schein. V. E. 1989: The relationship between sex role stereotypes and requisite management characteristics revisited. *Academy of Management Journal* 32, pp. 662–9.

Coe, T. 1992: *The Key to the Men's Club – Opening the doors to women in management*. London: Institute of Management.

Colgan, F. and Ledwith, S. 1996: Women as organisational change agents. In Ledwith, S. and Colgan, F. *Women in Organisations: challenging gender politics*. Basingstoke: Macmillan.

Collins, H. 1992: *The Equal Opportunities Handbook*. Oxford: Blackwell.

Cooper, C. and Davidson, M. (eds) 1983: *Women in Management*. London: Heinemann.

Davidson, M. and Cooper, C. 1992: *Shattering the Glass Ceiling: the woman manager*. London: Paul Chapman Publishing.

Dickens, L. 1994: The business case for women's equality: is the carrot better than the stick? *Employee Relations*, 16, 8, pp. 5–18.

Gibbins, C. 1994: Women and training: data from the Labour Force Survey. *Employment Gazette*, November: pp. 391–402.

Gooch, L. and Ledwith, S. 1996: Women in personnel management. In Ledwith, S. and Colgan, F. *Women in Organisations: challenging gender politics*. Basingstoke: Macmillan.

Gutek, B. A. and Larwood, L. (eds) 1987: *Women's Career Development*. London: Sage.

Hansard Society Commission 1990: *Women at the Top*. The Report of the Hansard Society Commission on Women at the Top. London: Hansard Society.

Harris, H. 1995: Organisational influences on women's career opportunities in international management. *Women in Management Review*, 10, 3, pp. 26–31.

Herriot, P. and Pemberton, C. 1995: *Competitive Advantage through Diversity: organisational learning from difference*. London: Sage.

Hirsh, W. and Jackson, C. 1989: Women into management: issues influencing the entry of women into managerial jobs. Institute of Manpower Studies Paper no. 158, p. 17.

Jackson, C. and Hirsh, W. 1991: Women managers and career progression: the British experience. *Women in Management Review and Abstracts* 6, 2, pp. 10–16.

Kandola, R. and Fullerton, J. 1994: *Managing the Mosaic*. London: Institute of Personnel and Development.

Kanter, R. M. 1977: *Men and Women of the Corporation*. New York: Basic Books.

King, C. (ed.) 1993: *Through the Glass Ceiling*. Sevenoaks: Tudor Business Publishing.

Legge, K. 1987: Women in personnel management: uphill climb or downhill slide? In A. Spencer and D. Podmore (eds) *In a Man's World*. London: Tavistock.

McBeath, G. 1990: *Practical Management Development*. Oxford: Blackwell.

McGuire, S. 1992: *Best Companies for Women: Britain's top employers*. London: Pandora.

Manpower Services Commission, 1981: *No Barriers Here?* Sheffield: MSC.

Margerison, C. 1992: *Making Management Development Work: achieving success in the nineties*. Maidenhead: McGraw-Hill.

Marshall, J. 1985: *Women Managers: travellers in a male world*. Chichester: John Wiley.

Marshall, J. 1995: *Women Managers Moving On: exploring career and life choices*. London: Routledge.

Mayo, A. 1991: *Managing Careers: strategies for organisations*. London: Institute of Personnel Management (now Institute of Personnel Development).

Mottram, P. 1987: Problems for the user in avoiding sex bias. *Occupational Psychologist* 3, pp. 6–7.

Mumford, A. 1993: *Management Development: Strategies for Action* (2nd edn) Institute of Personnel and Development.

Nicholson, N. and West, M. 1988: *Managerial Job Change: men and women in transition*. Cambridge: Cambridge University Press.

Opportunity 2000, 1994: *Third Year Report: executive summary*. London: Business in the Community.

Rosener, J. 1990: Ways women lead. *Harvard Business Review*. Nov–Dec pp. 119–25.

Rothwell, S. 1985: Is management a masculine role? *Management Education and Development* 16, 2, pp. 79–98.

Scase, R. and Goffee, R. 1989: *Reluctant Managers: their work and lifestyles*. London: Unwin Hyman.

Scase, R. and Goffee, R. 1990: Women in management: towards a research agenda. *International Journal of Human Resource Management* 1, 1, pp. 107–25.

Schein, V. E. 1973: The relationship between sex-role stereotypes and requisite management characteristics among female managers. *Journal of Applied Psychology* 57, 2, pp. 95–100.

Segerman Peck, L. M. 1991: *Networking and Mentoring: a woman's guide*. London: Piatkus Books.

Sheppard, D. C. 1989: Organisation, power and sexuality: the image and self-image of women managers. In Hearn, J., Sheppard, D. C., Tancred-Sheriff P. and Burrell, G. (eds) *The Sexuality of Organisation*. London: Sage.

Sly, F. 1993: Women in the labour Market (Office for National Statistics). *Employment Gazette*, November pp. 483–502.

Spencer, L. and Welchman, R. 1991: *Twice as Good to Go Half as Far: experiences and aspirations of women managers in local government*. London: Social and Community Planning Research.

Townley, B. 1990: A discriminating approach to appraisal. *Personnel Management* December pp. 34–7.

White, B., Cox, C. and Cooper, C. 1992: *Women's Career Development: a study of high-flyers*. Oxford: Blackwell.

Willis, E. and Daisley, J. 1992: *Developing Women Through Training: a practical handbook*. Maidenhead: McGraw-Hill.

Wilson, E. 1996: Managing diversity and HRD. In Stewart, J. and McGoldrick, J. *Human Resource Development: perspectives, strategies, and practice*. London: Pitman.

Woodall, J. Edwards, C. and Welchman, R. 1995: Winning the Lottery? Organisational Restructuring and Women's Management Development. *Women in Management Review and Abstracts* 10, 3, pp. 32–9.

Woodall, J. 1996: Human resource management and women: the vision of the gender blind? In Towers, B. (ed.) *The Handbook of Human Resource Management*, (2nd edn). Oxford: Blackwell.

Woodall, J., Edwards, C. and Welchman, R., 1997: Organisational restructuring: a challenge or a threat to equal opportunities? *Gender Work and Organisation* 4, 1, January pp. 2–12.

CHAPTER 12

Management Development for International Managers

•••• Introduction ••••

In the last quarter of a century international management development has shifted from being the exclusive preserve of multinational companies to a more general requirement for medium-sized and even small businesses in the UK. The volume of international business transactions has grown in an increasingly borderless world (Ohmae, 1990), and the range of strategies open to firms has broadened considerably to include joint ventures, licensing agreements, technology transfer arrangements and bidding consortia, as well as acquisitions, arrangements for export and direct overseas production. In addition, international business participation is not just the preserve of the large international business organization. Smaller domestic companies are pursuing new opportunities, not only within the Single European Market, but also increasingly in East Central Europe and the Pacific Basin which now includes the Peoples' Republic of China.

However, as we shall see, most organizations are ill-prepared to meet the demands that globalization places upon their management teams, and there is a discernible time lag between the recognition that requirements have changed, and the introduction of measures to meet them. There are endless exhortations in the popular management press for organizations to seek and develop the 'helicopter' outlook required to enable an international manager to think globally and act locally, but little practical exploration of what this means and how it can be achieved. In this chapter we shall outline some of the practical options available to all types of companies who wish to develop a capability in international management.

•••• Learning Objectives ••••

After reading this chapter you should be able to:

- Identify the main requirements of international managers in different organizational and strategic contexts.

- Appreciate that there is no common cross-cultural understanding of management, and that international managers have to be able to work within rather than against different cultural contexts.
- Identify a range of measures targeted at both the individual and the organization, which can help prepare and support international management development.
- Identify the labour market and domestic constraints preventing managers from taking an international role, especially women managers, and those in dual-career partnerships.

•••• What is Required of International Managers? ••••

There is a popular image of the international manager as being a mid-career expatriate who is located overseas in order to take up a key management position in a subsidiary. However, reality is much more complex and can vary from an extreme case, where an Anglo-Dutch company such as Unilever might have the majority of its employees located overseas, to a more modest medium sized business which has just broken into an overseas sales market. The many ways in which companies enter overseas markets can be classified into a broad three-fold typology of exporting, licensing and foreign direct investment, as outlined in exhibit 12.1.

From exhibit 12.1 it is clear that separate sets of managers will become involved at various stages, with diverse types of international activity, and that they will often require different skills (Bartlett and Ghoshal, 1992; Storey, 1992). Generally any international activity will require expatriate managers, parent country nationals (PCNs), from the home country, but these can be drawn from different specialisms and be at very different stages of their careers. In addition, host country nationals (HCNs), and even third country nationals (TCNs) are increasingly important members of international management teams, and they also require development.

It is quite helpful to view the forms of international business as lying along a continuum of stages (Dowling, Schuler and Welch, 1994), ranging from limited and

•••• Exhibit 12.1 ••••
Methods for firms to penetrate foreign markets

- **Exporting:** direct exporting; exporting through an agent; exporting through a distributor.
- **Licensing:** contract sales of knowledge; transfer of rights and responsibilities; sale of brand name, patents, and know-how; contract management; franchising; turnkey operations; subcontracting.
- **Foreign direct investment:** full production or service; green field development versus acquisition; wholly owned subsidiary versus joint venture.

Source: C. Hendry, 1994, p. 17

intermittent overseas relationships, such as export via an agent or foreign distributor, to the setting up of an overseas sales subsidiary or branch office. From the latter it is but a short step towards setting up a foreign production facility, usually in a special international division. These often subsequently develop into a divisionalized global structure, with worldwide international or regional product divisions, often managed through a matrix structure. The final stage is full globalization, where the whole business is organized along global lines, with strategic integration from headquarters. Of course, international companies do not always progress through all these stages in a unilinear fashion, and indeed can display the features of several stages at any one time. The important point is to be aware of this, as it will influence what is required of international managers.

Hence, we would argue that there is a growing need for managers to fill different roles at various stages of corporate international development. Thus, in limited relationships where the operation involves sales through export offices, sales representatives, joint ventures or distributor relationships, only those individuals directly concerned may need development. This is usually the position that most small businesses find themselves in when they enter international business arrangements. So in the case of export offices, the HCNs and the appropriate PCNs responsible may both need development. Sales representatives from the home company may not previously have contemplated an international role and will probably require intensive cultural awareness training, and possibly language training too. Also, in joint ventures, middle level technical and commercial specialists will suddenly find themselves exposed to international partners and greater responsibility. Not only is there the question of how to provide international management development in a quick fashion, but also of ensuring cost-effectiveness in the light of any risk associated with the future of the joint venture. If it is anticipated that there will be development beyond the temporary and limited nature of these relationships, then some development may also be extended to key managers from the business partner in the host country.

A second stage often leads the company to open up overseas subsidiaries in individual countries. This usually requires a senior expatriate management team at first, with gradual extension of management positions to host country nationals. At the next stage, setting up a regional business, managers from the various subsidiaries need to meet frequently to share ideas and information, and often to brainstorm and agree solutions. In a mature regional business there is a need for more responsive and long term succession planning to prepare potential expatriate managers, and host and third country nationals.

The final stage of transition towards a global business requires that managers be able to share worldwide information and be willing to work as team members across functional and country-regional lines. It is at this point that the helicopter quality becomes much prized – the ability to demonstrate cultural sensitivity and to rise above one's own cultural constraints.

International HRM specialists have tried to identify the qualities needed, and more recently have attempted to derive international management competencies (Barham and Wills, 1992; Wills and Barham, 1994). They identified four main action competencies around four main roles:

- championing international strategy by collaborating internationally to exploit and adapt learning between countries and markets;
- cross-border coaching and co-ordination by working with local management teams to build and lead multicultural teams;
- intercultural mediation and leading change; and
- managing personal effectiveness for international business, to cope with the demands and stress of international travel and managing at a distance.

This research reveals that success cannot be attributed to specific behavioural competencies or skills alone, but also to the cognitive and affective domains. Success in international management also appears to be dependent upon a deeper core competency based on cognitive complexity (the ability to see several dimensions of a problem, and be able to see patterns and relationships cross-culturally); emotional energy (to enable risk taking and dealing with uncomfortable or stressful situations); and psychological maturity (involving a strong curiosity to learn, strong personal morality and ability to live in the present rather than think about the next assignment).

All this raises the interesting question of how international managers acquire these competencies. Can they be developed by the organization or are early life experiences exposure to foreign travel and different cultures as important? The demand for greater international participation of managers at all levels means that development as well as selection processes become important.

As well as the traditional career expatriate and the rarer transnational manager, many domestic managers may also need to be internationally mobile for short periods. They may become drawn into international projects and joint ventures, or may themselves be either reporting to or working with a third country national from an overseas division or the parent company. In all cases they will at least need an understanding of the cultural differences in management.

•••• International Differences in Management, Education •••• and Development

The concepts of management and management development are culturally specific. Yet it is only over the last 20 years that more frequent and extensive international business activity has shown us that this is the case. In particular, the increasing number of international joint ventures and alliances throws this into sharper relief. Joint ventures between Western and Pacific Rim partners illustrate the contrast between the essentially short-term focus and high turnover of staff in the former relative to the latter. The concept of management is essentially of American origin, as is the idea that it is teachable via business management education (Lawrence, 1992). Indeed much of management theory is of American origin as in the case of motivation, leadership, group dynamics, studies of supervisory effectiveness, and insights into informal behaviour within organizations. The assumption has been that the principles are transferable across cultures and apply universally. However, this is now questionable. Nancy Adler (1991) has shown how important cross-cultural differences are in respect of leadership, motivation, and decision-making, and that the application of major theories of management science can be inappropriate because they arise from an American ethnocentric viewpoint.

In relation to motivation theory, for example, security rather than self-actualization may be the higher motivator in countries such as Spain or Italy, or hygiene factors may also be important motivators, as in Scandinavia. In China, self-actualization only has a meaning in the context of service to society at large. Expectancy theory will only work in cultures which emphasize internal attribution of work outcomes, and so in China and Japan where it is important to acknowledge team contribution and the role of senior staff, it is less likely to be effective. Charismatic leadership styles are not prized in Germany, and a visionary prima donna leadership style is anathema in Japan. With respect to performance management and appraisal there is no universal good practice. Cultural differences arise over the acceptability of objective versus subjective judgment; over measuring performance in relation to targets or behaviour; over taking account of team versus individual performance; and over the acceptability of frank as opposed to indirect feedback. The speed and location of decision making styles also varies with different emphases upon seniority and group decisions. So, the Swedish decision-making style of indecisiveness and slow consensus building, accompanied by systematic and detailed problem solving, and avoidance of open conflict (Brewster, 1993) might cause difficulties for British or American partners. In east central Europe, the legacy of central planning affects both current managerial behaviour and attitudes towards managerial learning (Woodall, 1994). In the light of this it is fair to conclude that what is considered to be effective management varies across cultures.

There is also a considerable variation in what is understood to be the legitimate sphere of human resource management and the way human resource management activities are carried out, such as in recruitment, selection, training and development and also the legal framework which surrounds it (Brewster et al., 1992). Whereas the USA takes for granted the value of strategically focused HRM and formal management development (Lawrence, 1992), the opposite could be said of much of Europe. In particular, the legitimacy and scope of management development in France is much more restricted. Here the education system provides a filter by means of a highly competitive entry into a meritocratic elite from which both business managers and senior public servants are drawn. As a result, French management careers frequently cross the public-private sector boundary. Early screening according to ability and aptitude, the importance of the grade achieved in the school leaving certificate (baccalauréat) taken at age eighteen, and a two-tier system of higher education dominated by the *grandes écoles*, ensures that those emerging into public and commercial life are extremely well-prepared for their managerial task. In this situation not only is there a distinctive understanding of the management task as being about rational analysis and decision-making, but all the most important qualities the successful manager should possess are already in place, and have been publicly certified by the education system (Lawrence, 1992). For this reason, management development is understood as a validating and grooming exercise of career management whereby new managerial recruits will progress through a regular prearranged set of postings leading directly to senior management. This also explains why traditional methods of identifying high potential (such as assessment centres and psychometric tests) are perceived as having hardly any relevance to the challenges identified by executive career managers in France (Bournois and Roussillon, 1992).

The practice of HRM in Germany provides a similar contrast to the UK. The German approach is much more reactive and legalistic, and indeed it is questionable as to whether this conforms to what is conventionally understood as HRM in the UK and USA. For a start, a wider range of employment issues are legally regulated, there is a comprehensive system of labour courts and wage agreements have the force of law. In this situation HRM is less about being proactive than about ensuring compliance with the law and implementation of formally negotiated policy (Lawrence, 1992). Above, all in the German system the personnel department has an important role in servicing the *Betriebsrat* (works council), which all tends to detract from any role as change agent. In addition, a weak understanding of general management, as opposed to technical and professional specialism, affects the way managers are developed and make their careers. As in France, the secondary and higher education systems seek to provide a broad foundation with subsequent specialization leading to a very high level of academic achievement combined with spells of relevant work experience. Until very recently, there was little general management education, and German companies still view their management as consisting of a variety of departments and functions requiring specialized knowledge and experience. For this reason, German managers expect that mobility will take place within the same function, and within the same industry.

In the German model there is a larger role for apprenticeships using similar methods to those identified in the Japanese model, followed by functional careers, with expertise based competition, unlike the Anglo-Dutch model, which is altogether less managed and structured with greater use of performance and potential reviews for highflyers.

Finally, we will make some mention of Japanese management practice and development. It is perhaps here that the cultural differences have been most widely aired in the West, largely because of the American fascination with the secrets of Japanese business success since the mid 1970s. By now the assumptions underlying Japanese management practice are well-known. Japanese managers within the large corporations and public service are generally held to be better educated than the British equivalent; stay with one firm throughout their career; experience systematic training in operational matters, and therefore enter management relatively late; and tend to be exposed to a wide variety of functional experience (Storey et al., 1991, p. 34). Different cultural traditions in management development exist so that for example in Japan an elite is identified in recruitment for long-term careers, followed by job rotation, intensive training, mentoring and regular performance monitoring, leading to multifunctional mobility, and good jobs for the best. The importance of deference to seniority in decision-making and the celebrated 'ringi' system whereby a junior manager drafts an initial proposal that other managers eventually amend and endorse are established features of Japanese management practice. This can mean a low tolerance of diversity, which is evident in the high degree of global integration within most Japanese companies. It is also generally assumed that Japanese management development practice is extensive and systematic. However, recent survey evidence (Storey et al., 1991) has shown that the form this takes places a great deal of responsibility upon the individual to seek out work-related developmental opportunities, rather than formal off the job training, and that the impact of the early 1990s recession in Japan has led to cutbacks in training, freezes in career progression and sometimes, redundancy.

···· Approaches to Developing International Managers ····

The preceding brief sketch of different cultural perceptions of management in general, and human resource management and management development in particular, would suggest that a strategic approach to international management development is necessary that takes into account both the scope of international activity entered into by the firm, the type and level of manager involved, and the cultural context of its operations. In addition, there needs to be an appropriate balance between formal didactic measures and exposure to experiential exercises combined with on the job learning (Iles, 1996). The choice will depend upon the degree of interaction expected with HCNs or TCNs, the degree of cultural similarity or distance between home and host country, the degree of job mobility required, and the prior cultural exposure of the managers involved (see figure 12.1). There are indeed a number of ways in which international management development might be achieved, and these are outlined below.

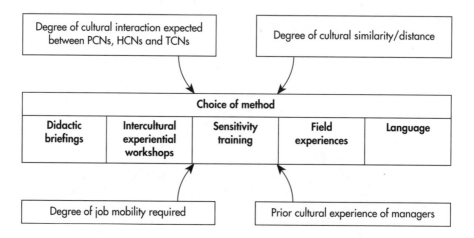

Figure 12.1 Factors influencing choice of method to develop international managers

···· **Exhibit 12.2** ····
Preparation for expatriation

Prior to departure:
- ensure adequate advance preparation rather than a last minute rush;
- provide an initial briefing;
- begin with an audit of skills and knowledge;
- focus on learning styles – especially encouraging the ability to learn from others;
- involve different types of trainers (academics and existing expatriates and host country and third country nationals);
- involve family members.

During the overseas assignment:
- arrange for continuous development by means of distance learning;
- provide opportunities for return leave for debriefing and reassessment;
- ensure regular monitoring;
- use appraisal to set up international learning contracts;
- use mentors in both the home and host country;
- adopt a global strategy of coordinated management development;
- hold international conferences and workshops to network international managers;
- promote multicultural team working.

PREPARATION FOR EXPATRIATION OF HOME COUNTRY NATIONALS TO FOREIGN WORLD OFFICES

Preparing home country nationals for expatriation involves considerable advance preparation. Sheila Rothwell (1992) has proposed a practical approach that starts by building on candidates' awareness of living and working abroad, and then moves on towards developing cultural awareness and interpersonal skills, and finally focuses upon providing knowledge and information (see exhibit 12.2).

INTERNATIONAL SEMINARS FOR IN-COMPANY PERSONNEL

International seminars are an important means for senior level expatriates to keep in touch with the wider business. They are also useful for other groups of staff, as a means to develop general management skills, to generate a common corporate identity and culture, and for general team-building. They can be particularly useful for middle level managers working in specialist functional or technical areas, such as HRM or product development. This is especially so when the organization requires greater global collaboration between managers from different cultures as in a joint venture (Regan, 1994). Such programmes usually work best if they are highly practical, are integrated with an in-company project, involve extensive networking and feedback, and are linked to other corporate communication strategies. They can also be used as an orientation mechanism to prepare younger managers for international assignments by covering national cultural differences, briefings on local politics and the law, and by assisting families to adapt.

OPENING UP OPPORTUNITIES FOR FREQUENT SHORT TERM TRAVEL

Providing short term travel opportunities is particularly useful for internationalizing senior level managers who may never have worked abroad, or may have acquired international experience a considerable while ago. At the other end of the scale short business visits and secondments abroad are a very important development tool for the young manager at the start of his/her international career.

DEVELOPING INTERNATIONAL TASK FORCES AND MULTICULTURAL PROJECT TEAMS

International task forces and project teams become a necessity for design, marketing and product development, and are universally agreed to be better for innovative rather than routine tasks. However, they require very careful attention to their operation in terms of set tasks, resources, and process. In addition, the composition of the group can affect the group dynamics; whether it is a bi-cultural group, for example with 50 per cent each British and Japanese, a token group where all but a few members are from the same background, or a true multicultural group where members represent three or more ethnic backgrounds (Adler, 1991). Multicultural group working is simultaneously capable of delivering considerable advantages while being susceptible to tremendous problems (Adler, 1991, pp. 128–35), in the same way that demographic heterogeneity acts as an asset and disadvantage for the top team (see chapter 13). The diversity of membership often leads to greater creativity and greater limitation on groupthink. However, group formation can be beset by attitudinal problems of mistrust, dislike, and stereotyping. It can lead to inaccuracy, inefficiency and misunderstanding in communication, and a general rise in stress level. Overall cultural diversity can diminish effective group functioning, which is why in general, compared with single culture groups, the performance of multi-cultural teams is much more likely to be either extremely effective or extremely ineffective (Adler, 1991).

Thus multicultural group working requires a great deal of HR professional support. One company which has attempted to find a systematic approach is British Petroleum (Neale and Mindel, 1992) which brought together a team of 40 people from 13 different nationalities working in a new environment. BP adopted two approaches. The first one stressed the importance of a person understanding their own culture, and the process which shaped their values, beliefs, preferences, ways of behaving and perceptions of others. This was seen as a priority before they attempted an understanding of other cultures. This is because cultural self-awareness provides a benchmark against which to compare unfamiliar situations, in order to gain more insight into where the differences lie. The other approach was teambuilding and group working. Here BP focused on the stages of uncovering national assumptions in order to identify multicultural action points as a basis for moving towards consensus. Once formed such multicultural teams need to be sustained by avoiding cultural dominance, and by ensuring mutual respect and frequent feedback, both within the group and from outside. As Iles (1996) notes, such approaches to multicultural working have a great deal in common with approaches to multiethnic working and diversity management within domestic organizational HR activity.

Another company that has adopted international task forces is Phillips which uses them for special study assignments lasting between six and eight months. They are preceded by a two week seminar at which senior management hand out projects and are rounded off by group presentations to the same senior management team. Multicultural task forces and working parties need not just be confined to the organization. For example, British Telecommunications plc is part of a European consortium of companies examining management development in telecommunications. Unfortunately both of these approaches have come mainly from international businesses based in the West. Japanese and other business from the Pacific Rim are not inclined to let go of cultural dominance.

BRINGING FOREIGN NATIONALS TO WORLD HEAD OFFICE

Many companies have realized that going international does not necessitate all managers having overseas experience. In fact such a colonial view of international management development ignores the fact that global organizations now increasingly rely upon HCNs and TCNs. So, to the contrary, it is important to sensitize many domestic middle level managers to multiculturalism. This can often be done by importing foreign expertise into the head office. These people then become a key force in assisting international development of the home team, and then themselves return overseas as part of a career move. Of course this needs sensitive treatment, taking account of local custom and practice in selection of these HCNs and TCNs, and also providing a support mechanism for them while they are away from their home country.

TAKING ADVANTAGE OF INTERNATIONAL EDUCATION PROGRAMMES

There are a number of other methods of international management development. The growing number of new graduates with linguistic fluency and cross-cultural ability reflects the change in higher education programmes. A number of programmes sponsored by the European Commission such as the ERASMUS network launched in 1989 (Fox, 1992; Easterby-Smith, 1992) have increased the number of business undergraduates with linguistic skills and experience of study in another country. There are also a large number of business schools and management colleges which provide international management education and training for mid-career managers. The most prestigious of these are INSEAD near Paris, and the International Management Centres around the world. There are signs that an international job market is opening up for such graduates, and many global companies are starting international management development programmes. Ironically, mainland European companies are more inclined in this direction than UK or USA organizations.

Other options include direct recruitment of mid-career managers with prior international experience; expatriating regional nationals to regional offices; bringing foreign nationals into regional offices; sponsoring international seminars jointly with staff from other companies (often in collaboration with business schools); encouraging membership and participation in international networks and associations, and appropriate language training.

USE OF AND SUPPORT FOR INTERNATIONAL MANAGEMENT DEVELOPMENT ACTIVITIES

A recent survey of 105 international cutting edge businesses (Derr and Oddou, 1993) revealed that most companies focused on developing expatriates, holding international seminars, and increasing opportunities for more frequent but short travel. However, they anticipated that in the future they would be making greater use of international task forces and project teams and bringing more foreign nationals into world head offices.

Thus there are many methods of international management development open to organizations. However, the one factor in common is that most involve individuals experiencing a personal transition. For those embarking on some form of foreign assignment not only is there the problem of their own individual culture shock on arrival (and often on re-entry back home), but also potential problems surrounding everyday living. For this reason, the responsibility for international management development involves HR specialists in a broader administrative and welfare role. It has been argued that international human resource management involves HR in more functions and activities, adoption of a broader perspective and greater involvement in individuals' lives (Dowling, Schuler and Welch, 1994). Expertise is required in international taxation, relocation, employment law, managing relations with the host country government and bureaucracy. Head office and regional HR teams are not just concerned with the needs of expatriates, but also of host country nationals and third country nationals. For all those on any form of overseas assignment welfare issues loom large, examples include employment needs of spouses, housing arrangements, children's education and health. For this reason the overhead costs of international management are high. Yet, notwithstanding the effort that organizations devote to international management, problems do arise at the organizational and individual level.

•••• The Constraints upon Developing International •••• Managers

LACK OF A STRATEGIC APPROACH

Despite considerable resources devoted to developing international managers, a recent survey (Price Waterhouse/Cranfield, 1991) revealed that 57 per cent of large European companies lacked a strategy for gaining international expertise for their managers. This was particularly worrying given the growing demand for employees to be involved in joint ventures and alliances. Another study (Scullion, 1992) revealed that two-thirds of a sample of British and Irish companies continue to rely heavily on expatriates to run their foreign operations, despite mounting evidence of a shortage of managers with the necessary international experience and orientation. At the same time, these companies cited weaknesses in the training and development they provided for host country nationals and third country nationals. Indeed, a key role of the expatriate manager was to coach these individuals.

PROBLEMS WITH REPATRIATION

Unless the expatriate assignment is part of an agreed career development strategy, then expatriates can confront problems on re-entry. Finding a job with an appropriate level of responsibility can be difficult for the repatriated manager. In addition the opportunity to use the skills acquired abroad is not always available, as many expatriates perform a broader role than they would at home with greater responsibility and decision-making autonomy. This can lead to unnecessary frustration, demotivation, and a waste of expertise, which at the very least could be used to train home country nationals. However, companies report that the main reasons that expatriates experience difficulty in reintegration are loss of status, loss of autonomy, reduced responsibility, loss of career direction, and lack of recognition of the value of international experience by the company. Recent results for the UK (Johnston, 1991) confirm earlier findings in the USA. Although repatriation can be a particular problem for those returning from the less developed world where they enjoyed a higher standard of living and a more relaxed pace of life, it is increasingly problematic for those on assignments within the West. The frequency of corporate restructuring can mean that not only will the job to which expatriates return have changed, but that on return they may even be facing redundancy.

RELUCTANCE TO CONTEMPLATE INTERNATIONAL MOBILITY

There is much evidence that, despite the increasing demand for expatriate managers, many managers are reluctant to contemplate an extensive overseas assignment. Besides anxiety about uncertain prospects at the end of the assignment, there are growing concerns over the impact on domestic arrangements. At the centre of this is the problem of the 'trailing spouse'. The notion of the expatriate assignment is grounded in a social reality that has been out of date for over 20 years; male managers with a dependent spouse who did not have a career of her own. Contemporary domestic partnerships at managerial level more usually consist of two highly educated people, each with a career from which it is not easy to take a break. In addition, the disruption to the education of school age children or the undesirability of separation involved in placing them in boarding school reinforces this reluctance to relocate overseas. Some companies have adjusted to this by either using shorter, more frequent, assignments, or by trying to arrange employment for a spouse. However, at a professional or managerial level the latter is not always easy. This probably explains why many companies are resorting to executive search for potential expatriates outside their own organizations. Apart from a growing pool of single or divorced executives, they are unlikely to attract the talent they require from those in modern domestic partnerships.

LACK OF SUPPORT FOR WOMEN IN INTERNATIONAL MANAGEMENT

Women are very much under-represented amongst expatriates and third country nationals. It has been estimated that, worldwide, women make up only between 2 and 15 per cent of international managers (Harris, 1995), and in both the UK and the USA the proportion of expatriates who are female is around 3 per cent (Scullion, 1992), a startling contrast to their position elsewhere in management. It has been assumed that societal norms, domestic arrangements, and women's preferences are the obstacle. However, Adler's explosion of these and other commonly held myths about women in international management (Adler, 1984; Adler, 1987), is backed up by more recent research which indicates the critical nature of home country organizational influence on women's prospects within both domestic and inter-national management positions (Harris, 1995). This applies in particular to the nature of the interplay of formal company policies and informal processes, and their effects upon women's perceptions of opportunities (see chapter 11). While a majority of UK companies with overseas operations have officially espoused equal opportunity policies, this certainly does not translate into a growing proportion of women in international management. This is ironic in the light of recent research (Barham and Devine, 1991) indicating that women are more sensitive to cultural differences and are therefore more able to work effectively with managers from other countries. While in the USA there have been successful efforts to increase the number of women expatriates, this has not yet been given serious attention in the UK.

Thus embarking upon, or furtherance of, international management development requires a strategic assessment before any action is taken. The following questions need to be answered in order to ensure that policy will meet both organizational and individual needs:

- What precisely is the nature of the organization's current international involve-ment, and in what ways is this likely to develop?
- What is required of international managers, both now and in the future?
- What are the current policies and practices for developing international managers, and to what extent do they meet current and future needs?
- What alternative methods could be considered, and why?
- How do arrangements for international management development fit in with organizational career management practices?
- Are there any current or potential problems that might affect the supply of international managers?

•••• Summary ••••

This chapter has emphasized the growing significance of international management development for all organizations, and a range of different managers, rather than just the selection and preparation of career expatriates. In particular, it has stressed the importance of developing a cultural awareness of the different understanding of the scope of management, management styles, and the acceptability of management development activities in the countries concerned. The task of supporting international management development is made difficult by the persistent assumption within the corporate sector that the focus should be home country male nationals (unattached or with a dependent spouse), who should be willing to relocate in an uncertain business environment. We have shown that, ultimately, this is self-defeating. For many individuals short assignments and secondments are preferable at some point in their lives, and longer ones at others. A uniform system of arrangements will not meet the needs of executives at different stages of their career life cycles (see chapter 3). Finally, big global companies need to consider whether their international management objectives are best served by a policy mainly targeted at expatriates, rather than host or third-country nationals.

EXERCISES

Examine the way in which managers are prepared for an international role in an organization that you know well:

(1) Is there sufficient strategic focus to ensure that the emerging needs of the organization will be met?

(2) Are practices sufficiently sensitive to changes in employment patterns and domestic lives that have taken place over the last 20 years?

•••• References ••••

Adler, N. 1984: Women do not want international careers and other myths about international management. *Organizational Dynamics* 13, 2, pp. 66–79.

Adler, N. 1987: Pacific basin managers: a 'Gaijin', not a woman. *Human Resource Management* 26, 2, pp. 169–92.

Adler, N. 1991: *International Dimensions of Organizational Behaviour.* 2nd edn. California: PWS-KENT Publishing Company.

Barham, K. and Devine, M. 1991: *The Quest for the International Manager: a survey of global human resource strategies.* London: Economist Intelligence Unit.

Barham, K. and Wills, S. 1992: *Management Across Frontiers: identifying the competencies of successful international managers.* Berkhamstead: Ashridge Management Research Group.

Bartlett, C. and Ghoshal, S. 1992: 'What is a global manager?' *Harvard Business Review* September–October pp. 124–32.

Bournois, F. and Roussillon, S. 1992: The management of 'highflier' executives in France: the weight of the national culture'. *Human Resource Management Journal* 3, 1, pp. 37–56.

Brewster, C. 1993: The paradox of adjustment: UK and Swedish expatriates in Sweden and the UK. *Human Resource Management Journal* 4, 1, pp. 49–62.

Brewster, C., Hegewisch, A., Holden, L. and Lockhart, T. 1992: *The European HRM Guide.* London: Academic Press.

Derr, C.B. and Oddou, G. 1993: Internationalising managers: speeding up the process. *European Management Journal* 11, 4, December, pp. 435–42.

Dowling, P. J., Schuler. R. S., and Welch, D. E. 1994: *International Dimensions of Human Resource Management.* 2nd edn, Belmont California: Wadsworth.

Easterby-Smith, M. 1992: European management education: the prospects for unification. *Human Resource Management Journal* 3, 1, pp. 24–36.

Evans, P., Lank, E. and Farquhar, A. 1989: Managing human resources in the interntional firm. In Evans, P., Doz, Y. and Laurent, A. (eds) *Human Resource Management in International Firms: change, globilization, innovaton.* Basingstoke: Macmillan.

Fox, S. 1992: The European Learning Community: towards a political economy of management learning. *Human Resource Management Journal* 3, 1, pp. 70–91.

Harris, H. 1995: Organizational influences on women's career opportunities in international management. *Women in Management Review* 10, 3, pp. 26–31.

Hendry, C. 1994: *Human Resource Strategies for International Growth.* London: Routledge.

Iles, P. 1996: International HRD. In Stewart, J. and McGoldrick, J. (eds) *Human Resource Development: perspectives, strategy and practice.* London: Pitman.

Johnston, J. 1991: An empirical study of the repatriation of managers in UK multinationals. *Human Resource Management Journal* 1, 4, pp. 102–9.

Lawrence, P. 1992: 'Management development in Europe: a study in cultural contrast'. *Human Resource Management Journal* 3, 1, Autumn, pp. 11–23.

Neale, R. and Mindel, R. 1992: Rigging up multicultural teamworking. *Personnel Management* January, pp. 36–9.

Ohmae, K. 1990: *The Borderless World: power and strategy in the interlinked economy.* London: Collins.

Regan, M. 1994: Developing the middle manager for globalization: the case of Electrolux. In Kirkbride, P. (ed.) *Human Resource Management in Europe: perspectives for the 1990s.* London: Routledge.

Rothwell, S. 1992: The development of the international manager. *Personnel Management.* January, pp. 33–5.

Scullion, H. 1992: Strategic recruitment and development of the 'international manager': some European considerations. *Human Resource Management Journal* 3, 1, pp. 57–61.

Storey, J., Okazaki-Ward, L., Gow, I., Edwards, P. K., and Sisson, K. 1991: Managerial careers and management development: a comparative analysis of Britain and Japan. *Human Resource Management Journal* 1, 2, pp. 33–58.

Storey, J. 1992: Making European managers: an overview. *Human Resource Management Journal* 3, 1, pp. 1–10.

Wills, S. and Barham, K. 1994: Being an international manager. *European Management Journal* 12, 1, March. pp. 49–58.

Woodall, J. 1994: The transfer of managerial knowledge to Eastern Europe. In Kirkbride, P. (ed.) *Human Resource Management in Europe: perspectives for the 1990s.* London: Routledge.

CHAPTER 13

Executive Development and the Top Team

•••• **Introduction** ••••

In this chapter the justification for the top team engaging in developmental activity is presented, but we also acknowledge the lack of activity which is undertaken in practice. The barriers to development are presented, including the lack of visibility of the work, the lack of clarity of the various top team roles, and the little time available, all of which make the remit for top team development particularly challenging. The chapter includes a framework for examining the development needs at four different stages – grooming, induction, developing individual competency, and processes for team based development. This is then applied by examining board level shared team roles in order to identify appropriate processes for team based development, and to focus here on shared and team based learning needs. Then the diverse development needs in terms of grooming, induction and in-role development for chief executives and chairpeople, executive and non-executive directors, are explored. The tension inherent within the various roles, between that of leader or manager, insider or outsider, developer or evaluator are shown to cause particular difficulties for the board members, which can also be addressed by the development agenda. When designing the process of top team development it is suggested that experience-based, facilitated development, using networks, mentoring and support, are more likely to lead to productive development interventions.

•••• **Learning Objectives** ••••

As a result of reading this chapter you should be able to:

- identify the need for development of the top team, and organizational examples of where it might be required;
- explain the reasons why many organizations ignore senior executive development;
- distinguish between the various roles of the top team, and appreciate the difficulties inherent within each;
- describe some of the key competencies which are needed by the top team;

- outline appropriate development methods for various members of the top team.

···· The Role of the Top Team ····

TOP TEAMS, BOARDS AND EXECUTIVES

The role of the top team is to devise, implement and evaluate strategy. Where the prime role of the board is to ratify and evaluate strategy, that of the management team accountable to the board is to devise and implement it. In addition senior management are responsible for policy development, interaction with the external environment and accountability.

Typically a board contains a chairperson, a chief executive, several non-executive directors and several executive directors of the organization. The executive directors may be functional based – such as directors of finance, marketing, engineering, research and development and human resources – products based, market, region or division based. For example exhibit 13.1 provides an outline of the board composition and members' responsibilities for Marks and Spencer (taken from their annual report). This illustrates the four main roles: chairperson; chief executive (or joint managing director in the case of Marks and Spencer); and various executive and non-executive directors. The composition illustrates the complexity of inter-organizational networks, particularly through the role of non-executive directors, a point made later in the chapter. At Marks and Spencer, their non-executive directors are represented on the boards of banks, in finance, engineering and manufacturing companies, newspapers, government quangos, committees and have even held government office, as well as being involved with universities and a range of other multinational organizations.

In large corporate multinational organizations there are often main and divisional boards. For American corporations, the directors on the main board are often called vice presidents, and also represent functional areas such as sales and marketing. There are also usually committees of the board. Some of the typical ones include the audit, remuneration/compensation, and nomination committees. Less typical is an environment committee such as at British Steel, and Marks and Spencer have also, in recent years, set up capital expenditure and information technology review committees.

To some extent each board has its own distinct structure and composition and differing balances of centralization and decentralization. The Body Shop for example separates out accountabilities at the national level from those at head office, and makes a distinction between the activities of manufacturing, wholesaling, marketing, sales and administrative functions – which are overseen by the main board – and managing franchises and shops which are the responsibility of the local level management. However these responsibilities invariably overlap, and the influence of the main board depends very largely on the organization. Thus at the Body Shop, information from the annual report and elsewhere show that the chief executive, Anita Roddick, plays a huge role in creating and reinforcing the values of the

•••• Exhibit 13.1 ••••
Board structure of Marks and Spencer

Board of Directors

Executive Directors

Sir Richard Greenbury Chairman Age 60 Non-executive director of Zeneca Group plc.
Keith Oates Deputy Chairman and Joint Managing Director Age 54 Responsible for international operations, finance, M&SFS, information technology and physical distribution. Non-executive director of Guinness PLC. BT and MCI Communications Corporation. Member of the English Sports Council.

Guy McCracken Joint Managing Director Age 48 Responsible for food division. Director of CORDA.
Peter Salsbury Joint Managing Director Age 47 Responsible for group estates, store development, operations, personnel (as of 1/4/97 also corporate and external affairs). President of Institute for Employment Studies. Non-executive director of TR Property Investment Trust PLC from 29/5/97.

Andrew Stone Joint Managing Director Age 54 Responsible for general merchandise division. Chairman of British Overseas Trade Group for Israel. Governor of Weizmann Institute of Science. Non-executive director of Thorn plc.

Non-Executive Directors

Brian Baldock Age 62 Appointed 1 October 1996. He was Deputy Chairman of Guinness PLC until June 1996 and prior to that Group Managing Director. He is a non-executive director of Cornhill Insurance plc and Dalgety plc.
Sir Martin Jacomb Age 67 Appointed in 1991. He is Chairman of the British Council, the Prudential Corporation plc and Delta plc. He is also a director of RTZ Corporation plc.
Denis Lanigan CBE Age 71 Appointed in 1987. He served 34 years with JWT Worldwide and was Vice-Chairman and Chief Operating Officer between 1982 and 1986. He was Chairman of MM&K Ltd between 1988 and 1991 and a director of the TSB Bank from 1987 to 1990. He is a member of the British Overseas Trade Board. (Retires July 1997.)
Sir Michael Perry CBE Age 63 Appointed 1 October 1996. He served 39 years with Unilever PLC and was Chairman between 1992 and 1996. He is Chairman of Dunlop Slazenger Group and Deputy Chairman of Bass plc and Centrica plc.
Dame Stella Rimington DCB Age 61 Appointed 1 January 1997. She worked for the Security Service (MI5 for 27 years and was Director General from 1992 to April 1996. She is a non-executive dfirector of BG plc.
Sir Ralph Robins Age 64 Appointed in 1992. He was appointed Chairman of Rolls-Royce plc in 1992 after 37 years with the Group. He is a director of Standard Chartered plc. Schroders plc and Cable and Wireless plc. He is Chairman of the Defence Industries Council

Lady Young PC DL Age 70 Appointed in 1987. She was a member of the Cabinet for two years. Leader of the House of Lords between 1981 and 1982 and Lord Privy Seal between 1982 and 1983. She was Minister of State at the FCO from 1983 to 1987. (Retires July 1997.)
Roger Aldridge Age 50 Group estates, store development and equipment, and head office premises. Member of Industrial Development Board of NI. Director of National Retail Planning Forum.
James Benfield Age 47 Childrenswear, home furnishings, including operations and marketing. (as of 1/4/97 also Direct Mail.) Non-executive director of Whittington Hospital Trust.
Nigel Colne CBE Age 56 International franchise group. (Retired 31/3/97.) Non-executive director of Halifax Building Society. Non-executive director of Woolworths, South Africa.
Robert Colvill Age 56 Finance, financial services. Non-executive director of Witan Investment Co plc. Chairman of Money Advice Trust.
Clara Freeman Age 44 Personnel (as of 1/4/97 also Corporate and External Affairs.) Director of Roffey Park Management College.
Derek Hayes Age 48 Retail operations Europe. (as of 1/4/97 also International Franchise Group.)

Chris Littmoden CBE Age 53 Retail operations The Americas. Special adviser to the Ministry of Defence, Director of British-American Chamber of Commerce. Director of Food Marketing Institute of America.
Barry Morris Age 49 Food group, liaison with Israel. Vice-Chairman of British-Israel Chamber of Commerce. Chairman of the British Friends of the Shenkar College.
Joe Rowe Age 49 Ladieswear. Member of Advisory Board, Warwick Business School.
John Sacher CBE Age 56 IT, physical distribution. Chairman of Whitehall & Industry Group. Chairman of Westminster Forum.
The Hon David Sieff Age 58 Corporate and external affairs. (Non-executive from 1/4/97.) Chairman of National Lottery Charities Board. Member of Board of Business in the Community.
Paul Smith Age 56 Retail operations Far East. Fellow of Institute of Personnel Management. Chairman of the Board of Trustees of Befrienders International.
Don Trangmar Age 57 Menswear, general merchandise technology. Trustee of Sick Children's Trust.

···· **Exhibit 13.1 continued** ····

Divisional Directors

Keith Bogg Information technology and physical distribution
Mike Burger Childrenswear and home furnishings
Geoffrey Dart Seconded as Chief Executive of NAAFI
Jeff Denton Corporate finance
Bob Fee Food operations
Jean-Marc Genis European retail (as of 1/4/97 European liaison)
Brian Godbold Design
Graham Harvey European government liaison (Retired 31/3/97)
Russell Hodgkinson Ladies' formalwear
Mike Johnson General merchandise operations and marketing
Alan Lambert European merchandise
Chris Lewis Overseas procurement – Far East

Jim McAllister London stores
Jim McCallum Store operations
Vince McGinlay Men's casualwear
Clive Nickolds European store operations and personnel
David Norgrove Men's formalwear
Alison Reed Financial control
Philip Sellwood Foods – long life and bakery
John Stanley Corporate affairs
Jim Stocks General merchandise technology and packaging development
Michael Taylor Foods – produce and protein
David Towell Marks & Spencer Financial Services
Hugh Walker Foods – prepared dishes
Nigel Whinnett Lingerie, footwear, hosiery, accessories, toiletries and cosmetics

Kim Winser Ladies' casualwear
Gordon Yeoman International franchise group
Martin van Zwanenberg Food technology

Company Secretary
John O'Neill (Retires 31/7/97)
Graham Oakley (From 1/8/97)

Chief Accountant
Tony Lenz

President and CEO. Brooks Brothers
Joseph Gromek

President and CEO. Kings Super Markets
Jim Meister

Source: Marks and Spencer Annual Report and Financial Statements 1997

organization. There is also more flexibility in the board level roles at the Body Shop, which is illustrated by the board members being listed in the annual report by their names without reference to role or job title, beyond that of chief executive, chairperson, managing director, directors and non-executive directors.

Boards are also now much more common within the public sector, for example in the NHS, local government, utilities and TECs representing the increased prevalence of business practices, culture and terminology, accompanying marketization and privatization of the public services. (Figure 13.1 provides a chart of the board composition for an NHS Trust.)

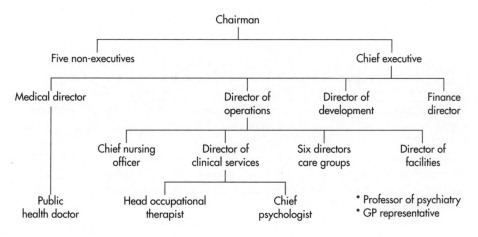

Figure 13.1 The board composition for one NHS Mental Health Trust

In the NHS there is a mandatory requirement to include a medical or clinical director and a nurse director on the board. Increasingly the medical director is chosen for his or her interest in management and ability to take the wider view, rather than being merely a representative of clinicians. Often the nurse director is also responsible for quality. Trusts generally have some finance, human resources, contracting, and operational services representation on the board as well (Dawson et al., 1995, pp. 38–9).

Even some major private companies utilize boards, as do small and medium sized enterprises. Here the achievement of a functionally supportive top team around an owner-manager/founder can be very problematic, both because of a reluctance to delegate, and fear that other managers might leave, having poached the business. Most research to date has been on board level top teams in the corporate sector. There has been less on the public and small and medium sized enterprise (SME) sector.

Boards differ in size: some small firms have as few as two directors, although a typical board may contain around six individuals, and boards can extend to ten or more members for larger, more complex, organizations. Larger boards enable directors to develop by taking on more specialist roles, whereas smaller boards are more likely to succeed through greater social integration. In multinational companies and public limited corporations a distinction can also be made between the main board and the divisional boards, as in exhibit 13.1.

What then is the role of a board? Cadbury (1990) summarized the functions of boards as follows:

- to define the company's purpose;
- to agree the strategies and plans for achieving that purpose;
- to establish the company's policies;
- to appoint the chief executive and to review their performance and that of the top executives;
- in all this to be the driving force of the company.

The term 'corporate governance' reflects the primary role of the board, which is to govern (Coulson-Thomas, 1992). Governance includes determining the purpose and establishing objectives for the organization, identifying a strategy, ensuring the appropriate management processes exist to implement the strategy, and monitoring, reviewing and reporting on performance. This is confirmed by one piece of research where 70 per cent of chairpeople describe the function of their board in terms of establishing objectives and strategy, and subsequently monitoring and reviewing their achievement (Coulson-Thomas and Wakelam 1990, 1991). This cycle is reproduced in figure 13.2.

An alternative model of the role of boards can be found in figure 13.3 (Audit Commission, 1995) which identifies their main roles in the public sector as being: steering in terms of priorities and resource allocation; monitoring performance and accountability; and responsiveness to government and the local population. Clearly, in the public sector, there is a greater requirement for accountability and responsiveness due to the use of public funds which are intended to be used for providing essential public services in the most cost-efficient and effective way.

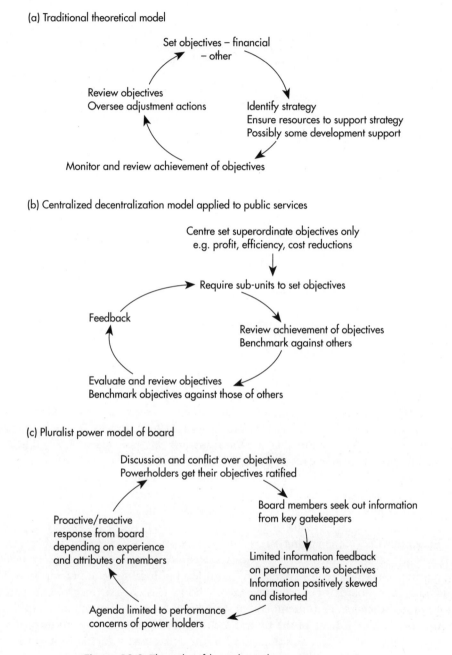

(a) Traditional theoretical model

Set objectives – financial
– other

Review objectives
Oversee adjustment actions

Identify strategy
Ensure resources to support strategy
Possibly some development support

Monitor and review achievement of objectives

(b) Centralized decentralization model applied to public services

Centre set superordinate objectives only
e.g. profit, efficiency, cost reductions

Require sub-units to set objectives

Feedback

Review achievement of objectives
Benchmark against others

Evaluate and review objectives
Benchmark objectives against those of others

(c) Pluralist power model of board

Discussion and conflict over objectives
Powerholders get their objectives ratified

Board members seek out information
from key gatekeepers

Proactive/reactive
response from board
depending on experience
and attributes of members

Limited information feedback
on performance to objectives
Information positively skewed
and distorted

Agenda limited to performance
concerns of power holders

Figure 13.2 The role of boards and top management

Even private sector boards are required to show some accountability, and they are legally required to serve the shareholder interests, where shareholding exists. In fact,

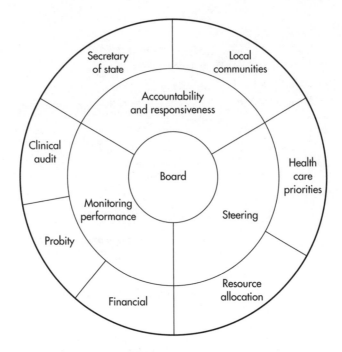

Figure 13.3 The role of boards in the NHS
Source: Audit Commission, 1995

corporate decision makers pursue corporate survival as much as shareholder wealth, as described in a study by Donaldson and Lorsch (1983). Private sector boards are also required to be accountable by following various procedures for publishing annual reports with monies accounted for and including an audit of accounts. This financial accountability is not always easy, as has been evident in two recent cases, the Maxwell pension fund fraud case and the British Airways alleged dirty tricks campaign against Virgin Atlantic, where the board claimed it did not know of the tactics of the ticket sales team.

Boards also have a changing and mixed composition, which in the public sector reflects the need to incorporate various stakeholder interests. Thus many health authorities now have representation at board level of local general practitioners, for example. The boards of locally managed schools (LMS) also incorporate parent governors, teachers, and members of the local business community and local education authority. Even in the private sector, boards often attempt to incorporate relevent stakeholder interests, for example in the appointment of Sue Birley in 1996, a university professor in entrepeneurship and expert on small business venturing, onto the main board of National Westminster Bank, in order to incorporate better knowledge of small business needs at the board level. The recruitment of new non-executive directors in particular can be a developmental experience for other board members, as they bring in and share fresh ideas and skills.

HOW BOARDS FUNCTION: BALANCING INTEGRATION, DIVERSITY AND POWER

The diversity of background and function of board members can be a great strength in terms of breadth of skill and experience, but it can also be a destructive dynamic when resulting in sectional infighting and power games (see Pettigrew, 1992 for a pluralist view of the top team). Pfeffer (1983) suggests that: 'Socialization and informal control will be more effective where members are more homogenous, because their similarity of background, joint experience and shared perspective provide a common vocabulary and the basis for mutual understanding.' This point is affirmed by others (for example Katz and Kahn, 1978, p. 423) and Smith et al. (1996, p. 41) who believe that members of socially integrated groups experience higher morale and satisfaction and, most importantly, exhibit greater efficiency in the co-ordination of tasks, whereas heterogenous top management teams are expected to be more difficult and expensive to co-ordinate and control, and that 'generally, researchers have argued that team heterogeneity is negatively related to social integration and communication.' (Smith et al., 1996, p. 46). This is confirmed in their research which found that team social integration was positively related to return on investment and growth in sales.

Norburn (1989) found significant differences between the views of CEOs and top management teams on this topic with respect to the homogeneity of experience through the recruitment of insiders, versus heterogeneity of experience. CEOs believed it best for rising executives to stay with one company and work their way up the managerial ladder, whereas top management teams saw this as leading to patronage. Norburn's results indicate that CEOs would replicate their own experience in terms of grooming the next generation, a possibility which suggests that we could end up with corporate clones, more matched to qualities required in the past than to future needs.

We therefore have a quandary when we come to development related to the constitution, attitude and behaviour of management boards. On the one hand the literature suggests recruitment and development should be steered towards achieving more homogeneity, or at least to overcome the problems of heterogeneity, in terms of education, background, skills, experience and attitudes. On the other, it is suggested that recruitment should not be 'in one's own image' and development should be more geared towards overcoming the problems of too much homogeneity resulting in groupthink (Janis, 1972).

The solution Smith et al. (1996, p. 64) provided is that: 'Behavioural change efforts directed at enhancing informal team communications, and social integration, such as teambuilding, are likely to have payoffs in terms of team efficiency and total organizational performance.' Equally, we suggest that top manager development should lead to developing independence, a point supported by the Audit Commission (1995). This is due to the need for critical appraisal and evaluation of performance, and the role of non-executive directors as independent advisers. These two different forms of development are not necessarily contradictory, but derive from the very different demands on the top team to work together for the organization, and to stand back and evaluate the organization.

There is a similar quandary over the issue of the use of power within top teams and boards, and whether development should be geared to promoting it or diffusing it. Pettigrew (1992) mentions the work of Pfeffer and Salancik (1978) on the formation of inner circles of corporate power, and what is sometimes known as the 'kitchen cabinet' where a clique of two or three directors may essentially take the most important decisions within the organization with little consultation. An example of a powerful triad is the chair, chief executive and finance director, which can effectively leave others feeling powerless in the organization, and expose it to lack of 'reality checking'. Likewise there may exist other powerful inter-organizational networks of power with linkages, for example, through interlocking directorships or multiple board membership. When developing directors for effectiveness, it needs to be decided whether these networks serve a purpose, and whether it is desirable that directors as part of their development, strengthen these linkages. This can occur, for example, through secondment swaps, dual membership and so on. Alternatively, linkages can be weakened to prevent conflicts of loyalties, nepotism and insider dealing. Currently not enough research has been done to enable us to delineate such issues clearly. Pearce and Zahra (1991) suggested that powerful, independent boards were associated with superior corporate financial performance, and played a crucial role in creating corporate identity, especially in the establishment and maintenance of a code of ethics. They also suggested that powerful boards provided useful business contacts, thus strengthening the link between corporations and their environments.

There are also problems with becoming too focused on qualities or competencies of senior executive directors as a basis for identifying development needs. As well as under-emphasizing issues of power and networks, the literature in this area tends to rely on a methodology which utilizes self-report questionnaires. There is the danger that we are getting received wisdom and the post-hoc rationalization rhetoric of directors, contaminated with personal biases, 'I have succeeded therefore we should recruit and develop in my own image', so that all we are doing is institutionalizing subjectivity and those very views that the competencies approach was designed to overcome by more systematic methods. Very few studies take a longtitudinal case study approach to fully investigate and observe boardroom behaviour, decision-making and its effects. Likewise research into the development needs of boards, such as that commissioned by the Institute of Directors, is plagued by the biases of self-report questionnaires, with some reporting findings from as few as 8 per cent of those directors contacted (see for example Coulson-Thomas, 1990).

•••• The Justification for Senior Executive Development ••••

Given senior executives' position within the organization, a very strong case needs to be made for the use of development for it to have a chance to be used at all. There is a case for separating the development needs of senior executives from those of others. The top team's role and development needs are different from those of other managers, in that being at the strategic apex of organizations, they devise and evaluate strategy. They also have legal requirements and evaluative and reporting responsibilities, particularly with relation to financial probity.

Despite decentralization, the work of Gould and Campbell (1987) demonstrates that whatever the different structures and approaches to managing the centre – local arrangements in large firms, there continues to be a role for the centre, which needs support. As Schuler and Jackson (1987) point out, human resource practices at the top levels of an organization are different from those at lower levels, and the different roles and practices suggest that their development needs are therefore likely to be different, requiring our separate attention. Their role is clearly changing. We have suggested in chapters 1 and 2 that the changes taking place point to flatter, less hierarchical, organizations, where more decisions are being taken at lower levels. This is not to say that there is no longer a separate role for senior executives, far from it, but it does suggest that their roles need to be re-assessed. For example Smith and Kofron (1996) suggest that the role of senior executives is changing from planners and directors to coaches and supporters.

One critical distinction which is made between the top team and other managers is between direction and management. However this distinction should not be overstressed, and there is some evidence that the distinction between different levels of the managerial hierarchy is becoming blurred. There are those such as Coulson-Thomas (1991, 1992) who make a distinction between managing and management and the director level roles of direction and leadership. They suggest that directors are more outward looking and focus on the external business environment and long-term strategic and policy issues, whereas managers are more focused internally on the here and now and the short term and are more implementation oriented. For example Coulson-Thomas suggests that the top qualities which distinguish direction from management are: strategic awareness and planning; objectivity; ability to see the company as a whole; long-term vision; ultimate responsibility for the company; commanding respect/leadership; decision/policy making; anticipation of changing trends; delegation; lateral thinking; and responsibility to shareholders. If this were true then the challenge for moving people through the career progression from middle to top management would be extremely difficult indeed. However, these leadership qualities are increasingly being required in senior and even middle management as well as by international managers (see chapter 12). If we re-read Coulson-Thomas's list of direction qualities, how many in truth are not part of the remit of other managers? If the qualities and competencies desired of a manager are closer than we thought to those of director, then also in practice the reverse may be true. For example, many directors have also to consider the short term survival and development of a company, particularly for smaller companies.

Another reason to focus on top managers is that upper-level managers have an important impact on organizational outcomes because of the decisions they are empowered to make for the organization. This relates to Hambrick and Mason's upper-echelon theory (1984). Werther (1993) suggests: 'Given the leverage of executives to design and execute the strategies, structures and systems which become the organization's sources of competitive advantage, development among this group suggests significant potential returns.'

There are also knock on effects when managers at this level engage in developmental activity. Top managers are role models, when they engage in an activity it sends powerful signals to others that his or her activity is worthwhile and important. For these reasons it is argued that senior management commitment is needed to give credibility to organizational initiatives, including that of management development. The converse is also true. Failure to solicit others' active engagement reduces the credibility of management development. The 'do-as-I-direct-not-as-I-do' approach to management development also suffers from sending out mixed messages, one of the techniques which shore up Argyris's (1990, p. 27) organizational defences, discussed in chapter 7.

As well as the organizational needs for senior managers to engage in development, there are strong personal needs which may be met. For example, development may enable senior managers to extend the scope of functional responsibilities in preparation for boardroom appointments and director development, and thus to advance their own career to obtain a seat on the board.

This suggests that top team development is an activity which begins long before membership of that team does, and that is why we mention grooming as the first stage in the development process. The notion of continuing professional and management development, so much a part of our view of contemporary development, as explained in chapter 10, is dented once managers approach the senior levels. Practice suggests that there is a ceiling firmly in place, so that grooming is the last, not first, point of engagement in senior executive development.

Before proceeding to outline the approaches to executive development it is important to sound a note of warning. There is mixed evidence on the extent to which development targeted at this group can lead to improved organizational performance. Coulson-Thomas's (1992) argument that training is one of the two most commonly cited means of improving the effectiveness of a board (the other being changing its composition), must be treated with caution. Although this belief is widely shared, there is at least one study which suggests the contrary, (Martell et al., 1996). Martell et al. suggest that the lack of a relationship with business unit performance could be related firstly to the inappropriateness of the process or content of the training and development being provided, or secondly that the training in itself is not a worthwhile activity. It should not therefore be assumed that development is always required.

Moving away from research based on surveys and towards organizational case studies, there is more evidence of the impact of top manager training on effectiveness. For example Smith (1992) suggests that at ICL the training programme for top managers had forced the pace of change with immediate impact on the bottom line.

With the cautionary notes sounded above, it is important to be particularly sure that any develement is highly relevent to a senior executive, and is delivered in a timely and appropriate way. We suggest that this is made possible by focusing on the various roles of the top team, and by examining those areas where senior executives feel they are ineffective in their performance.

Few directors, despite the arguments for it, engage in development. It is worrying that surveys by the Institute of Directors find that fewer than 1 in 10 directors have been involved in any training or developmental activities since they were appointed to the board (Merrick, 1994). Where development in the boardroom does take place it is fairly typical for it to be handled directly by the chairperson or chief executive, without outside expertise. Human resource professionals are often perceived by the chairperson as having little to offer within the boardroom environment (Coulson-Thomas, 1992). Likewise, when non-executive directors take up their posts, they generally know very little about the organization.

So why does development fail to get on the board agenda? It is probably not due to the lack of evidence of its contribution to organizational effectiveness (mentioned above) but to other constraints (discussed below).

•••• Barriers to Senior Executive Development ••••

There are five main potential barriers to senior executive development: lack of visibility and clarity of roles; attitudes; identifying appropriate facilitators; time; and numbers.

First, the work of senior executives is even more opaque and ill-defined than that of other managers, and therefore it poses a problem when identifying relevant activities for development. Next there is the perception that if you have made it to the top of the organization, you have somehow succeeded so far, and therefore must have the skills and qualities necessary. There is the associated problem of finding a facilitator with sufficient credibility and 'clout'. Who should conduct the development? Despite potential credibility problems of internal consultants less senior within the organization, Mumford (1995) still argues for an expansion of the role of the human resource specialist. Another alternative is to use an outside facilitator, although as we shall see, in reality much developmental help falls to other incumbents, and the chairperson, chief executive or non-executive directors can play their own role in developing and coaching others.

There is also a time barrier to development as getting on with the job requires long hours and few holidays, combined with the multiple decisions and roles that have to be conducted. The available time is highly important, particularly if it is costed out and related to senior executives' impact on the organization. Therefore there has to be a good demonstrable case for using it in development. The time issue is particularly pertinent for non-executive directors, who have a specific term of office, often around three years, and usually come to the organization from outside with little of the organizational-specific knowledge of 'how things are done around here'. This lack of information and short learning curve can either act as a dynamic for development, or else a deterrent as the director immerses him or herself in the role. The top team also has few members, and so does not justify the expense of designing huge development programmes that are given to graduate trainees, for example, where the investment is reaped in terms of the numbers benefiting.

These factors combine to convince many senior executives that they are a breed apart and so are exempt from good practice advocated elsewhere in the organization. All of these deterents require careful planning and identification of development needs and appropriate methods for development to be seen as worthwhile at all. To explain these needs, a framework for examining the various development needs is used.

•••• A Framework for Identifying Development at •••• Different Stages

It is possible to identify four main stages in the development process for senior executives:

- grooming,
- induction,
- competencies within role,
- team effectiveness.

These stages are applied in exhibit 13.2 which identifies appropriate developmental activities at each stage.

Grooming is the preparation required to prepare senior managers for the transition into the next level in the organization, and the move from being a manager to becoming a director. Kakabadse and Margerison (1988) stress the need for preparing senior executives by giving them responsibility and wide managerial experience at an early age.

As grooming takes place prior to their appointment as a director, it can be difficult for an organization to instigate this, particularly if they recruit from outside the organization at the highest levels. There are many different approaches to succession planning and grooming a manager for the top (for example see Gratton and Syrett 1990, Gratton, 1990). The approaches of IBM, Amstrad, Hanson and BAT are very different: ranging from highly structured internal development through the identification of potential early on and coaching, and grooming and integration between career plans and available jobs at one extreme; and ad hoc informal approaches in the middle; to succession based on acquisition and local responsibility on the other.

Ultimately this requires higher level directors to act as sponsors and mentors and take a special interest in those beneath them, and although the organization can encourage this in its HR processes (for example in appraisal) and culture, it is all too easy for it to degenerate into nepotism and favouritism. As we shall see, grooming is an area which has to some extent gone out of fashion, and in any case was only practised by those large corporate organizations with highly structured internal labour markets, many of whom have rethought their HR approaches in the light of downsizing, for example IBM (Peach, 1992), or with privatization and contracting out, as with the civil service.

There needs to be some induction process for all senior roles, to support the individual in making the transition. Bennett (1996) shows how the lack of a comprehensive induction programme prevented new senior directors from getting more quickly into the business. This is particularly relevant for those who are recruited from outside the organization and who need to be inducted into its

•••• Exhibit 13.2 ••••
An overview of developmental activities for the top team

Grooming – Aimed at preparing managers for senior positions, through the following methods:

- being mentored;
- being sponsored;
- being coached;
- given special assignments;
- given early responsibility;
- given wide managerial experience (e.g. through job rotation);
- given visibility (e.g. through high profile presentations).

Induction – Aimed at familiarizing directors with new roles, organizational contexts and cultures, to enable them to adjust and make an early contribution, through the following methods:

- structured briefing and familiarization with the organization and its practices, tours (especially for NEDs);
- opportunities for less structured briefings according to individual requirements;
- getting support in appraising development needs;
- being counselled in taking the broader view or changing direction;

Competencies within role – Aimed at supporting skill acquisition (e.g. in the area of strategy formulation, performance evaluation, change management), and developing personal competency in role through the following methods:

- counselling to identify role relationships;
- counselling to identify specialisms;
- deputizing and acting-up (e.g. a director deputizing for the chief executive);
- networking (with those in comparative roles outside the organization);
- giving and attending seminars and presentations;
- asking for internal or external briefings from specialists or experts;
- doing special projects, individually and jointly with others, using internal coach or external facilitator;
- attending formal courses targeted at this level;
- facilitated learning from experience and on the job;
- mentoring and being mentored;
- coaching and being coached;
- seeking out 360% performance feedback;
- engaging in self-development;
- writing and using personal development plans.

Team effectiveness – Aimed at building creative synergy and complementary skills within the management team, and identifying common goals and priorities, through the following methods:

- facilitated away days;
- developmental sessions at end of board meetings;
- facilitated team building and evaluation of team effectiveness;
- facilitated team role clarification eg. using individual counselling;
- team questionnaires and personality profiles.

culture, objectives, strategy, processes and practices. This is the case for non-executive directors who may need extra help to understand the way the organization works speedily, in order to make an effective contribution. If an executive has been promoted, he or she needs reorienting in terms of what activities to throw off and what new strategic leadership and evaluative activities to engage in. If they have moved from being the director of leisure, for example, to become the chief executive of a district council, they will need help to move further from the detail, and also to take a broader view beyond that of their previous directorate.

Once in role, the third area of developmental activity is in relation to identifying and developing an individual's capabilities to fulfill that role. In the next section, when we turn to the individual development needs for different roles, we highlight processes such as learning from experience and on the job, mentoring and being mentored, special projects, networking, and externally facilitated learning.

The final aspect of developmental activity for the top team is team effectiveness, including the collective development needs which may be delivered to the team together rather than separately. It involves identification of the interaction of team roles, team effectiveness and strengths and weaknesses as a basis for development interventions. This is discussed after an investigation of the issues of grooming, induction, and individual development needed for the various roles at the top.

•••• Individual Roles and Development Needs ••••

THE CHAIRPERSON

The role of the chairperson is part independent and evaluative, and part supportive. Generally the chair plays a role in selection of non-executive directors, and also in performance evaluation of the chief executive. This begs the question as to whether or not the position of the chairperson and the CEO should be occupied by the same individual or not, and increasingly there is the argument that it should not (Cadbury Report 1992, Rechner and Dalton 1991).

The chair is also responsible for the working of the board, for its balance of membership subject to board and shareholders' approval, for ensuring that all relevant issues are on the agenda, and for ensuring that all directors are enabled and encouraged to play their full part in its activities (Cadbury Report, 1992). Thus, in development, they have their own development needs and also play a role in developing others, for example induction and ongoing coaching of non-executive directors as discussed below.

Stewart (1991), in her work on chairpeople and chief executives in the National Health Service, identified the very varied way in which the role of chair could be played out in practice, despite her finding common external guidance on their role in leading the authority, leading the officers and managing external relations through representation and negotiation. In discussing the relationship of the chairperson and district general manager (akin to a chief executive), for example, she identified five different roles for the chair as outlined in exhibit 13.3.

• • • • Exhibit 13.3 • • • •
The five roles of the chairperson with relation to the chief executive

Stewart (1991), in her work on the top teams in the NHS, identified five different ways the role of the chairperson could vary with relation to the chief executive (or at that time the district general manager – DGM):

- *Partner* – a sharing of the role of managing by the chairperson and the DGM akin to a 'marriage'.
- *Executive* – where the chairperson instructs the DGM and other managers to take action.
- *Mentor* – where the chairperson acts as a coach and counsellor, seeking to influence positively the DGM's behaviour, which was particularly in evidence where the DGM had been recently appointed, or did not have much NHS experience.
- *Consultant* – where the chairperson waits to be approached for advice.
- *Distant* – the chairperson's role is predominantly that of chairing authority meetings and attending obligatory external meetings and functions.

Source: Stewart, R., 1991, pp. 0022–2380

Stewart uses the concept of domains in her model of demands, constraints and choices, to explain how the chair and the general manager have distinct but also overlapping roles, for instance, they may both be needed to attend protest meetings over the closure of a hospital. Although they may both have domains of their own, each may deputize for the other – for example in the role of external figurehead, if the chairperson cannot attend a briefing of members of parliament – and this may be one way in which developmental opportunities are offered to both. One role for an external facilitator of development may be for them to help the chairperson and chief executive identify what is the nature of the role relationships between them, what might be an appropriate model, and how they can work together more effectively. Individual counselling may be the best way to put this into practice.

With relation to grooming, induction and in-role competencies, the main point to make about the chairperson is their role in developing others. As we shall see in the next section, their role is vital in induction in helping new non-executive directors to clarify their roles and identify their development needs and potential areas for specialization. Once in role, they continue to provide support through coaching, and also in setting a culture which enables a constructive contribution to create an environment in which it is easier for non-executive directors to speak out. They can also provide ongoing feedback on performance, both formally and informally, to non-executive directors, and generally it is their job to appraise and mentor the chief executive.

Elsewhere in this book we have highlighted the benefits of mentoring systems for the mentored (chapter 9). However it can equally be commended for the benefits to the mentor. Such a process can reinforce and develop appropriate behaviour in others, and provide opportunities to reflect on their own style and approach to decision-making. The process of making explicit the tacit and covert skills of management can in itself help an individual to assess and appraise him or herself. Yet there are challenges here for development. Is the chairperson equipped with the requisite skills to engage in mentoring, coaching and support? Where it is practised inappropriately, it can be resented and perceived as interference.

NON-EXECUTIVE DIRECTORS

Non-executive directors can provide boards with fresh ideas and approaches in the same way as can an externally appointed chief executive. Thus, in some organizations, they play a role in developing managers and the organization, as in the case of the AA (Bennett, 1996).

Non-executive directors' main role is one of independence, which is one rationale for their holding part-time, short term, appointments, so that they can continue to have considerable links with other organizations. Non-executive directors are hampered in their effectiveness by those very aspects which ensure their independence. As external appointments, they lack detailed knowledge of the organization and its practices, and having a fairly short tenure they have to learn fairly quickly on the job. It is not surprising then that two-thirds of non-executive directors in private sector companies identify insufficient knowledge of the business as one of the main factors inhibiting their effectiveness (BDO, 1994).

For them, development needs to be targeted in the first place at induction and familiarization geared at learning the ropes. This is likely to need to be fairly closely tailored to the needs of the individual and the type of organization, and one role for the chairperson or chief executive could be discussion with new non-executives with a view to identifying their particular learning needs and knowledge gaps, and ensuring that an induction process is put in place to meet these. The use of personal development plans can help in this process, and non-executive directors need to be encouraged to manage their own learning and use their own resources to put these into practice.

After the initial induction, non-executive directors can become more effective by learning a specialism which fits in with their own background and interests, and with the other members of the team. Again, a chairperson or chief executive can help to identify an area for development, and facilitate membership of the appropriate groups and committees. For example, a non-executive director could specialize in audit, and be encouraged to sit on the audit committee; or alternatively in consultation and communication with the local population or customers, through convening or being a spokesperson for the organization at public meetings, or representing the organization on public bodies. Development activity, rather than being a blanket approach after the process of induction, should be steered towards their chosen area of contribution.

There are, however, two key areas where non-executive directors do need to have some developmental support, at least initially. One is to give them the confidence to take the independent view, and ask probing questions, particularly in the face of dominant or insecure chief executives. This requires them to be skilled at identifying and using relevant information, and at contributing to meetings, a role which can be developed through a chairperson who encourages open questioning and debate.

Another key role for a non-executive director is in networking, and in providing a link between the organization and others. Networking can be a valuable form of development, for example through setting up or being involved with formal or informal meetings, or even learning sets of non-executive directors across organizations, where they can swap ideas and information.

Longer term development is steered towards the possibility of their taking on the role of a chairperson, either at this or another organization. Again the chairperson's ability to act as a coach, mentor and role model is crucial. Thus in general, non-executive directors need development which is built into the remit of their work, which is geared towards quick familiarization with the organization, highly tailored to their individual needs, and supported through coaching from a chairperson.

An example of some of the questions which can be asked to review the current developmental activity for non-executive directors, and as an agenda for creating a development programme, can be found in exhibit 13.4.

THE CHIEF EXECUTIVE

A major factor which affects the development needs of the chief executive is whether they come from inside or outside the organization. Clearly the process of grooming is more easily tackled if they have been promoted up through the organization. The study of CEO succession and organizational performance has a long history but lacks cumulative knowledge. Zajac (1990) suggests that outsiders suffer from 'information asymmetry', and despite the assumption that organizations with poor performance might be more likely to choose an outsider, Dalton and Kesner (1985, p. 751) claim that they are more frequent in firms with moderately good prior performance. Outsider CEOs are also likely to have similar induction needs to non-executive directors (above) requiring fast exposure to organizational knowledge and practices, and the ability to sift through huge amounts of information to focus on the most important strategic issues.

Once in role, their development requirements relate to two main areas: developing their strategic decision making and change management skills on the one hand; and keeping well informed about company and competitor developments on the other. The former can be improved through formal short courses directed at small groups of comparative executives, supplemented by regular feedback, coaching, mentoring and support. It can be extremely lonely and stressful at the top, and the chairperson is able to observe a CEO's strengths and weaknesses, provide advice, draw on their different background and experience to give it, and provide support through times of difficulty, for example in a dispute. With relation to their latter needs, of seeking and digesting the important information they need for decision making, and keeping informed and abreast of current issues, they can to some extent steer their own development by asking for regular briefings from various directors and experts within the organization. Alternatively the chief executive can look outside the organization for support, from networks of similar senior executives, and from attending seminars

•••• Exhibit 13.4 ••••
Non-executive directors: a checklist for developmental action
(Example taken from the NHS)

Questions	Priority	Lead person
Understanding the health service		
1 Have non-executive directors received training in the operation of the NHS nationally?		
2 Is there a formal induction programme tailored for individual non-executive directors?		
3 Has the chairperson outlined key responsibilities in consultation with non-executive directors and drawn up success criteria for non-executive directors?		
4 Does each non-executive director have an informal plan for developing their role?		
5 Is there mutual feedback on performance between chairpersons and non-executive directors?		
6 Is there a group enabling non-executive directors to share experience with those on other boards?		
7 Are non-executive directors encouraged to draw on views from outside the executive group?		
8 Are non-executive directors encouraged to have independent access to the Trust (or to providers in the case of purchaser non-executive directors)?		
9 Do non-executive directors use the audit committee to build good working relationships with their external auditors, enabling auditors to bring problem areas to their attention?		
Behaviour		
1 Does the chairperson lead by example, questioning executives and asking them to account for progress made?		
2 Is there an appropriate balance of contribution between executive and non-executive directors?		
3 Do the chief executive and other executive directors welcome questioning and discussion by non-executive directors?		
4 Does the chairperson lead non-executive directors in a robust review of performance?		

•••• Exhibit 13.4 continued ••••

Questions	Priority	Lead person
5 Does this review take place within the context that the culture of the board is to work together as a team?		
6 Is adequate time allowed for discussion at board meetings, as well as for information giving?		
7 What mechanisms are in place to enable the board to monitor the quality of medical care?		
8 Does the board receive feedback on the implementation of major decisions?		
9 Does the audit committee follow up audit reports to ensure that recommendations are being implemented and action taken?		
Boards' working practices		
1 What processes are in place to enable non-executive directors to be involved in formulating the strategy from the start?		
2 Do non-executive directors in practice influence the allocation of money?		
3 Do non-executive directors monitor the implementation of the strategy through:		
– receiving regular progress reports?		
– weighing up executive proposals against it?		
4 Has the board decided what performance reports to see, and how frequently?		
5 Do financial reports have the five good practice hallmarks?		
Responsiveness to the community		
1 Do boards have policies for all key components of responsiveness to the community:		
– informing the public?		
– taking account of the public's views?		
– answering the public?		
2 Are non-executive directors exposed to a range of views from the community?		

···· Exhibit 13.4 continued ····

Questions	Priority	Lead person
3 Do non-executive directors ensure that public opinion is taken into account when formulating the strategy?		
4 Do chairpersons invite non-executive directors to lead a discussion with the board on the implications for the community of major decisions?		
5 Do public meetings meet the good practice criteria?		
6 Is feedback from public meetings reported to the board?		
7 Where public meetings do not provide a forum for boards to answer to the public, do non-executive directors stimulate discussion of alternative strategies?		

Source: Audit Commission, 1995

and briefings. Some of the learning needs and development methods discussed below for senior executive directors are also relevant.

SENIOR EXECUTIVE DIRECTORS

Most directors are recruited from within the organization, unlike non-executive directors and chairpersons who by their nature come from outside the organization. However, merger and acquisition activity does increasingly lead to external appointments, and there is growing evidence that delayering is increasing this trend.

It is suggested that there are different competencies required by senior executives on the one hand and board level directors on the other. Sharrock et al. (1993) suggest that the transition process is a time when people are particularly vulnerable and most likely to make mistakes, and therefore what is needed is development counselling to extend skills and deal with the isolation they may feel, and to enable them to make the transition. This does suggest support at the grooming and induction stages, utilizing the help of either other senior executives, or independent consultants.

One difficulty for newly promoted board members is identifying which activities need to be developed further and which need to be relinquished or delegated to other managers. This is one area where coaching can be an appropriate development tool. The succession route to the top becomes particularly problematic for those who have taken a functional chimney career route. Hambrick and d'Aventi (1985) in the US found that companies who performed badly had a greater preponderance of top executives with throughput functional experience (such as production and accounting) rather than output functional experience (such as marketing and sales).

Problems of work overload and lack of strategic vision develop when new directors do not leave operational issues and the work of their old department behind. There is therefore a role for induction to director level which enables senior executives to change direction and refocus on their new level of work.

One way of doing this is to adopt a programme which focuses on strategic thinking, and Zabriskie and Huellmantel (1991) outline a programme which contains six elements of strategic thinking. Likewise, Seibert et al. (1995) assess the issue of how executive talent can be nurtured in a way which reinforces the strategy of the firm. They highlight the techniques used by 3M and Motorola in focusing on global strategy for developing international and European managers. As with many other such programmes, they stress the importance of job experience, and experience based learning, as well as timeliness in the delivery of such programmes.

Others have also tried to identify sets of standards for boards of directors, for example Henley Management College were commissioned by the Institute of Directors to do so (Merrick, 1994). They identify 37 personal competencies which include integrity, decisiveness, the ability to listen, and a willingness to take a helicopter approach and rise above problems facing the company. The standards identify board processes such as organizing and running a board of directors and developing the directors as a group. Among the tasks they address are vision and values, strategy and structure, and responsibility to stakeholders.

If we move from identifying the competencies required to examining the process through which development can take place in the job, we find another minefield. It is possible to identify some of the main learning processes cited in the literature, for example, learning from informal processes and experience and on the job, mentoring and being mentored, special projects, use of networks, career counselling, 360 degree feedback, and facilitated learning (see exhibit 13.2).

Mumford in many of his works (for example 1987, 1988, 1991) and others (for example Seibert et al., 1995), stress the need for more emphasis on informal processes and development through tasks which occur within a manager's job, so that there is an integration of learning experience with work. The fact that directors are motivated by achieving results for their organization and that they see learning as a discretionary activity, as we have discussed above, has implications for the approach to development; the approach is more likely to be successful if it focuses on the learning opportunities through activities in which they are engaged, thus focusing on opportunistic learning and opportunities for learning, in, around and through the job. Mumford (1991) suggests that this can be done intuitively, incidentally, retrospectively, and prospectively. To learn intuitively, a learning orientation must be deeply ingrained, and incidental learning is largely a matter of making the most of opportunities as and when they arise. Retrospective learning, such as in debriefing oneself over how one handled a meeting, for instance, and prospective learning, through planning how to make the most of a learning opportunity, are more likely to require the help of a mentor. Mentoring and being mentored, as we have seen in relation to the role of the chairperson in supporting non-executive directors, can play a very useful part in development at this level, if used carefully and supportively.

Identifying special projects can be a particularly effective way of developing top managers, both individually and within teams. The ICL programme reported by

Smith (1992), brings together three teams working on separate projects, but they also do a joint project. A team leader has the sole function of the removal of barriers and implementation of team plans.

An alternative approach is to help a manager gain perspectives from beyond their own organization. As with non-executive directors, directors benefit from the use of networks of people to whom they can turn for an external perspective on key issues. One way is through formal courses and programmes, and a plethora of these are springing up. Directors need to be careful to avoid those which are a repackaging of more general management courses, not least because of the peculiarities of their role and issues to do with the time available which have been raised above.

Career counselling is another way to gain a new perspective and support to enable a senior director to work through his or her progress, and through their plans for the future. An IRRR Bulletin (1993) reports on the use of career counselling consultants at the TSB, Christies and the London Stock Exchange to help directors identify the development they need to achieve their own objectives, presenting options on how the director could manage his or her own career.

There is also increasing emphasis on incorporating other stakeholders' views onto the development agenda, and one way is through utilizing 360 degree feedback in the development programme. The Benefits Agency (Donaldson, 1995, Terry and Hadland, 1995) utilizes 360 degree feedback in a programme which is accompanied by personality tests, (using Myers Briggs and Firo-B), a session with a psychologist, and time for personal reflection, as well as a videoed exercise. The programme, which utilized a competencies assessment approach, found that participants had reasonable logistics skills, but few had adequate skills for managing the emotional aspects of change. It is not surprising that the participants on this development programme found this process quite daunting.

Many facilitated director learning programmes incorporate all or some of these processes. Common design features of facilitated director learning programmes are:

- to contain an element of flexibility, to explore the opportunities and problems for learning as an individual and as a group;
- use of personal development plans to help identify appropriate learning interventions;
- the identification and conduct of a project which has personal significance and crucial importance to the organization;
- learning sessions at times to suit busy executives, for example breakfast meetings (for example see Werther, 1993).

Mumford (1995) is a particularly useful sourcebook which provides advice on how to build a director level developmental programme, including such features as personal development plans, ways of evaluating the training, and detailed case studies. Elsewhere Mumford (1987) has claimed that the most important thing in designing a successful programme is clear and appropriate job objectives and the identification and measurement of outputs. Mumford highlighted the most common reasons for the failure of such programmes. These include poor diagnosis of culture and business needs.

•••• Top Team Development for Board Effectiveness ••••

When someone is appointed as a new director or non-executive director, it is usual for them to join an existing team. Therefore their ability to contribute to the work of the board and have attributes which complement the qualities of existing board members are important. Developmental help can be useful to induct new team members as well as to help focus on team issues, to engage in team building and to clarify the different roles and responsibilites of the team, to help evaluate team effectiveness, appraise team strengths and weaknesses and identify any competency or role gaps which need to be addressed. One of the problems is that on the whole the qualities which help striving individuals to become directors are also the qualities which can make team work difficult.

Getting access to the top team is difficult, however, and team developmental activities draw heavily on time and resources, and therefore need to be clearly focused and time constrained. It is also difficult to get all the directors together at once, for example to attend an away day on priorities and effectiveness. One way is to 'piggy-back' on the end of board meetings. Another is to use an external consultant to see team members individually, and from that construct the team issues.

Many of these methods involve engaging an outside consultant to spend time with the team and explore their strengths and weaknesses. Personality profiling, job scanning, team role questionnaires and team effectiveness exercises are sometimes used to support this process (see chapter 6). The success of such approaches depends largely on the skill of the consultant in confronting the team members in a way that is both assertive and authoritative and on their ability to drive through insights and changes which get acted upon over time, rather than forgotten about after the event. Exhibit 13.2 outlines some of the methods used for developing top team effectiveness.

•••• Learning for Specific Sectors and Types of •••• Organization

Finally, there is a need to identify the development needs of senior executives within particular contexts. For example, the learning needs of international managers within large organizations are very different from those of owner managers within small local businesses. A survey conducted by Mann and Staudenmier (1991) found that the most important training needs of international directors were perceived as the management of change and global strategy and competition. It is not just the learning needs which are different, but also the learning process which needs to be adapted. Facilitated team projects may be very useful for international development programmes in large organizations, but for smaller firms it may be easier for a manager to work on their own project within a learning set, supported and facilitated from outside the organization.

In the small firm, although training is seen as a powerful agent of change, it is often vulnerable to the whim of the owner-manager, and Jennings et al. (1996) argue for the importance of building links with other institutions such as local universities, trade associations and TECs. Goss (1989) suggests that in terms of process, developmental support should be packaged in discontinuous and discrete ways, in order to fit in with owner managers' busy schedules. Johnson (1995) claims that stress is one of the greatest problems because owner-managers often work long hours, cause disruption if they are absent, usually keep poor records, and may carry the weight and the fate of the business and its employees on their shoulders. Therefore it is argued that techniques for handling stress should be built into the programme.

•••• Summary ••••

We have shown how difficult is the task facing anyone trying to design developmental programmes and activities for the top team. We have shown that their roles and responsibilities vary, and therefore both the content and process of development need to vary according to both the organization, and whether the role is of a director, non-executive director, chairperson or chief executive. We suggest that there are both individual and shared learning needs, and ones which require team based approaches. Development is an activity which takes place before, at a new appointment, and in the role.

Due to the difficulties of time, and also gaining credibility for those providing the learning opportunity, we suggest that off-the-job learning has to be highly tailored and supplemented by considerable mentoring and coaching internally, and by involvement in senior executive networks, externally.

EXERCISES

(1) Take the top team of an organization known to you. Ask how much you actually know about their work, and research the following questions. If it is possible try to interview a member of the top team, or find out the answers through human resources or management development personnel.

   (a) How are the different roles and responsibilities of the top team divided up?

   (b) How much do they accord to the delineation of the roles and responsibilities outlined in this chapter? If you can, try interviewing one of the top team on their perception of their role.

   (c) How visible is their work?

   (d) How can we measure their effectiveness?

(e) What career path have they followed to get to where they are?

(f) What developmental activities do the top team engage in?

(g) What (or who) do the members of this team believe to have been positive and important influences on their ability to perform well?

(h) If you can ask a member of the top team to fill in the form provided in exhibit 13.4.

(2) Assume the role of chief executive officer has fallen vacant in an organization known to you. Identify:

(a) How the organization should go about specifying the job description and person specification for the new post holder.

(b) How they should go about recruiting and selecting a new CEO (what channels and methods should be adopted)?

(c) What developmental activities should the new CEO engage in as part of his/her induction to the organization?

(d) What ongoing developmental activities and sources of support should the new CEO utilize to continue to maximize his/her effectiveness?

•••• References ••••

Argyris, C. 1990: *Overcoming Organizational Defenses.* Boston, MA.: Allyn and Bacon.

Audit Commission, 1995: *Taken on Board: corporate governance in the NHS: developing the role of non-executive directors,* London: HMSO.

BDO, 1994: *Non-Executive Directors: watchdogs or advisers?* BDO Binder Hamlyn Special Briefing No. 91.

Bennett, H. 1996: Tuning up for life in the fast lane. *People Management,* 2, 12, pp. 34–5.

Cadbury, A. 1990: *The Company Chairman.* London: Director Books.

Cadbury Report 1992: *Report of the committee on the financial aspects of corporate governance.* Chaired by Sir Adrian Cadbury, and Code of Practice. London: Gee and Co.

Coulson-Thomas, C. 1990: *Professional Development of and for the Board.* A Survey undertaken for the Institute of Directors. London: Adaptation Ltd.

Coulson-Thomas, C. 1991: Competent directors: boardroom myths and realities. *Journal of General Management* 17, pp. 1–26.

Coulson-Thomas, C. 1992: Developing competent directors and effective boards. *Journal of Management Development,* 11, 1, pp. 39–49.

Coulson-Thomas, C. and Wakelam, A. 1990: *Developing Directors.* A survey, funded by the Training Agency, conducted by Adaptation Ltd and the Centre for Management Studies, University of Exeter.

Coulson-Thomas, C. and Wakelam, A. 1991: *The Effective Board, current practice, myths and realities.* An IOD discussion document. London: Institute of Directors.

Dalton, D. R., and Kesner, I. F. 1985: Organizational performance as an antecedent of inside/outside chief executive succession: an empirical assessment. *Academy of Management Journal,* 28, pp. 749–62.

Dawson, S., Winstanley, D., Mole, V. and Sherval, J. 1995: *Managing in the NHS: a study of senior executives.* London: HMSO.

Donaldson, L. 1995: Leading change in a challenging environment - the benefits Agency's new MDP. *Competency,* 2, 4, pp. 17–18.

Donaldson, G. and Lorsch, J. 1983 *Decision-Making at the Top: The Shaping of Strategic Direction.* New York: Basic Books.

Goss, D. M. 1989: Management development and small business education: the implications of diversity. *Management Education and Development,* 20, 2, pp. 100–11.

Gould, M., and Campbell, A. 1987: *The Role of the Centre in Managing Diversified Organisations.* Oxford: Blackwell.

Gratton, L. 1990: *Heirs Apparent: succession strategies for the 1990s.* Oxford: Blackwell.

Gratton, L. and Syrett, M. 1990 Heirs apparent: succession strategies for the future. *Personnel Management,* January, pp. 34–8.

Hambrick, D. and d'Aventi, R. 1985: Top team deterioration as part of the downward spiral of large corporate bankruptcies. *Management Science,* 38, pp. 1445–66.

Hambrick, D. C. and Mason, P. A. 1984: Upper echelons: the organization as a reflection of its top managers. *Academy of Management Review,* 9, pp. 193–206.

Industrial Relations Review and Report 1993: Executive development through career management: increasing the effectiveness of top managers. *IRRR Employee Development Bulletin,* 546, pp. 2–6

Janis, I. 1972: *Victims of Groupthink.* Boston: Houghton Mifflin.

Jennings, P. L., Banfield, P. and Beaver, G. 1996: Human resource development in small firms: a competence based approach. *Strategic Change,* 5, 2, pp. 89–105.

Johnson, D. 1995: Stress and stress management among owner-managers of small and medium sized enterprises. *Employee Counselling Today,* 7, 5, pp. 14–19.

Kakabadse, A. and Margerison, C. 1988: Top executives addressing their management development needs. *Leadership and Organization Development Journal,* 9, 4, pp. 17–21.

Katz, D., and Kahn, R. 1978: *The Social Psychology of Organizations.* New York: John Wiley and Sons.

Mann, R. and Staudenmier, J. 1991: Strategic shifts in executive development. *Training and Development (USA),* 45, 7, pp. 37–40.

Martell, K., Gupta, A., and Carroll, S. J. 1996: Human resource management practices, business strategies and firm performance. *Irish Business and Administration Research,* 17, 1, pp. 18–35.

Merrick, N. 1994: Taking training to the top. *Personnel Management,* December, pp. 51–2.

Mumford, A. 1987: Myths and realities in developing directors., *Personnel Management,* 19, 2, pp. 29–33.

Mumford, A. 1988: Developing managers for the board. *Journal of Management Development,* 7, 1, pp. 13–23.

Mumford, A. 1991: Developing the top team to meet organisational objectives. *Journal of Management Development,* 10, 5, pp. 5–14.

Mumford, A. 1995: *Learning at the Top.* London: McGraw Hill.

Norburn, D. 1989: The chief executive: a breed apart. *Strategic Management Journal,* 10, pp. 1–15.

Peach, L. 1992: Parting by mutual agreement: IBM's transition to manpower cuts. *Personnel Management,* March, pp. 40–3.

Pearce, J. A. and Zahra, S. A. 1991: The relative power of CEOs and boards of directors: association with corporate performance. *Strategic Management Journal,* 12, 2 pp. 135–53.

Pettigrew, A. 1992: On studying managerial elites. *Strategic Management Journal,* 13, pp. 163–82.

Pfeffer, J. 1983: Organizational demography. In Cummings, L. L. and Straw, B. M. (eds) *Research in Organizational Behavior.* Greenwich, CT: JAI Press.

Pfeffer, J. and Salancik, G. 1978: *The External Control of Organizations: a resource dependence perspective,* New York: Harper and Row.

Rechner, P. L. and Dalton, D. R. 1991: CEO duality and organizational performance: a longtitudinal analysis. *Strategic Management Journal,* 12, pp. 155–65.

Schuler, R. S. and Jackson, S. E. 1987: Organizational strategy and organizational level as determinants of human resource management practices. *Human Resource Planning,* 10, pp. 125–41.

Seibert, K., Hall, D. and Kram, K. 1995: Strengthening the weak link in strategic executive development: integrating individual development and global business strategy. *Human Resource Management* 34, 4, pp. 549–67.

Sharrock, R., Grant, P. and Acker, B. 1993: Developing peak performers. *Directions,* May, pp. 14–19.

Smith, A. 1992: Fast off the blocks. *Personnel Today* 13–26 October, 25.

Smith, K. A. and Kofron, E. A. 1996: Toward a research agenda on top management teams an strategy implementation. *Irish Business and Administrative Research* 17, 1, pp. 135–52.

Smith, K. G., Smith, K. A., Olian, J. D. Sims, H. P., O'Bannon, D. P. and Scully, J. A. 1996: Top management team demography and process: the role of social integration and communication. *Irish Business and Administrative Research* 17, 1, pp. 36–70.

Stewart, R. 1991 Chairmen and chief executives: an exploration of their relationship. *Journal of Management Studies,* 28, 5, pp. 0022–2380.

Terry, A. and Hadland, M, 1995: Reaping the benefits from development. *People Management,* 1, 15, pp. 30–2.

Werther, W. B. 1993: A university/corporate solution to closing the executive development gap. *Journal of Management Development,* 12, 4, pp. 29–36.

Zabriskie, N. and Huellmantel, A. 1991: Developing strategic thinking in senior management. *Long Range Planning,* 24, 6, pp. 25–32.

Zajac, E. 1990 CEO selection, succession, compensation and firm performance: a theoretical integration and empirical analysis. *Strategic Management Journal,* 11, pp. 217–30.

Index